Benjamin McAlester Anderson

Effects of the War on Money, Credit and Banking on France and the United States

Salzwasser

Benjamin McAlester Anderson

Effects of the War on Money, Credit and Banking on France and the United States

1. Auflage | ISBN: 978-3-84604-678-4

Erscheinungsort: Frankfurt, Deutschland

Erscheinungsjahr: 2020

Salzwasser Verlag GmbH

Reprint of the original, first published in 1919.

Carnegie Endowment for International Peace

DIVISION OF ECONOMICS AND HISTORY

JOHN BATES CLARK, DIRECTOR

PRELIMINARY ECONOMIC STUDIES OF THE WAR

EDITED BY

DAVID KINLEY

Professor of Political Economy, University of Illinois
Member of Committee of Research of the Endowment

No. 15

EFFECTS OF THE WAR ON MONEY, CREDIT AND BANKING IN FRANCE AND THE UNITED STATES

BY

B. M. ANDERSON, JR., PH.D.

NEW YORK

OXFORD UNIVERSITY PRESS

AMERICAN BRANCH: 35 West 32nd Street

LONDON, TORONTO, MELBOURNE, AND BOMBAY

1919

EDITOR'S PREFACE

Professor Anderson's study of " Effects of the War on Money, Credit and Banking in France and the United States " needs no commendation. It is full both of information and of suggestions, and will be valuable not only to bankers but to other business men, to students, and to the general reader.

The account of occurrences and policies in the United States is so full, accurate and clear that editorial comment on them is unnecessary. Certain matters stand out in the confused history of the early days of the war which should be guiding posts for the future. For he would have been held a foolish prophet who, before the war, would have predicted that the economic structure of the world would have withstood as well as it actually did the shock of the military cataclysm. The closing of the stock exchanges, the moratoria, the strength and wise action of central banks and the provision of emergency currency, are the great master strokes of policy that kept the economic " ship of state " from shipwreck.

The history of the action of the French banks will be, in the main, new to most American readers. The policy showed in many ways the shortsightedness that characterized our own banking policy in times of stress before the establishment of the federal reserve system. Cooperation among the private banks of France seems to have been difficult and a generous public policy unthought of. To be sure, the conditions of French life have made France a capital lending and an agricultural country, rather than an industrial one. It may well be that those responsible for the conduct of the French private banks thought it their first duty to conserve these classes of interests, not being able to see far enough ahead to know that neglect to support their government strongly would inevitably be the ruin even of those interests.

The advantages of our own new system, the federal reserve system, have been brought prominently to notice. For the first time in our history we have had an organization powerful enough to control the disturbing factors of the credit situation. The war leaves us the strongest country in the world in the matter of gold holdings and in the extension of our credit. Nevertheless, we must not draw too optimistic conclusions as to our monetary strength from these facts. We shall have to work hard to retain the advantages which these two conditions give us.

I am glad that the subject of this study has been in such masterly hands as those of Dr. Anderson.

DAVID KINLEY.

Urbana, Illinois,
February 19, 1919.

FOREWORD

A four year period in the history of money, credit and banking in France and the United States might ordinarily be covered satisfactorily in a slender essay, easily written in a short time. Almost every week of the war period, however, has brought events of the first magnitude in both countries. A definitive history of money, credit and banking during this period must be the work of several years. There is not merely the problem of reading and digesting an immense mass of materials, but there is also the certainty that many episodes, carefully disguised for political and military reasons, can not be justly evaluated until a later time. The writer trusts that other students will bear these difficulties in mind in passing judgment on the book. Errors it must contain, both in statements of fact and in interpretations.

It is a pleasure to acknowledge various obligations to others. Mr. Harvey E. Fisk of the Bankers Trust Company of New York kindly supplied several of the charts, as did Dr. M. Jacobson, statistician of the Federal Reserve Board. Both gentlemen have given advice and information. The United States Bureau of Labor Statistics, the Service Department of the National Bank of Commerce in New York, the New York Times *Annalist,* the library of the Carnegie Endowment for International Peace at Washington and other organizations have been very generous. The author is indebted for many ideas to his colleagues of the Committee of the American Economic Association on the Purchasing Power of Money with Reference to the War, Professors Irving Fisher, W. C. Mitchell, E. W. Kemmerer and W. M. Persons and Dr. Royal Meeker. Mr. Basil P. Blackett, financial representative of the British Government, has given information and advice, as have Professors O. M. W. Sprague and H. P. Willis. It is, perhaps, unnecessary to say that the writer alone is responsible for the views here expressed.

B. M. ANDERSON, Jr.

November, 1918.

v

CONTENTS

EFFECTS OF THE WAR ON MONEY,
CREDIT AND BANKING IN FRANCE
AND THE UNITED STATES

CHAPTER I

Introduction

In its details, the effect of the war upon money, credit and banking is bewilderingly complex. It is, therefore, necessary at the outset to sketch in broad outline certain of the main movements and tendencies as a skeleton about which some of the details may be grouped. This outline is, in fact, fairly simple and the writer is content to present it in a form even simpler than the facts will warrant as a first approximation in the study of a complex body of details.

We must view the effects of the war first on their physical side: what has the war brought about in production and consumption, in the course of manufactures, shipping, agriculture and mining? The first step taken at the outbreak of the war was, of course, the mobilization of the armies. Throughout France, Germany, Austria, Russia, Serbia and Belgium, the outbreak of the war led millions of laborers to drop their tools and go to the front. Production was thus instantly enormously curtailed. At the same moment, there began an incredible increase in consumption, as these millions of men not only consumed more food and wore out more clothing than in ordinary times, but also devoted themselves to the most wasteful kind of destruction of the products of labor in the form of explosives, costly machines of war and the like. The consumption of the governments and the armies increased much more rapidly than civilian consumption could contract, and the reservoirs of supplies existing in the belligerent countries were rapidly diminished.

In ordinary times the world lives from hand to mouth. With all our accumulation of wealth we are never far removed from famine or from shortages of consumption goods. The stored up wealth of the world, railroads and bridges, buildings, factories, machinery, farm improvements, household furnishings, museums and art galleries, and the like, are not available for direct consumption, and with the stoppage of the current flow of goods from farms and factories, fisheries and mines, the world is speedily placed on short rations. It was, therefore, vitally necessary that new supplies should be secured promptly by the belligerent powers, and for this there were several sources.

The matter was accomplished most simply in Germany, which was early blockaded and unable to draw in very much from the outside world. There were labor reserves, old men, women and children, and for the labor that was not mobilized there was the possibility of overtime work. This resource was not the first in France, but, none the less, in France by November, 1917, with 24 per cent of the normal labor force mobilized in the army, there was 98 per cent of the normal labor supply at work—which meant a heavy draft on the women, children and old men, and also a draft on colonial and foreign labor brought into France.

France and England commanded the seas, and their first resource for the immediate increase in the volume of goods and supplies required for the war was in neutral countries, notably the United States. The one big outstanding fact in the course of international trade during the war has been the gigantic increase in American exports to England, France and others of the Entente Allies—an increase of exports not met by an increase of imports and constituting consequently a net addition to the physical resources of the Entente. This addition to the power of the countries opposed to Germany was no doubt crucial in saving them from defeat.

To a much less extent, neutral resources of goods and supplies were available for Germany. Germany has drawn on the Netherlands, Switzerland, Norway, Sweden and Denmark—to some extent on Italy and Roumania in the early period of the war—and on some other countries. Some supplies from America went, in the early part of the war, to Germany, by means of transshipments through the Netherlands, Sweden and other neutral markets. This, however, has been exaggerated on the basis of the figures for imports from the United States of certain neutral countries, notably the Scandinavian countries. It is worth while to point out that in the ordinary course of trade before the war a considerable volume of American goods was sent first to the Free Port of Hamburg and subsequently trans-shipped to the Scandinavian countries. When Hamburg was blockaded, these goods were shipped directly to the countries of their ultimate destination, thereby swelling the import figures of these countries from the United States, but not proportionately increasing their actual imports from the United States. To a very large degree, the Central Powers have been self-sufficing during the whole course of the war.

Viewing the matter in physical terms, therefore, it is fairly easy to see the main transformations that the war has brought about in industry and trade. On the side of money, credit, banking and finance, the outlines are not so clear and easily drawn. The first effect of all of the outbreak of the great war —indeed an effect that manifested itself with the mere prospect of war—was a greatly increased significance attached to a special function of money, namely, money as a " bearer of options " and as a " store of value." In tranquil times, men are often content to keep their wealth in nonliquid forms. Men can make long run plans and long time investments, and are often glad to get such investments which combine high yield with slight liquidity. But when danger, uncertainty and emergencies come, men prefer gold to real estate. The effort is made, even at the price of a heavy sacrifice, to accumulate economic resources in form suitable for immediate use. Not knowing which way to turn, men seek to prepare themselves to turn in any way that the future may indicate to be most advantageous. The effort to sell real estate or other absolutely fixed forms of investment at the outbreak of the war was futile. There were no buyers. But it was possible, to a very considerable extent, to turn securities quoted in the great stock exchanges into cash in the form of bank deposits or bank notes, and it was possible, to a considerable extent, to turn bank notes and bank deposits into gold; and the first indications of coming war manifest themselves in these two operations.

The effort to turn bank credits into gold manifested itself

first as German bankers, as early as 1912, began to take steps to increase their gold supply. In order to take gold out of the hands of the people and carry it to the reserves of the Reichsbank, fifty and twenty mark bank notes were issued to take the place of the gold in circulation. German agents regularly appeared as bidders for gold at the London auction rooms. Gold was shipped from the United States to Germany, and the famous Spandau treasure was transferred to the vaults of the Reichsbank. By 1914, Germany ceased to take much gold, having presumably decided that her resources were adequate.[1]

France and Russia made strong efforts to increase their gold reserves during the spring and summer of 1914. In eighteen months preceding the outbreak of the war, the gold holdings of the central banks of Germany, France and Russia were estimated to have increased by $360,000,000. This drift of gold to these great central reservoirs led to a tightening of the money markets of the rest of the world, and led to an unusually large drain on the gold supply of the United States.

So far the movement was silent and unaccompanied by excitement. It increased the tendency to gloom and depression which most of the financial centers of the world felt in any case, but it was skilfully managed and did not occasion great alarm. Following the assassination at Sarajevo on June 28, 1914, however, and the alarms that followed, the effort to convert securities into bank credit began to assume great proportions. Starting with heavy selling on the bourse of Vienna, with a fall in the prices of stocks of from 10 to 12 per cent on July 13, it spread rapidly to the other great markets, culminating in panics in the bourses of Vienna, Berlin, Paris and other continental centers and forcing them to suspend operations. The selling spread to London and New York, and, by the time war became certain, all Europe was selling in New York, without limit of price, such securities as it held as were listed in the New York market. Europe, particularly Great Britain, had invested heavily in American securi-

---

[1] Goodhue, E. W.: "Some Economic Effects of the European War on the United States." *Journal of the American Bankers' Association*, May, 1916, page 1034; Conant: "American Finance in the War Tempest," *Review of Reviews*, vol. 50, page 326.

ties, and the efforts to realize upon these investments finally forced even far away New York to close its stock exchange on July 31, a few hours after the London stock exchange closed.

In connection with this effort to get wealth into the most liquid possible form, there manifested itself promptly in the continental countries a strong preference for gold as compared with bank notes or bank credit, a preference reflecting distrust of the paper money, and reflecting a general belief that the central banks would not preserve the convertibility of their notes into gold. Gold quickly disappeared from circulation; central banks quickly suspended gold redemption; and continental Europe went promptly to a paper money basis. The preference for " hard money " over paper even extended to the silver coin, whose bullion value was less than the value of the bank notes which the people distrusted. This preference for " hard money " has even extended at times, particularly on the part of peasants, to copper, so that copper coins have been hoarded where bank notes have been paid out. We shall later discuss this phenomenon in detail in connection with the medium of exchange in France.

The strong preference for wealth in liquid form is in itself an evidence of a demoralization of credit, but there were inevitable factors which would have demoralized the credit fabric even in the absence of this dramatic psychological change. At the outbreak of war, with belligerent cruisers seeking to capture the merchant ships of their enemies, ocean trade was suddenly interrupted. The shipments of gold from one country to another became impossible. The shipment of goods from one country to another became impossible. Unable to ship either gold or goods, unable to sell securities because the stock exchanges were closed, unable to borrow at foreign banks because of the uncertainties of the credit situation and because of the weakness of many banks, men in one country who had bought goods from another country and who had payments to make in that other country, were unable to meet their obligations. This situation centered in London, which, by long standing custom, is the center for making international payments. The whole world was indebted to London and the world was unable to meet its debts. London institutions, unable to collect from their various debtors, were similarly unable to pay their creditors. The credit situation was necessarily demoralized. The declaration of war, moreover, at once made it impossible that creditors in England could collect from debtors in Germany or *vice versa.*

The credit system is dependent upon a steady flow of funds from debtor to creditor. Each business man in general is both debtor and creditor; funds starting from an ultimate consumer may go through many hands, canceling many debts in the process. An interruption anywhere in this chain of payments may demoralize the credit system.

There was further the collapse of security values and the inability of those who had borrowed at the banks on stock and bond collateral security, often on call, to pay their obligations at the banks. The volume of such stock and bond collateral loans is in normal times enormous and the banks were greatly weakened by the situation.

The demoralization of industry by mobilization of labor, and through much of France and Belgium by actual invasion, again made it impossible for great numbers of debtors to meet their obligations. For all these reasons, it is clear that a difficult situation was created for banks and the whole credit system. When to this is added the fact that France had been in depression and even crisis for two years preceding the war; that the great private banks of France were demoralized by losses in the period preceding the outbreak of the war, growing largely out of bad foreign investments; that the private banks in France and joint stock banks in England showed themselves unexpectedly cowardly—in France much more than in England—it is perfectly clear that the situation called for extraordinary remedies.

The first of these extraordinary remedies we have already mentioned, the closing of the stock exchanges. This was done in considerable degree for the protection of the banks. By long standing tradition, banks are accustomed to reckon the price of the stock exchange collateral on which they lend, during the hours that the stock exchange is closed, at the closing price of the last session. With the certainty that stock exchange prices would go indefinitely lower if the stock exchanges remained open, there was also the certainty that the margin of protection which the bankers require in connection with collateral loans would be more than wiped out. The usual remedy which a banker can apply when his margin on a collateral loan is in danger was not available. In such a situation, a banker commonly calls on the borrower to provide more security, and if the borrower is unable to do this, the banker sells the collateral for what it will bring in the market, applies the proceeds to paying off the collateral loan and turns over the balance, if any, to the borrower. But in this great emergency, neither bankers nor anyone else could have any reasonable expectation of selling securities in considerable amount for enough to protect the loans they were supposed to secure. When the stock exchanges closed, the banks could continue to reckon the securities at the last closing price and thus avoid the technical admission that their assets were impaired, and brokers could be protected against the danger of the banks' " selling them out " at a loss.

But more drastic measures were applied in England and France, and for that matter, despite denials,[1] in Germany. *Moratoria* were applied. By decree of the state, debtors were relieved in varying degree of the necessity of meeting their obligations at the time they fell due and were given time to gather their wits, to set their houses in order and to make such use as they could of slow assets in protecting their solvency. There were no moratoria in the United States, but in New York and other financial centers, by general agreement of the banks, clearing houses, stock exchanges and other financial institutions, the debtors were protected from pressure by creditors in connection with stock exchange engagements.

Another means of meeting the collapse of the credit system was aid from the central banks in Germany, France and England. This aid in Germany, England and France took the form of rediscounting the paper held by the private banks and other dealers in bills and notes and in a great expansion of

---

[1] *Vide* Laughlin: *Credit of the Nations.* New York, 1918, pages 224-227.

the notes or deposits of the central banks. In New York, where there was no central bank, there was still an informal pooling of bank resources and close cooperation among the banks.

Another remedy applied very generally was the issue in one form or another of emergency currency for general circulation: in the United States the Aldrich-Vreeland notes, in Great Britain a special emergency currency issued by the government, and in France a great flood of notes of the Banque de France with some special emergency currency. A further form of extraordinary remedy was concerted action to handle the foreign exchange problem.

One of the first great problems which the outbreak of the war occasioned, and a problem of the very first magnitude throughout the war, has been that of obtaining funds for the gigantic war expenditures by the governments, a fiscal problem. In general, there are five main ways in which states may provide for war expenditures:

    (a) By taxation
    (b) By long term bonds
    (c) By short term Treasury bills
    (d) By advances from a state bank of issue in the form of bank notes
    (e) By a direct issue of paper money by the government

The last method was used to a considerable extent by the Northern government during the American Civil War. It is commonly recognized as the least desirable form of financing a war, and in form has been avoided by all the major belligerents in the present war. Practically, however, the distinction between government paper and note issue by the national banks of Russia or Austria is hard to draw; while the legal tender notes of the German loan bureaus (*Darlehnskassenscheine*), available as legal reserve for the notes of the Reichsbank, are also practically not to be distinguished from a paper money issued directly by the government, with legal tender privilege, to meet the fiscal needs of the state. The notes of the Banque de France also have been issued largely in response to fiscal needs. The government paper issued by Great Britain has apparently been kept carefully divorced from the fiscal operations of the state and apparently has been issued by the government to the banks to meet the needs of circulation.

On the whole, Great Britain and the United States have made large use of long time loans and taxes, and have called on the banks chiefly in connection with short time Treasury bills or certificates, although, of course, banks in Great Britain and the United States have purchased long time bonds and have made substantial loans with such bonds as collateral security. To a much greater extent, however, than in continental Europe, Great Britain and the United States have financed the war by real subtractions from the incomes of the people rather than by mere additions to bank credit.

It is less easy to speak with confidence of the situation in France. France has done little with taxation, and, to a very large extent, has relied on short term loans. But the short term loans appear to have been taken in France largely by the people, and, with the exception of the Banque de France itself, there has probably been an actual contraction of bank credit in France during most of the war. It is probably true that France, as well as Great Britain and the United States, has secured the major part of her fiscal resources during the war from the current income of the people.

We have already seen that the changes in foreign trade are, on the physical side, matters of outstanding significance. The European Entente Allies, purchasing heavily in the United States and from other neutrals, have had an ever increasing adverse balance of trade, which at the present aggregates many billions of dollars. This fact has given rise to some of the most critical and interesting financial problems of the war. Ordinarily, within fairly short intervals, a country's exports and imports roughly balance. If, through considerable periods, the physical items of exports and imports do not balance, it is usually easy to find invisible items that complete the balance sheet: interest payments, freights, insurance premiums, banking commissions, travelers' expenditures, investments. Items of this sort can usually be counted on to explain such differences between imports and exports as occur. Balances still unmet are commonly settled with small shipments of gold.

The credit resources of France, England and other European belligerents have been strained in meeting such an adverse trade balance as the past four years have brought about. The outbreak of the war saw England and France favorably placed. New York was indebted to them partly because of shipments of commodities earlier in the year, but more because of the heavy selling of securities on the New York stock exchange. For a time the exchange rates in New York ruled in favor of Paris and London and New York exported gold, not indeed to London because of dangers at sea, but to Ottawa, where the Bank of England established a depository. With December, 1914, the tide turned, however, as a consequence of increasing shipments of goods from the United States to the Allies and from the beginning of 1915 to March, 1917, when the United States broke with Germany, there was a steady stream of gold coming to the United States, chiefly through England, amounting in all to over a billion dollars.

This gold, however, paid for a minor fraction of the adverse trade balance. The rest was paid for partly by the return of securities to the United States, partly by direct government borrowings by France and Great Britain in the United States, and partly by adjustments of short term mercantile credits. With the entry of the United States into the war, the adverse trade balance has been met by direct loans by the federal government to its allies. In connection with the loans made before the entry of the United States into the war, it is interesting to note that some of them have been based upon American securities owned by European investors, mobilized by the governments of France and Great Britain, and hypothecated in New York.

The progress of the war has been marked by more and more direct governmental control of prices, industry, shipping, basic raw materials, railway transportation, etc., as the world's physical resources have been progressively strained. The course of prices during the war has attracted great attention and has been one of the dramatic features of it. There has been a worldwide rise of commodity prices, the inevitable consequence of a world-wide scarcity of commodities, due to the fact that 50,000,000 men have been withdrawn from industry and have been put to work in the most destructive kind of consumption of the products of industry, to the fact that transportation resources have been diminished and made precarious, and to the fact that industry, where not directly destroyed, has been demoralized and rendered less productive by the general interruption of the ordinary course of trade. In terms of gold, therefore, commodities in general have risen in price.

To this rise in gold prices, there has been superadded in various countries a further rise in prices occasioned by the depreciation of paper currency no longer convertible into gold. This is true in an overwhelming degree in Russia, in large degree in Austria and Germany, in considerable measure in France, and to some extent in Great Britain.

The change in prices, however, has not been all in one direction. A few commodities have not risen. Coffee and India rubber in the United States would be cases where commodities were as abundant for ordinary civilian consumption during the war as they were before the war. They did not rise in price in the United States. In countries where currency depreciation is not a major factor, the prices of stocks, bonds and real estate have shown a large decline. This is due partly to uncertainty as to the future of certain securities, but chiefly to a rising discount on the future, as the pressure of present needs forces governments and peoples to mortgage future incomes increasingly to obtain the means of carrying on the war and sustaining life. The correlatives are of course rising long time interest rates and rising commodity prices. This is strikingly true in the United States and Great Britain. It appears to be true also in France, at least so far as the securities on the French bourse may be taken as typical.

In general, the war has been accompanied by a large expansion of bank credits. This has been true in Great Britain; it has been true in the United States; it has been true to a very great degree in Germany. In France, however, although the Banque de France has expanded credits enormously, the whole increase being in credits to the state, the other banks have, on the whole, contracted their lending operations and their volume of deposits subject to check or draft, at least through most of the war period.

In Great Britain, France and the United States, the savings banks have all been in some measure alarmed by the shrinkage in the market quotations of their investments and by the tendency during the earlier period of the war of depositors to withdraw funds. In all three countries there has developed the understanding that public action will be taken to the extent that is necessary to protect savings banks from insolvency. The problem seems to have cleared for the savings banks of the United States without much positive action. More serious in Great Britain and France, the problem now appears to be a manageable one.

The position of the savings banks is typical of all recipients of fixed incomes in a period of rapidly rising prices and rapidly rising interest rates. Railroads and municipal public utilities, whose charges are fixed and whose costs are rising, have suffered during the war; the gold mining industry has suffered; men on fixed salaries or retired capitalists living on investments have found their real income steadily reduced with the rising prices. In England, France and the United States, some form of government guarantee of railroad credit has been found necessary.

Partly as a consequence of the heavy drains made by the warring states upon the loanable funds of the various countries, it has been increasingly difficult to finance private enterprises. In part, this has been desirable. It is not well that new enterprises producing luxuries or other things that the people can get along without should expand, competing with the governments for labor and supplies in the market, but the necessity for financing the new war time industries has been very great. On the whole, private capital has been adequate for this in Great Britain and the United States, though some state assistance has been necessary. In France, however, state aid on a considerable scale has been extended to necessary enterprises, including agriculture.

The enormous volume of war time expenditures has led to great industrial activity throughout most of the world, and the huge profits resulting from the rising prices connected with the war have in large degree buried the financial difficulties which the outbreak of the war occasioned. The credit system has come to life again, moratoria have largely been dispensed with, and pending insolvencies largely averted. To a very considerable extent, it seems, moreover, particularly in the United States, that business men, foreseeing a shock when the war is over, anticipating a drastic drop in prices with the falling off of war orders and with the return of labor to ordinary pursuits, have buttressed their positions with large reserves, have charged to depreciation the extraordinary expenditures for new buildings and equipment in connection with the war time industries, and are prepared to readjust themselves to a lower level of commodity prices without bankruptcy.

The problem of the huge debts of the warring states, which we shall deal with in later chapters, has given concern to very many students. It appears probable, however, that there need not be in these war debts any insurmountable dangers to solvency after the war.

In what follows we shall undertake to treat these major topics and others necessarily connected with them, with considerable fulness in the case of France. The discussion of money, credit and banking in the United States will be much briefer. The reason for putting the chief emphasis upon France in our discussion is that the war time developments of the United States are much more familiar to American readers than are those in France.

PART I
FRANCE

CHAPTER II

Money, Credit and Banking in France

It would be hard to find a sharper contrast among the great banking systems of the world than that between France and the United States. The difference is so great that it is not always easy for trained students whose background is primarily French, and trained students whose background is primarily American, to find a common language or to realize that beneath the differences in forms there are many common principles in operation. The American takes for granted many practices, and theories regarding those practices, of which some of the best informed French bankers seem to know little; while the French student takes for granted doctrines and practices which must be very carefully explained indeed to the American student of this subject.

One difficulty in the way of understanding the French system is the paucity of statistical materials in usable shape.[1] With the exception of the Banque de France, the Caisse des Dépôts et Consignations, and some minor semi-public institutions of banking character, French banks are wholly private institutions. If incorporated at all, they are incorporated under the general corporation laws, and subject to no more state control than a manufacturing corporation would be. The state requires no reports from them in uniform style, or, indeed, any reports at all, in general, except for taxation purposes. Commonly they make annual reports to their stockholders, and frequently they publish some sort of balance sheet statements at intervals between the annual reports. But it is not easy to get information from

---

[1] *Cf.* opinion expressed in *Statesman's Year Book,* 1912, page 794, where figures for the private banks are declared to be so unsatisfactory as not to justify republication.

these reports as to their actual operations. Take, for example,
the statement of the Crédit Lyonnais of December 31, 1905. The
statement of assets is as follows:

ACTIF DU CRÉDIT LYONNAIS
December 31, 1905

Espèces en caisse et dans les banques	Fr. 171,554,052.82
Portfeuille	1,030,060,878.68
Avances sur garanties et Reports	395,685,193.93
Comptes courants	535,566,961.42
Fortfeuille-titres (actions, bons, obligations et rentes)	5,446,754.89
Comptes d'ordres et divers	1,422,772.67
Immeubles	37,000,000.00
	Fr. 2,176,736,614.41

Just because of the uncertainty as to the meaning of certain
of these items, it has seemed best to give them in the French
version. The first item, cash on hand and in the banks, will seem
familiar enough to those used to the accounts of English joint
stock banks. French bankers attach little importance to cash
reserves. If their portfolios contain plenty of liquid paper, rediscountable at the Banque de France, they find their real reserves
there, and the question of actual cash in their vaults is purely a
matter of convenience. *"Espèce"* obviously can not be translated " specie," which would mean, in English, gold and silver
coin. Presumbably *"espèces"* means, simply, " ready funds "
in the money market sense, including gold and silver coin, notes
of the Banque de France, and deposits with the Banque de
France and other banks. American bankers supply much more
detailed information on this point in their reports. French
bankers other than the Banque de France—and for that matter
English bankers—free from the absurdity of legal minimum
reserves, and free to a large degree from the difficulties of getting cash in an emergency which American bankers, until recently, have faced, have been accustomed to regard the matter
as relatively unimportant.

Real question arises, however, as to the second item, " portfolio," which contains over a billion francs! What is included
in this huge lump sum? The bank does not say " commercial
portfolio." A common understanding would seem to be that

the item contains discounted commercial bills of exchange, with short maturities, but critics of the great private banks have suggested that many other things may be there, including securities owned, and paper drawn in connection with stock market operations. In any case, a subdivision of this huge item among the branches of the great company would be illuminating.[1] During the war, as we shall see, " portfolio " has been combined with other elements in the statement of this bank, in a very confusing and baffling manner.

" Advances on reports " is definite enough. It means stock market loans made till the next settlement day on the security of stock and bond collateral. The whole item " advances on ' garanties ' and reports," is translated as " loans against securities and contangoes "[2] by the London *Economist* of May 17, 1913, while in English statements published by the Crédit Lyonnais itself, it appears (June 30, 1915) as " loans against collateral and time loans," and (October 31, 1908) " call loans and time loans." It may be safely taken as chiefly, if not exclusively, a figure for loans in connection with bourse transactions.

"*Comptes courants,*" current accounts (on the assets side), is an item which would find its nearest counterpart in American banking under the head of " overdrafts," though it is, perhaps, misleading to say this. It is misleading, first, because with us overdrafts are represented by actual checks drawn on the bank, and held by the bank. In the second place, in American banking, overdrafts are generally illegal, or at all events regarded as bad banking, while there is no such stigma attached to this item in

---

[1] The Crédit Lyonnais stated to the National Monetary Commission that only commercial and industrial bills, chiefly commercial bills, were included here, and denied that its security holdings were larger than shown in its published statement. See Senate Document 405, 61st Cong., 2d Sess. Compare with this statement the contentions of Lysis: *Contre d'Oligarchie financière en France*, 12th ed., Paris, 1908 (*La Revue*), pages 31, 53-86.

[2] "Contango" and "report" are, respectively, the terms used in London and Paris to describe the loans made on collateral security till the next settlement day, on the stock exchange or the bourse. Fortnightly settlements prevail in these centers instead of the daily settlements made in New York. "Contango" is also applied to the interest rate at which these loans are made. For details, see H. C. Emery: *Speculation on the Stock and Produce Exchanges in the United States.* The term "report" is also used in Berlin. Neither of these expressions is used in New York.

French banking.   The term "current accounts" appears also on the liability side—in the statement of the date in question it stands on the liability side at 856,272,484.76 francs.   It is a form of deposit, with overdraft privileges.   The active business man is likely to have a "*compte courant*" rather than a "*dépôt*" (deposit).   If he overdraws this account, he becomes a debtor of the bank to the extent of the overdraft, and pays interest on the amounts overdrawn for the time that his account remains overdrawn.   His overdrawn account then appears as an asset of the bank.   If his account shows a positive balance, it appears as "current account" on the liability side of the bank's statement. There is a prior understanding as to how much he may overdraw —a sort of "line of credit" understanding.   Often securities or other collateral may be deposited in advance.   Such a practice has been well known in some of our southern States and on the Pacific coast and similar practices are well established in Scotland and in England, outside of London.   It is perfectly sound banking, if properly understood and safeguarded.   For our present purposes, however, it is enough to note that not much information regarding the bank's business is contained in the figure.   For what purposes were overdrafts to the extent of three hundred and ninety-five million francs permitted?   Critics, unable to find elsewhere in the bank's statement figures which could account for the supposed operations of the bank in "high finance," have suggested that "*comptes courants*" may in no small part represent accounts of agents of the bank itself, operating on the bourse.[1]

The remaining items on the assets side are small, and need no comment, except that the very smallness of the item "*portfcuille-titres*" (stock and bond portfolio) would strongly suggest that most of the holdings of the bank in securities must be somewhere else!   As will later be made clear, banks of the character of the Crédit Lyonnais have had as a very great part indeed of their business the handling of securities, particularly foreign issues which were to be marketed to their depositors, and whose values meanwhile must be protected by bourse operations.

---

[1] *Cf.* Lysis, *op. cit.*, pages 58-59.

On the liability side, three items aggregate the great bulk of
the whole:

```
Dépôts et bons à vue...................................Fr. 705,650,500.36
Comptes Courants ........................................    856,272,484.76
Acceptations ......   .....................................    180,559,616.46
                                                          ──────────────
                                                      Fr. 1,742,482,601.58
```

Of total liabilities of 2,176,736,614 francs, 1,742,482,614 are
contained in these three items.

It is not alone the paucity of items, the lack of details, in such
reports that baffle us. If American banks gave no more details
than this, it would still be possible to trace many general movements by watching their changes, because we could localize
them, compare variations in different States, in different cities,
and in different sections of the country. But, as will be made
clearer later, the figures for the few great banks like the Crédit
Lyonnais cover all sections of France, where their branches are
widely scattered, and, especially in the case of the Crédit Lyonnais, numerous foreign branches as well.

But there are further difficulties. How accurately made up are
the figures presented? There is no public auditing. The statement has been repeatedly made in France that the figures for
profits of the Crédit Lyonnais are fictitious, that they generally approximate the actual amount declared in dividends,
with some hundreds of thousands of francs added to give veri-
similitude.[1]

These considerations need not have a sinister significance. The
first thought of an American depositor who is told that his banker
is " doctoring " his balance sheet would be that the bank is
insolvent, and that *losses* are thereby being concealed. It would
appear more probable that the French banks were concealing
profits to the extent that such considerations moved them at all.
In 1900, an officer of the Crédit Lyonnais, replying to a stock-
holder's question, declined to give out figures on the ground that
the banks were subject to heavy taxation, and it would not be

---

[1] *L'Information*, April 12, 1905; *ibid.*, May 9, 1905. Quoted by Lysis,
op. cit., page 62.

wise to reveal them![1]   But probably the fundamental reason is one which great private bankers in many countries would sympathize with: banking is a delicate matter; it is not well for the uninitiated to know too much about it; secrecy and privacy are the banker's right.   Much is said in France about the necessity of guarding secrets from competitors—a defense that evokes a good deal of sarcasm from those critics of the French " money trust " who maintain that all the great private banks work in perfect accord.

Enough has been said to make it clear that, in general, statistical materials for the study of French banking must be inadequate, and that to a very unsatisfactory extent we must rely on information which lacks quantitative exactness.   This is especially true during the war period, as the method of making up the balance sheets has been altered, so that comparison with previous figures is very difficult.

Certain general contrasts between American and French banking will perhaps serve best to get the French system before us. This contrast will be more effectively made if we think of both systems as they stood in 1914, before France was torn by war, and before our federal reserve system was inaugurated.   Subsequent pages will deal with the four years that have passed since then.

A familiar contrast is that between centralized and decentralized banking.   French banking is highly centralized, while in America there were over twenty-five thousand independent banking institutions—most of which were and are really independent. The great central bank, the Banque de France, holder of the great gold reserve, monopolist in the field of note issue in France, standing ready to rediscount the paper of the other banks at any time, dealing chiefly with the banks rather than directly with the people, closely allied with the state, the reliance of the state in

[1] Lysis, *op. cit.*, pages 80-81.   It is very difficult to make much out of the annual reports to stockholders.   They deal largely in banal generalities —a practice not unknown to American corporation officials.   Lysis quotes Paul Leroy-Béaulieu as follows: " Il faut bien le dire, la méthode ordinairement suivie en France et peut-être ailleurs pour les rapports de la direction avec les actionnaires est une méthode toute illusoire.   Elle ne donne aucune garantie de bonne gestion."   Page 89.

times of emergency—this feature of French banking, wholly lacking in 1914 in the United States, is familiar enough to American students. But French centralization goes far beyond that. Apart from the Banque de France, there are some four or five other great private banks which do most of the banking business of the country. Chief among these are the Crédit Lyonnais, the Société Générale pour Favoriser le Développement du Commerce et de l'Industrie en France (commonly known as the Société Générale), the Comptoir d'Escompte, the Crédit Industriel. The first three really stand in a class by themselves, as *the* great credit houses. These banks all have numerous branches scattered all over France (except that the Crédit Industriel confines itself to Paris). The Société Générale has 1,000 branches. The Crédit Lyonnais has branches, not only in France but in Russia, where "Lyonski Kredit" is a familiar name, in the Balkans, in almost every part of Europe, and in other continents. Other French banks also have foreign branches. In recent decades, these great credit houses have rapidly absorbed or driven out of business the independent provincial and local banks, although there remain strong institutions among these, whose relative position has been somewhat strengthened by the events of the war.[1] In general, however, a local bank in France is a branch of a great Paris institution, receives instructions from Paris, is manned by men sent out or chosen from Paris, and is subject to little control by local business men or local authorities.

The institutions so far named deal directly with the people, and especially receive deposits of almost all sizes from the general public. There is, however, another institution, less conspicuous than those named, but probably as powerful as any of them, namely, the Banque de Paris et des Pays-Bas. This institution does not receive the deposits of the general public or discount commercial paper as a regular business. Its nearest counterpart in the United States would be J. P. Morgan and Co. Its power, very great, is commonly exerted indirectly, through its relations with other houses. Its own operations are largely in the field of foreign exchange, security underwriting and marketing, handling

[1] See the summary in the London *Economist* of August 11, 1917, page 209, of an interesting study of French provincial banks by Léon Barety.

the deposits of certain great corporations in whose securities it deals, etc.

Most of these institutions are supposed to be bound together by close understandings, and to work in close harmony. No such charges of a "money trust" have ever been brought in the United States as have been made by French critics of these institutions. The nature of this cooperation will best be considered when we take up the kinds of banking business done in France.

But the centralization has gone much further than this. In America, there are many thousands of independent savings banks, each, under general laws and some State supervision, free to make its own investments. In France, virtually all the local savings banks (*caisses d'épargne ordinaires*) are required to turn over the funds deposited with them to a great central state institution, La Caisse des Dépôts et Consignations, which makes the investments for them, chiefly in the *rentes,* the long time obligations of the French Government.

In the midst of this centralization, the independent local banks have themselves felt it necessary to combine. Many of the provincial banks are themselves possessed of numerous branches. There are altogether some 2,700 or more of local and provincial banks, many of them insignificant in size. In 1905, 325 of them formed a protective union, the Société Centrale des Banques de Province, which also carries on in Paris a banking business, chiefly concerned with the huge security operations which are concentrated there.[1]

One great institution, the Crédit Foncier, with branches throughout France, does most of the mortgage loan business in the cities. It was anticipated, at the time of its organization, that it would supply agricultural credit largely, but this it has done to a very slight extent. Agricultural mortgages in France are chiefly taken by individuals, rather than by institutions, and French agricultural lands are not heavily mortgaged.[2]

[1] Laughlin: *Credit of the Nations*, New York, 1918, page 147.
[2] I am indebted to Dr. J. E. Pope for information regarding agricultural credit in France. Dr. Pope states that it is virtually impossible, with data now accessible, to give an account of war changes in this field.

Next to its highly centralized character, we should perhaps mention the important rôle of bank notes in French banking as a feature marking it off from American banking. Notes of the Banque de France have been the main means of making payments in France. Checks drawn against deposit accounts have had a very limited use. This generalization is one to which we are accustomed. The situation is, however, more complicated than this simple generalization would imply, and there seems to be some misunderstanding even among French writers who have been advocating an extension of the check and deposit system during the war as to the significance of the contrast.

In America, we are accustomed to the doctrine that deposits grow out of loans, in very large degree. A bank, making a loan to a depositor, gives him, not cash or bank notes, as a rule, but a deposit credit. Against this he draws a check, which is deposited by the one to whom he gives it, leading to a transfer of the deposit credit on the books of the bank, if both are depositors of the same bank, or, through familiar clearing house machinery, to a deposit credit in some other bank, without actual transfer of cash between the banks to any considerable percentage of the amount involved. Deposits with us, in other words, are a fabric built up largely by the creation of new bank credits, transferred by check, rather than due to the actual " depositing " across the bank's counter of actual " money " (gold, silver, greenbacks, national bank notes, gold and silver certificates, etc.). If we did not use checks, if we could borrow from the banks only coin or bank notes, and if only one bank in the country had the power to issue bank notes, it is not easy to see how deposit banking could be a very important matter in this country. And yet, deposit banking is very important in France. In France proper, only the Banque de France can issue notes. (The Banque de l'Algérie, chartered by the French Government, is also a bank of issue, privileged to issue about 300,-000,000 francs in notes before the war.) But the great private banks have, in their " deposits " and " *comptes courants* " (on the liability side) many billions of francs. For the Banque de France itself, on February 12, 1914, the " *comptes courants* " (liability) [1] in Paris and branches amounted to 695,000,000 francs. This looks small when compared with the 5,845,000,000 francs of note issue shown by the same statement of the Banque de France, and would make it appear that the main form in which that bank extends credit is clearly in note issue. But it must be remembered that to a large extent the notes of the Banque de France were before the war really little more than gold, or coin, certificates. On the date in question, the Banque de France held a metal cover for the notes of 4,222,000,000 francs, the great bulk of which was gold. Only the " uncovered " part of the note issue could thus represent a real extension of new bank credit. This uncovered note issue amounted to only 1,623,000,000 francs on the date in question, an amount larger, indeed, than the current accounts of the Banque de France by nearly a billion francs, but still a very small amount when compared with the deposits and current accounts of all the French banks, including the Banque de France itself. The Crédit Lyonnais alone, for example, at about the same time (December, 1913) [2] showed deposits and current accounts (liability) combined aggregating about 1,220,000,000 francs, an amount which is only four hundred millions short of the uncovered note issue of the Banque de France, and which, combined with the current accounts of the Banque de France, exceeds the uncovered note issue by nearly three hundred millions. If deposit banking can represent real extensions of new bank credit only in connection with checks, and if the chief form of credit extension in France is by means of the bank note, we have some curious phenomena to explain.

There is a real problem here, from the standpoint of one familiar only with American or English banking, if the statements commonly made about checks and bank notes in France are to be accepted. And first, it must be observed, that the use of checks in France, even before the war, was by no means so limited as many have supposed. To be sure, the *concièrge* and

---

[1] Unlike many of the French banks, the Banque de France shows no "*comptes courants*" on the assets side. The term " deposits " would be used by an American bank to describe this item in the Banque de France statement.

[2] London *Economist*, May 23, 1914, page 1254.

the small tradesman would commonly have nothing to do with checks. To be sure, the general practice, in paying house rents, in paying retail bills, in paying wages, in paying taxes, and in many other places where an American would unhesitatingly draw checks, was to pay with bank notes or coin. Even large payments were often made by bank notes. The use of checks was, and is, a thing little known among the masses of the people in France. Indeed, the " woolen sock," in which gold itself, rather than bank notes, was hoarded, is a long standing tradition in France, and hard money, rather than either notes or deposits, has been a large factor in French life. But it by no means follows from this that large business transactions, and stock market transactions, have not freely availed themselves of the convenience of the checking system. To a very large extent, they have done so. No such study has been made in France of the use of credit instruments in payments as that which has been made in this country by Dean David Kinley.[1] One can only rely on general statements made by men who can speak authoritatively from first hand knowledge of French banking. But the author, on the basis of such information, is quite confident that the use of checks has been much more extensive in France than has been generally stated in English and American books upon the subject.

In the United States, as Kinley's figures show, over 90 per cent of all payments are made by check, rather than coin or paper money. Over 50 per cent of all retail payments are made by check; about 30 per cent of wages are paid by check; and over 90 per cent of wholesale business is done by check. No such high proportions could be found for wholesale, retail or wage payments in France. But Kinley's figures also make it clear that retail and wholesale payments combined constitute only about one-fourth of the payments made in the United States. The bulk of our payments is listed in his figures under the head of " all other," and these " all other " payments are found, on analysis, to be concentrated in the great centers of

[1] *The Use of Money and Credit Instruments in Payments in the United States,* National Monetary Commission Report.

speculation and finance, notably New York City itself.[1] France is also a country where financial and speculative operations are carried on on a vast scale, and the men who carry them on are by no means ignorant of the convenience of the checking system.

In the second place, it must be pointed out that the check is by no means the only instrument for mobilizing deposit credits, and making it possible to utilize the deposit as a means for extending new bank credit. In Germany, where also it has been supposed that the bank note, rather than the deposit, is the chief means of payment, we find the " giro system," under which a depositor instructs his bank to transfer to some other person, perhaps in a different city, a deposit credit, performing a service similar to the checking system. It is dependent in part on branch banking, although it can be worked out through independent correspondent banks as well.

In 1907, the Banque de France made transfers between clients to the extent of 180 billion francs.[2] The Banque de France makes transfers all over France for the government for its private depositors and for the other banks which deposit with it. The other banks will commonly make transfers between branches in a given city, but for transfers between their own branches in different cities they will normally use the machinery of the Banque de France.[3] Here, then, is an enormous body of payments made by deposit credit by a method which is quite as effective as the check for the purpose, without the use of checks.

The annual income of the people of France before the war has been estimated at about thirty billion francs.[4] The total annual retail trade of the country must be substantially less than that.

---

[1] *Cf.* the present writer's *Value of Money*, Macmillan, 1917, chaps. 13 and 19, for an analysis of Kinley's figures.

[2] National Monetary Commission Report: *Interviews on the Banking and Currency Systems of England, France, etc.*, Senate Document No. 405, 61st Cong., 2d Sess., pages 204 and 240.

[3] To a considerable extent, these transfers take the place of clearings among the other banks and their volume explains the insignificant volume of operations of the Paris clearing house. *Cf.* Patron, *Bank of France.* National Monetary Commission Report, pages 71-75.

[4] Helfferich's estimate, quoted by Laughlin, *op. cit.*, page 194.

In America, Kinley's studies,[1] referred to above, would show that wholesale trade is about twice as great as retail trade, in pecuniary magnitude, if payments are a test. If this should be true also of France, the total of French wholesale and retail trade before the war could not exceed ninety billion francs per year and hence these bank transfers would be double the total wholesale and retail trade of France. To assume that the five billions of bank notes in France made as many payments as the 180 billions of transfers made by the Banque de France alone during the year, one would have to assume that the bank notes have a " velocity of circulation " of thirty-six times per year.[2]

Deposit and current account banking, then, is obviously a large factor in France, and the notion that notes constitute the chief medium of payments must be seriously challenged. That notes and coins are used in the major *number* of transactions is doubtless true. It would probably be true in the United States. But that notes and coins are used in making the major part, *in pecuniary magnitude,* of the payments in France is probably untrue. Transfers, by check or bank transfers, of deposit credits and current account credits, were probably quantitatively greater than note payments before the war.

But there is yet another highly important, even though unmeasurable, substitute for notes and coins in payments in France, little used for a generation in the United States (though very important here two generations ago) and that is the bill of exchange or acceptance. The wholesaler, sending a shipment of goods to a retailer, instead of receiving a check or cash in pay-

[1] This comparison is rough and inexact, partly because of the assumption that the proportions of wholesale to retail trade are the same for France as for the United States, and partly because of uncertainty as to the relation of *payments to trade. Cf. Value of Money,* chaps. 13 and 19. For the purpose in hand, however, the figures given do not understate the magnitudes of wholesale and retail trade, because the whole national income is allowed to be spent at retail, and because it is assumed that payments bear the same relation to wholesale trade that they do to retail trade. In fact, payments are more likely to represent duplications, speculations, and loans and repayments, in wholesale than in retail business.

[2] *Cf.* the studies in velocity of circulation of Kemmerer, Fisher and Pierre des Essar. Fisher places the " velocity of money " for the United States at from nineteen to twenty-two times a year. Kemmerer's estimate is about twice as high. Fisher appears to me to have made the better estimate, though the whole problem is a baffling one.

ment, draws a bill on the retailer, either " at sight " or on thirty, sixty or ninety days' time, and this bill, "accepted " by the retailer, becomes the latter's promise to pay. It may then be used by the wholesaler in making payments to some one else—a practice probably more common in Germany than in France, and much more common with "bank acceptances " (to be described in a moment) than with "trade acceptances " (the transaction just described). In any case, the drawing of the bill, and the accepting of the bill, in themselves constitute final payment for the goods.[1] Frequently the wholesaler will draw, not on the retailer himself, but on the retailer's bank, and the " acceptance " of the retailer's bank makes the instrument a " bank acceptance." In the figures given above for the balance sheet of the Crédit Lyonnais, *"acceptations"* appear at 180 million francs—a liability of the bank, much of it, presumably, on customers' account. An acceptance of the Crédit Lyonnais can be used by the drawer for many purposes. He can discount it with his banker, and get a deposit credit, or bank notes, in return. It can be freely rediscounted by the banker at other private banks, or at the Banque de France. The wholesaler himself, if a depositor with the Banque de France, can discount it there. Or, the wholesaler may use it directly as a means of paying his own debts to other business men, passing it on at the market discount—a discount which may not always be required. An acceptance by a well known bank, with only a few days to run, would be virtually a certified check, so far as serving as a medium of exchange is concerned.

Our problem, then, ceases to be quite as baffling as it at first appeared. There is a wide extension of new bank credit under the deposit system in France. Checks are used. And deposits can be made mobile without them by bank transfers. The bank acceptance, and even the trade acceptance, are in part credit substitutes for notes and cash as media of exchange. In addition to the uncovered note issue of the Banque de France, there

---

[1] Of course, the bill itself has yet to be paid. This may require bank notes or a check. But it may be accomplished by an offsetting bill. And the bill may pass through several hands, paying for goods several times, before being paid.

is a very substantial body of real bank credit, growing out of bank loans, serving as the counterpart of our own elastic bank deposits.

But this is not the whole story. To an extent that is almost incredible at first blush to the American student, it is true in France that "deposits" really are deposits in the primitive sense—that they represent real savings put in over the counter, in the form of coin, bank notes and credit instruments, which come in payment of net income, rather than as part of the gross income of the active business man. It is true to a very high degree in France that loans grow out of deposits, rather than that deposits (as in England and America) grow chiefly out of loans. For individual banks, or even communities, this is often true in the United States. There is, for example, a bank in Cambridge, Massachusetts, whose depositors include few important active business men. The retail merchants at Harvard Square deposit with it, but for the most part, its deposits come from students and teachers of Harvard University, and from people whose incomes, often large, are chiefly derived from stocks and bonds or other investments. It can not possibly lend all its deposits to its own depositors. It goes outside, buys commercial paper from other cities, lends to Boston brokers on collateral security who are not among its depositors, buys securities, etc. To be sure, the checks deposited with it would not be nearly so great in volume if other banks, in other places, were not making loans. It is part of a larger system in which deposits grow largely out of loans. But by and large, so far as its own balance sheet is concerned, its loans result from its deposits, rather than the reverse.

Now France occupied before the war, in the general world credit system, much the position of this Cambridge bank in the general banking system of the larger community. The depositors of French banks are real capitalists, recipients of income from which they save substantial amounts, rather than active business men who rely on bank accommodation for carrying on their businesses. The French are notoriously a thrifty people, and their surpluses constantly overflow their own boundaries, seeking investment abroad. In France, the bankers do really lend out their deposits, instead of chiefly creating their deposits by lending. Indeed, the deposits of French banks in general are very much like the deposits of our savings banks. The active business man has a " current account," rather than a deposit. A careless reading of the balance sheet of the French banks, however, might lead one to overestimate the relative importance of " deposits " as compared with " current accounts." In America, when a business man borrows from his bank, he will receive a deposit credit for the whole amount covered by the agreement, which will appear as a liability of the bank in its balance sheet. In France, under the " current account " system, the more common practice will be for no entry to appear in the bank's books at all until he actually draws against his account, and he will only gradually draw the whole of his loan. This will lead to an asset item on the bank's books. The main way in which current accounts, as a liability, develop on the bank's books will be by the actual depositing of items coming in from outside the bank, canceling the borrower's indebtedness and building up a surplus to his credit. One difference between the two systems, therefore, is that the French method leads to smaller figures on the bank's balance sheet than the American system, for a given extension of credit, and that the importance of the loan and deposit business of French banks, as compared with American banks, is not adequately presented by a mere comparison of balance sheets. The difference is largely a matter of form and bookkeeping methods. The economic substance is not altered thereby. This consideration does not, however, remove the fact that French loans grow chiefly out of the capital and deposits of the banks, instead of the deposits growing out of the loans.

In the fact that the French in general deposit more than the banks lend in France, and in the consequent overflow of French funds into foreign investments, we have one of the most interesting and distinctive features of the whole French system. In the fate of these foreign investments during the present war, we have the most tragic episode in the whole financial chronicle of the war period in France.

For many years before the war, the French banks were marketing to their customers, through their numerous branches, enormous quantities of securities, largely foreign securities. It is not easy to get exact figures of the extent of this, but that a billion and a half francs of French savings were in one form or another sent abroad in an ordinary year is not improbable. This was perhaps two-thirds to three-fourths of the total annual savings of the French people. To an ever increasing extent, the outside world was becoming indebted to France. Annual payments of interest and dividends, steadily increasing, turned the balance of international payments more and more in favor of France. Part of this France took in the form of gold, and the Banque de France built up a vast gold reserve. This gold reserve stood at the outbreak of the war at over four billion francs. Partly this great reserve seems to have been built up, as a matter of deliberate policy, as a war chest. From 1899 to 1910, the Banque de France increased its gold reserve by 75 per cent, while its discounts and advances increased only 5 per cent. Part of her excess foreign credits France took in the form of goods—the physical " balance of trade " was regularly " against " France, which means, merely, that as a rich capitalist nation she was able to consume more than she produced at home. But a very considerable part of her income from abroad she reinvested abroad, adding ever to her creditor position, and constantly increasing the back flow of titles to goods produced by other peoples. In her huge gold reserve, and in her great store of claims on the wealth of the outside world, France felt herself well provided against the war which she feared her brutal and arrogant neighbor was preparing to force upon her. She could live and fight upon her capital accumulations. Her surplus, if she could weather the military shock, would enable her to outlast her formidable opponent economically. It seemed a strong position. France felt secure.

But the position had its weak points, which French critics, to say nothing of German and English critics, had vigorously pointed out before the war. Chief among these French critics was the redoubtable Lysis—a pseudonym which many have supposed represents the distinguished editor of *La Révue,* Jean Finot. At all events, Finot stands sponsor, in a preface, for the book "*Contre l'Oligarchie financière en France,*" [1] which first appeared as a series of articles in *La Revue,* running from November 1, 1906, to November 15, 1907. The book is certainly written by an ardent patriot, a clear thinker and a man wonderfully well informed about French money, credit and banking. It hangs together, and it carries conviction. It has been easy to verify many of its contentions by conversations with English and American financiers familiar with the operations of the ,French banks, and in every way friendly to France. The course of the war has itself been a sad fulfilment of many of Lysis' apprehensions.

Has it been well for France that so much of her savings were sent abroad, if French industry was thereby starved of the capital needed for its development? Was France better off, even with good foreign investments, than she would have been with a strongly developed industry, which would have enabled her to produce within her own borders the goods she needed for the war? Is it well with a nation that its people are largely capitalists and agriculturalists, instead of active *entrepreneurs* and factory laborers, when a great war comes?

It will not serve to answer that capital seeks the best market, that the thing is settled by impersonal economic law. That would be true in a country where banking is decentralized, and where many competitive agencies are offering investments to the people. But in France the decision has been made by a few great private banks, on whose judgment their numerous depositors almost wholly relied. And these great private banks, nominally competitors, have in fact been closely associated, following a common policy, and often sharing openly in the same marketing operations.

---

[1] Douzième Edition, Paris, 1908. Aux Bureaux de *La Revue.* See also Kaufmann, E.: *Das französische Bankwesen mit besonderer Berücksichtigung der drei Depositengrossbanken,* Tübigen, 1911 : and Mehrens, B.: *Die Entstehung und Entwicklung der grossen französischen Kreditinstitute,* Stuttgart, 1911, for the same general view.

Officials of the Crédit Lyonnais, testifying before the American National Monetary Commission, had this to say:

A. There are two kinds of such operations: first when the Crédit Lyonnais is alone interested in the operation; and second, when others of the Paris bankers are interested with us. The largest recent issue, in connection with other bankers, was the five per cent Russian loan of 1906 of 1,200,000,000 francs. What is very important in our way of floating a loan is that the sales are made in small quantities; the transaction is completed in a very few days, and each of our customers buys only the number of bonds corresponding to his investment requirement.

Q. As a matter of fact, anything you recommend they will buy?

A. Yes, and even with a very large issue; the bonds do not remain long in the market, because in our country savings are very extended. Everyone saves his money. The small savings of France are the wealth of the country. By examining the balances of accounts of our customers we can know whether they want to invest or not, and then we endeavor to have stocks and bonds to offer them as they require them: but that is variable, and sometimes we might have a large issue, forty or fifty million francs, taken up by the public in a few days.[1]

In reply to further questions, it developed that the French banks are much like bond houses in America, and handle virtually all the security business of France. Most of their operations are in securities which they sell on commission, rather than in securities they own. When asked as to the amount of the commission, the only information they vouchsafed was: "Naturally the commission varies."[2]

Lysis supplies more detailed information regarding the commissions. On the 800 million franc issue of Russian 5 per cent Treasury notes of 1904, the margin was 10 per cent. On the 62,500,000 franc issue of Morocco in the same year, the profit was at least 18¾ per cent. The profit is rarely less than 5 per cent of the selling price of the issues.[3] The Russian 5 per cents of 1906, the enormous issue which was mentioned in the testimony of the Crédit Lyonnais above, and whose fortunes during the war we shall follow in later pages, was sold at a profit of over 7 per cent. The Russian Government received

---

[1] National Monetary Commission Report, Senate Document No. 405, 61st Cong., 2d Sess., page 233.
[2] *Ibid.*, page 234.
[3] Lysis, *op. cit.*, pages 24-31.

eighty-three for a bond which the banks sold the people at eighty-eight. But the Russian Government received only eighty-two in reality, since it had to pay 1 per cent of the par value as a further commission to an intermediary of the banks![1]

Doubtless it may be urged that selling expenses are high. They are. They include a good many services which the banks through their numerous branches perform *gratis* for their customers. They include elaborate marketing campaigns. They include, as an American banker who has had dealings with French bankers in this connection states, not merely advertising charges in the press, but also, quite frankly, in one case at least, *subsidies* to the press. The selling costs are high—but need costs be so high for good securities? London can do the thing more cheaply. New York, despite past scandals in connection with underwriting operations, does the thing more cheaply. There can be little doubt that in many of these operations French bankers have shown themselves greedy to a marked degree, and that the greed has been largely at the expense of their confiding clients.

The direction of French investment, then, has been subject, not to the free movement of capital, sent piecemeal, under competitive conditions, by alert individual investors, to those lines of investment which promised the best yield for a given degree of safety, but has been controlled by a few great banks, working to a large degree in harmony, acting for a passive body of depositors, and controlling public opinion through the press. In choosing the investments, these bankers have in no small degree been moved by the fact that certain lines of investment gave them higher commissions than others. But the securities whose necessitous sellers will pay high commissions for are not the ones which a great investing people find it best to hold when the evil days come!

What has been the direction of French investment? To a very large degree, the issues of second rate foreign governments.[2]

---

[1] Lysis, *op. cit.*, pages 48-49, note.
[2] *Ibid., passim.* London *Economist, Supplement,* December, 1914, page 8.

Russian securities have been bought in enormous quantities. Bulgarian state issues have been bought in large amounts. Brazilian issues, not alone of the central government, but even of the municipalities, have been largely bought.[1] These were a poor resource for France when the great war came! Brazil, dependent largely on the price of a single commodity, coffee, for its public revenues, was not in a happy condition when the price of coffee dropped from a high of fourteen cents in 1913 to a low of 5¾ cents in March, 1914! Nor did extensive agricultural loans in Belgium and Austria, for which the banks are little responsible, prove to be the happiest source from which to secure funds quickly when emergencies arose.

In part, evils of this sort are found in every country. No great money market can feel itself wholly virtuous when scandals of this sort are mentioned. But the evils have been accentuated in France, in no small part by virtue of the very centralization of banking, the extensive development of branch banking and the disappearance of the local independent banker, who was interested in local industry, in touch with local needs, and who preferred to put funds where he could watch them, at home. The deliberate policy of many French banks—openly avowed by the Crédit Lyonnais[2]—of keeping local men out of the branches, accentuates this. The investment of banking funds in local commerce and industry requires watchfulness and local knowledge, as well as initiative on the part of the local banker. Branch banking can not be recommended to America on the basis of French experience. Very much of our vigor and economic progress must be attributed to our many thousands of independent local banks.

Of course there are other factors. France is a static country from other causes. The population, already relatively dense, has

---

[1] Professor O. M. W. Sprague states that the French bankers have the tradition that securities backed by the *taxing power*, even of an inferior government, are much superior to any industrial securities. For Professor Sprague's general endorsement of the criticism of French banking here given, see *American Economic Review*, March, 1912, pages 126-129.

[2] Interviews on the *Banking and Currency Systems of England, France, etc.*, National Monetary Commission Report, Senate Document 405, 61st Cong., 2d Sess., page 246.

not been increasing. The people are by tradition conservative in economic matters. Canada has not found that branch banking has stifled her rapid expansion. Canada borrows from her banks, instead of investing through them. Her people are willing to take chances, believing in the resources of an undeveloped country. The French investor has come to feel that only conservative securities should be bought. It is not wholly the fault of the French banker that when he buys securities which yield 7 and 8 per cent, he markets them to his people to yield 4 or 5 per cent. The French investor would distrust a security that yielded more than 5 per cent. He prefers a safe Russian state issue, yielding 4½ per cent, to a French industrial security yielding 6. He is like the New England investor who bought New Haven because the yield was so low that it *must* be safe!

Branch banking in a country which has little capital can exist only if it makes real credit extensions in the localities where the branches are found. But in a country like France, where surplus capital exists in abundance, and where the banks are primarily investing agencies for their depositors, branch banking, carried far, is almost certain to be pernicious. The policy must be worked out by a small set of men in Paris. The loans entrusted to the discretion of branch officials must be mechanically made, under the safeguard of rigid formulae. They are. In Paris great financial operations are planned and executed. But in the branches the operations are chiefly confined to two things: (1) selling to customers the securities [1] selected and recommended by the central office; (2) making the safest kind of discounts on short term commercial bills. French banks are loath to take manufacturers' paper. They are wholly unwilling to act as "sleeping partner" in a manufacturing enterprise (*commandite*). German banks will finance a manufacturing establishment, put a bank official on its board, and give it every assistance. They will buy its securities outright, and hold them as regular investments of the bank. American bankers com-

---

[1] Lysis states that promotion and salary for officials in the branches depend chiefly on their success in marketing securities. *Op. cit.*, page 31.

monly do not buy the securities of small manufacturing corporations, but they do lend to them heavily, often for the purchase of fixed capital, and give them a great deal of supervision and advice. In France the local independent banks and the provincial banks with branches have done this, but the great credit houses which dominate French banking refuse to do it. Within France, in the matter of loans and discounts, they play the safest sort of game. Some short time industrial paper they will take, covering a small part of the circulating capital of a manufacturer (work in process, raw materials), but chiefly they insist on true commercial paper, growing out of the actual movement of goods. Even mercantile credit is extended grudgingly. " Our theory is that every merchant ought to have capital enough to go on by himself in normal times, but there are times in the busy season— say three or four months—when he will need more capital, and then he comes to us and we lend him money under this item [*comptes courants*]." [1] No doubt the German banks have overdone this matter of financing manufacturers, and their assets were not as liquid as bankers' assets ought to be. But the French bankers in their extreme conservatism have gone to absurd lengths in the other direction, while taking wild risks for their customers in investments outside of France.[2] Part of it, no doubt, is to be explained by the simple consideration that it is easier for a small group of busy gentlemen to give attention to the annual budgets of foreign states, involving millions and billions of francs at a time, once a year, than to watch piecemeal weekly and monthly details of many smaller businesses scattered throughout France. The financing of industry requires care, attention, discrimination. But strict commercial banking based on documentary bills can be trusted to subordinates under rule of thumb.

French banks hold very much short time paper of foreign banks. They lend to the New Orleans banks to help move the cotton crop. They were, down to 1911, lending a great deal to German banks, which enabled the German banks to finance

<hr>

[1] Statement by Crédit Lyonnais, in *Interviews on the Banking and Currency Systems of England, France, etc., loc. cit.*, page 231.
[2] London *Economist*, Supplement, December 19, 1914, page 8.

German industry more generously, and led to the building of factories in Germany which could not otherwise have been built, which Germany has turned to good account in the present war. When France recalled these loans at the time of the Morocco trouble in 1911, Germany was financially embarrassed—but the physical factories and equipment remained on German soil! Had France continued the practice till 1914, Germany would not have been even financially embarrassed by a French effort to recall the loans—she would simply not have paid them![1]

It is proper to call attention to the fact that the Banque de France itself has been free from responsibility for these foreign investments. It has been a high minded public institution. It has limited its profits greatly by its huge gold accumulation. It has properly limited its assets to liquid items (including short loans on collateral security of specified types to the bourse). It has retained at every step the confidence of the French people. Indeed, one of the severest arraignments of the great credit houses in France for their policy of sending away French capital and starving French industry came recently, in a debate over the renewal of the Banque's privilege in the French Chamber of Deputies, from a leading defender of the Banque de France, M. Candace. Early in July, 1918, M. Candace reiterated virtually all of Lysis' main contentions.[2]

[1] The writer ventures to refer here to his discussion of the policy of English, American and German banks in the financing of industry, in the chapter on " Bank Assets and Bank Reserves " of his *Value of Money*.
[2] London *Economist*, July 13, 1918, page 42.

CHAPTER III

The Outbreak of the War in France

This long discussion of French banking before the war has
been necessary for an understanding of the course of events
since the war began. And it has been particularly necessary
since much of what has been written in America about French
banking has been based on an uncritical acceptance of the
encomiums which much of French financial literature has for
decades been pronouncing upon the French system. As regards
the Banque de France, these encomiums have been deserved. But
serious reservations must be made for not a few of the great
credit houses.

For two years before the war France had been suffering from
depression,[1] growing in no small part out of the general policies
which we have been discussing. French industry was languish-
ing. The bourse was sagging and breaking under the discovery
that many of the foreign loans were precarious. The Balkan
wars had weakened the market in Balkan securities and had led
to further apprehensions of war. The state too had had its
share in bringing about the depression. The French Government,
under the influence of radical parties, had been increasing its
budget rapidly, and the public debt was very heavy—well over
thirty billion francs—five times that of Germany and twice that
of England.[2] (This comparison is unduly favorable to Germany,
since German municipalities, especially the smaller cities, had
much heavier debt burdens than French municipalities.)[3] Further, there was great political instability throughout the first half
of 1914. Ministries were dissolving frequently. The passage of
the budget was delayed long beyond the normal time. The radical

---

[1] London *Economist*, August 15, 1914, page 321; *ibid.*, Supplement, December 19, 1914; *ibid.*, June 13, 1914, page 1444; *ibid.*, July 18, 1914, page 125.
Die Bank, June, 1914, page 703. Laughlin, J. L.: *Credit of the Nations*,
New York, 1918, page 156.
[2] Laughlin, *op. cit.*, p. 155.
[3] *Vide Die Bank*, September, 1914, page 895.

parties were insisting on bringing in the dreaded income tax, and additional taxes on securities, as a means of financing new social legislation without further reliance on public loans. It is not easy for an American or English student to understand how dreadful this proposal appeared to the more conservative elements in France. But one who will run through the editorials of Paul Leroy-Beaulieu in the *Economiste Français* for the first half of 1914 may well get the impression that the end of the world was at hand. At all events, fear of taxes was clearly a great factor in the depression, and it is well to understand this attitude in evaluating French financial policies during the war period which follows.

On July 1, 1914, there were only 116 blast furnaces in operation in France. Fifty furnaces were shut down.[1] Manufacturing output in many lines was curtailed. The weather in July was causing serious apprehensions regarding the crops. The Balkan state securities had fallen on the bourse. The March, 1914, option in coffee in New York fell to a low of $.0579 per pound, while similar prices prevailed at Havre (as against a range of from 8½ to 14 cents in 1913). This, with other difficulties, precipitated a crisis in Brazil, with great weakness in Brazilians on the Paris bourse, and there was weakness in Argentine securities as well. Mexican investments were held largely in France, and Mexico was in chaos. Late in May and early in June, largely as a consequence of the weakness of these securities, those banking houses which had been most responsible for them were in serious troubles. Runs were started. The Société Générale was hardest hit, though some other houses were also affected. Wild rumors were going about. In this situation, the Société Générale took the unprecedented step of asking the Banque de France to send its accountants to go over the portfolio of the Société Générale. This was done, and a reassuring statement was made by the Banque de France, which stopped the runs.[2] German

---

[1] London *Economist*, August 1, 1914, page 231.

[2] *Die Bank*, June, 1914, page 703; London *Economist*, June 13, 1914, page 1444. The Société Générale sent out a circular letter, in June, 1914, stating that by reason of the calumnies which had been spread abroad about them, they had requested the Ministers of Finance to ask the Banque de France to examine their accounts. The letter contains the reassuring statement by the Banque de France.

bankers took a ribald joy in this episode, recalling a similar occasion in 1911, when the Reichsbank had had to perform a similar service for certain of the German houses! Bank shares in France were very weak during this episode and continued weak, suffering heavily in the quasi-collapse that came in the middle of July, when the storm clouds began to threaten. The shares of one great credit house dropped one hundred francs in a single day. Government securities were also very weak, particularly the new 3½ per cents just issued, on which only a small instalment had been paid. These dropped ominously in July, as much as 1.50 francs on the hundred (to 86.62) in one day.[1] Throughout July, to the outbreak of the war, the bourse continued to break, and losses were enormous when the moratorium (which we shall later discuss) was finally proclaimed.

Such was the financial situation with which France entered upon the great war. But there was another side. The Banque de France itself had unshakable prestige. The French people, willing enough to quarrel bitterly over internal problems, and even divided fundamentally over the very foundations of the economic organization of society—for French radicalism goes deep, and the French socialist is often reckoned a conservative by the real radicals in France!—were none the less prepared, despite German intrigue and occasional French traitors, to rally loyally to meet the nation's extreme danger. The very crisis and depression meant that France had unusual supplies of hoarded funds, gold and bank notes, ready for the purchase of the short term obligations which the government early began to issue. In times of crisis and depression investors hold off, waiting for better days, and in France the " woolen sock " was unusually full in July and August, 1914. The initial burden of war finance fell chiefly on the Banque de France itself. The great credit houses played a sorry rôle at the beginning of the war, though they have to some extent redeemed themselves in the later parts of it.

The first shock of the war in Paris, as in London and New York, was felt on the bourse. As long as trading was per-

[1] London *Economist*, July 25, 1914, page 175.

mitted, frightened sellers sought to turn their securities into ready money at whatever price they would bring. The phenomenon was worldwide, and it will be more convenient to describe many of the international phases of it in connection with our account of New York. No great stock market can be weakened without affecting the others. For one thing, many securities are listed on more than one market and some of them on many markets. Selling in these securities, starting in one market, quickly spreads through the action of arbitraging brokers to others where the prices have not yet been broken. Brokers in all great markets have a network of credit relations with brokers in other markets, and if a selling wave in any market goes so far as seriously to jeopard margins, weakness manifests itself in other markets, and in other securities, as banks, uncertain as to the solvency of the brokers, call on them for larger margins, which leads them to call on their customers for more margins, which leads their customers to lighten the load of securities they are carrying, with a consequent decline in prices.

Part of the weakness of the Paris bourse through July was due to weakness in Vienna, in Berlin, in Amsterdam and other centers. Vienna appears to have felt the shock of approaching war first, a fall of from 10 to 12 per cent in stocks taking place there on July 13, preceded by four bear days beginning with July 2. Paris had troubles enough of its own before this, but seems not to have taken the assassination of the Austrian Crown Prince at Sarajevo on June 28 very seriously. From the very moment that this occurred, Vienna was disturbed.[1] In France, on the other hand, there appears to have been little more than a recognition that the situation called for tact and decorum. M. Paul Leroy-Beaulieu, in the issue of the *Economiste Français* next following the assassination, gives editorial expression of sympathy for Austria and her venerable ruler with a degree of courtesy and diplomacy that makes one feel that he was per-

---

[1] The assassination occurred on Sunday and the Monday following was a holiday in Austria. By Tuesday a panic had been averted on the bourse. But between July 2 and 13 there were four days of very heavy selling. *Cf.* London *Economist*, foreign correspondence, Austria-Hungary, Germany and France, for July, 1914.

forming an official duty. But French financial papers continued for a time the discussion of their local problems, particularly the new taxation on securities and incomes, and the causes other than Sarajevo affecting the bourse. On July 20 Vienna had a further heavy decline in stocks. It was July 23 before Paris and Berlin had their real war panic in the stock markets. There had meanwhile been reflexes in the stock exchanges in London and New York. By July 25 selling in both markets, on foreign account, was very heavy. On July 27 the Vienna exchange was closed. The next day Austria declared war on Serbia. Bourses were closed on July 28 in Montreal, Toronto and Madrid. On July 29 the Berlin bourse discontinued quotations. By July 30 the panic had reached London and bourses were closed in St. Petersburg and in all South American countries. The Coulisse (curb market) was closed in Paris on that day. On the same day the Parquet, the official bourse in Paris, virtually suspended selling, although it was not officially closed till September 3, when the French Government withdrew from Paris to Bordeaux. On July 31 the London stock exchange was closed and a few hours later on the same day, four minutes before time for opening the New York stock exchange, the authorities of that institution announced to the anxious brokers that it would not open. Enormous selling orders from Europe and from frightened Americans had accumulated in their hands overnight, selling orders " at the market " (meaning at any price whatever), the " bears " had already covered their short sales, and it was clear that New York alone could not stand the strain of the concentrated selling of a frightened world. On August 1, Germany declared war on Russia, and late at night on August 4, England declared war on Germany.

The decline in prices on the Paris bourse was very great. From July 30 to December 7, when the bourse was reopened, for cash trading only, in Paris, it is very difficult to get quotations that mean much. After the bourse was officially closed on September 3, quotations on the bourse of Bordeaux, and even the Lyons bourse, give some index of conditions, but neither these markets, nor the market at Paris between July 30 and December

7, represented a large enough volume of transactions to be really significant. The following Paris figures will show the effect of the outbreak of the war on certain leading securities:

	June 25	July 23	July 30	Dec. 7
Three per cent rentes	83.65	81.30	82.50	72.50
Russian 5's of 1906	102.00	101.00	95.09	88.20
Banque de France [1]	4,640.00	4,574.00	4,400.00	4,600.00
Banque de Paris et des Pays-Bas	1,520.00	1,295.00	1,160.00	1,000.00
Comptoir d'Escompte	1,029.00	994.00	907.00	650.00
Crédit Lyonnais	1,600.00	1,480.00	1,340.00	1,050.00
Nord Railway [1]	1,718.00	1,270.00	1,240.00	1,300.00

Comment may be made on the practically complete recovery by the Banque de France shares, and on the improvement in the shares of the Nord Railway, whose properties were in considerable degree in German hands, over the interval from July 30 to the reopening of the bourse.[2] As will later appear, the railway had relations with the government which served to protect its shareholders from loss. The further great decline in shares of banks other than the Banque de France will be abundantly explained by the developments between July and December, which we have now to give an account of. The decline in the three per cents of the French Government to 72.50 still leaves them selling at a high price, in consideration of the yield. These securities were slow in getting into line with other securities in the relation of yield to price.

With a bourse demoralized before the war by causes which were not connected with the war, with a two years' period of depression, which had grown progressively worse in the second year, just passed through, with banks weakened, with fiscal derangements of a serious sort, with political turmoil and ministerial instability, France entered the war. In a very short time her most important mining and manufacturing sections in the north and northeast were overrun by the Germans, and Paris

---

[1] Quotations of December 14. No quotations on December 7. *Cf.* London *Economist*, December 19, 1914, page 1070.

[2] There is no significance to be attached to the fact that both of these quotations come on December 14, while the others in this column are as of December 7. Quotations were few on both days and comparison between them reveals no general drift for the week. The main changes from December 7 to December 14 were a rise of fifty points in Comptoir d'Escompte, and a further drop of twenty-five points in Crédit Lyonnais.

was in serious danger. Industries of all kinds were further demoralized throughout France by the mobilization throughout of a large portion of the labor force and by the commandeering of railways for troop movements. It was impossible that the ordinary processes of credit should go on under such conditions.

The bourse was the weakest point. Next in point of helplessness and timidity were the great credit houses, such as the Crédit Lyonnais, Société Générale and others whose character and operations we have been discussing. The state had credit resources, particularly in view of the large sums of hoarded money which were ready for investment in the short term obligations of the state, and very especially because of its relations with the Banque de France. A pillar of strength in the situation, and, indeed, the one really solid element in it, were the unshaken prestige and courage of the Banque de France. Even that institution, however, fell back on extraordinary remedies, and despite its enormous gold reserve it suspended [1] specie payments, and issued its notes, under government authorization under the *cours forcé* (legal tender irredeemable notes). This step was taken on August 5, 1914.

Bankruptcy threatened almost everybody. Few indeed among men active in business or finance had the ready cash to liquidate their debts, when so many of their debtors were unable to meet obligations. The bourse had carried through its settlements readily enough in 1870. It seemed wholly unable to do so in 1914. With the cessation of bourse trading, loans on " reports " (stock and bond collateral loans) made in large quantity by the Paris banks, usually counted on as a liquid asset, became frozen. The banks, moreover, with substantial holdings in securities, particularly the Bulgarian, Brazilian, Mexican, Russian and other inferior securities, which they had been marketing to their depositors in the boom period preceding 1912, and even in the depression following, were faced with heavy losses if they tried in any way to use these assets—for which in fact there was no market at all. Nor was even commercial paper, supposed to be

---

[1] This is a traditional practice of the Banque de France in emergencies—as in 1848 and 1870. One wonders, however, why it deems it worth while to accumulate gold reserves, if it does not expect to use them.

always a liquid asset, in better plight. Industry was demoralized; commerce at a standstill. Few merchants indeed—not to mention those in occupied territory—could liquidate their acceptances at maturity. The pressure was most immediately felt at the bourse and next at the banks.

To meet this situation, a moratorium was proclaimed, first affecting the bourse and the banks, but shortly extended to cover commercial paper, house rents and a very wide range of debts indeed. The general initial scheme of the government for meeting the emergency is thus summarized by the London *Economist* of August 15, 1914:[1]

A. *Economic measures:*
  I. The suspension of import duties on wheat, barley, oats, maize, hay.
  II. Free importation for frozen meats and potatoes.
  III. Embargo on exports of salt.
  IV. Prohibition to export foodstuffs and contraband of war, including all army and navy materials, live animals, motors, explosives of all kinds, cold storage apparatus, nitrate of soda, lead, provisions, transport vehicles, etc.
  V. The organization of relief for the families of conscripts called to the colors.
B. *Financial measures:*
  I. Declaration of a temporary moratorium for bourse and coulisse transactions entered into before August 1, settlement being postponed till August 30. [This settlement was subsequently postponed many times, and remained a vexed and difficult question for a long time.]
  II. (*a*) Depositors in banks with deposits under 250 francs are allowed to withdraw the whole sum; (*b*) above this sum, depositors can withdraw only 5 per cent of the surplus, with a provision that employers of labor may draw what they can show to be necessary for paying the wages of employes on each pay day; (*c*) the moratorium to extend to insurance contracts; (*d*) certain relaxations of the instalment payments due from the subscribers to the French 3½ per cent loan just issued.
  III. Savings banks.—Withdrawals of deposits are limited to fifty francs per fortnight for each depositor.
  IV. The issue, by the government, of twenty franc and five franc legal tender notes.
  V. Suspension of specie payments by the Banque de France.

To these should be added certain further details: The law of August 5, which authorized suspension of specie payments by the

[1] Page 321.

Banque de France (and the note issuing Banque de l'Algérie), raised the limit of note issue for the former from 6,800,000,000 francs to 12,000,000,000 and of the latter from 300,000,000 francs to 400,000,000. These legal limits are always kept well in advance of the actual issue. So far as the Banque de France is concerned, they have never actually restricted issue.[1] During the course of the war they have been raised again and again. For the Banque de France the legal limit was raised to 27 billion francs on February 7, 1918, and on May 3, 1918, it was raised to 30 billions.[2] The limit for the Banque de l'Algérie was raised to 700 millions on May 28, 1918.[3] In these impressive figures for the Banque de France note issue, largely attained as we shall see by the actual note issue, most writers see one of the most ominous features in the course of the four years of the war for French finance, and we have at all events clear evidence of the extent to which the government has leaned on the Banque for its war needs. But this will receive later attention.

By August 9, 1914, the moratorium was extended to all negotiable instruments, except those issued by the public Treasury itself and except checks presented by the drawer. This moratorium, as the moratorium on bank deposits, expected originally merely to give thirty days' delay, was subsequently extended many times, and there remain large blocks of premoratorium bills in the assets of the Banque de France late in the summer of 1918. The problem of the rent moratorium was being debated by the Chamber of Deputies in the summer of 1918 and various schemes were being then proposed for bringing it to an end. The bourse moratorium remained a serious problem for a very long time. It is easy to declare a moratorium; France has found it very difficult to get rid of one! There have, however, been gradual steps taken, undoing the initial rigors, and we shall trace these steps in a later chapter.

The great private banks took full advantage of the moratorium

---

[1] Apparently the only reason for retaining a legal limit on the issue of the Banque de France is that the legislature is thereby enabled to wrest concessions from the Banque from time to time, as the limit is raised.

[2] *Bulletin de Statistique et de Législation Comparée*, May, 1918, page 853.

[3] *Ibid.*, page 887.

on deposits. They were weakened and they were frightened. Protected from the public by the moratorium, they still turned for additional safety to the Banque de France and turned their rediscountable assets into cash on a great scale. The following figures will show something of the extent of this:

CRÉDIT LYONNAIS

	June 30, 1914	May 31, 1915
Cash in hand or with banks	Fr. 231,000,000	Fr. 678,000,000
Bills discounted	1,648,000,000	901,000,000
Loans on securities	356,000,000	262,000,000
Current accounts (asset)	714,000,000	401,000,000

All the leading French private banks present similar figures.[1] The deposits and current accounts (liability) of these banks show a great shrinkage also, while their acceptances fall off very heavily indeed. During no small part of the first year of the war, the extra note issue of the Banque de France scarcely made good the gap left by reduced credit extensions by the private banks.

A fatalistic view of the situation will see in this policy of the French private banks merely the necessary consequence of the moratorium and the difficulties of the bourse. It may be almost as well argued, however, that the difficulties of the bourse and the moratorium were due to the policy of the banks. The banks were, as we have seen, in large measure indeed responsible for the flotation of unsound securities at inflated values, whose collapse placed the bourse in such straits. They may possibly have been so shaken by this that they were helpless when the crash came. If, however, their balance sheets tell the truth, if their " securities owned " were really all comprised in their figures for this item, then they should have been in a position to meet much better than they did the great emergency. It is the duty of banks to lend freely in panic times. It is their duty to pay their depositors on demand. It is only by these measures that panics can be checked and the credit machinery—on which industry and trade today depend—kept going. If depositors are sure that they can get their deposits on demand, they will not make heavy calls on the banks. If solvent business men are sure

[1] *Quarterly Journal of Economics,* November, 1915, pages 73-74. *Cf.* the chapter, *infra,* on the " Private Banks."

that they can borrow what they need to meet their obligations, they will not try to borrow in excess of their needs. It is precisely in such situations that more rather than less bank credit is needed. The banks of America in panics, hampered by absurd legal reserve laws and lacking a central bank at which they could rediscount their paper when reserves run low, have more than once had to suspend cash payment of checks and have had to curtail lending in panic times. But London has proved again and again that these things are unnecessary, that panics can be met and stopped, if only the banks will be courageous enough.

It is easy to sneer at the cowardice of these private banks in France. It may be urged, and with force, that London found this policy hard to carry out in the great emergency of 1914, and that the London joint stock banks likewise curtailed loans, hoarded gold and rediscounted heavily with the Bank of England. It may be noted, however, that the London banks quickly recovered from their fright and, further, that one great trouble in England at this time came from France itself—many London brokers who had funds due from French brokers were unable to pay their debts because of failure to get remittances from France.[1] In London as in Paris the stock market was the weakest point, and the English moratorium, which was soon largely dispensed with, came initially from this weakness. Possibly the shock was so great, the disaster so appalling, the loss from German invasion so great, that no amount of courage on the part of the French banks could have averted the moratorium. But surely it is possible that more could have been done.

M. Alfred Neymarck, in his paper on " French Savings " in the National Monetary Commission Report,[2] makes a comparison of the American and French systems very adverse to us, based on our experience in 1907. If we had had a central bank of issue, he thinks that our crisis could never have occurred. And not a few writers have compared our system with the French system, very much to the advantage of the latter from the standpoint of meeting crises. Americans have taken these lessons

[1] J. M. Keynes: "War and the Financial System," British *Economic Journal*, September, 1914, page 462.

[2] Senate Document No. 494, 61st Cong., 2d Sess., pages 180-181.

humbly and have profited by them.   Surely we have little to be proud of in this matter prior to 1914. But it is exceedingly interesting to see a distinguished French financial authority proposing as a means of mitigating the absolute tie-up of French deposits the remedy which we have repeatedly made use of in panic times—the use of clearing house certificates in payments between banks and the use of checks "good only through the clearing house" as a means of mobilizing deposits! This proposal was made by M. Raphaël-Georges Lévy in *Figaro* of August 22, 1914, and was endorsed by the *Economiste Français*.[1] Nothing apparently came of it, but something has since been done in developing further the Paris clearing house (Chambre de Compensation des Banquiers de Paris), which under a new name has become a factor of some importance. The use of checks has also been sedulously encouraged, as we shall see.

The *Economiste Français* has from the first been of the opinion that the moratorium went to wholly unnecessary extremes. It thinks that the bourse moratorium could have been avoided and that special arrangements, with an assistance fund, the granting of delays in special cases, with informal cooperation of banks and bourse, would have sufficed. The bourse tie-up involved the whole system and stifled industry generally. But the *Economiste* denies that even the moratorium on the bourse and the moratorium on commercial paper justified the moratorium on deposits, because the banks could rediscount with the Banque de France, which could issue notes under *cours forcé*.[2] It seems pretty clear that the banks, other than the Banque de France, showed themselves cowardly and helpless, sought only their own safety, refused to take good checks in dollars or sterling, demanded wholly unreasonable margins and other protection in such loans as they made, and even proved a positive burden, rather than an aid, in the difficult situation. They availed themselves of the rediscount privilege to an exaggerated degree,[3] and then hoarded the proceeds.

---

[1] Vol. 2, 1914, pages 276-277.
[2] *Economiste Français*, August 8, 1914, page 203.
[3] London *Economist*, September 26, 1914, page 529.

One obvious evil growing out of the moratorium, with its complete lock-up of deposits and of the bourse, was the inability of the government to rely on the usual machinery of securing loans. The funds needed for the war came for many months either from the Banque de France directly or else from the notes and gold hoarded by the people, who bought short term notes of the government (*bons de la défense nationale*) partly because there was nothing else they trusted in which to invest.

Some sort of moratorium, at all events, some very extraordinary remedies, were demanded by the wholly unprecedented situation. But France seems to have overdone the thing at every step, and tied herself up in coils from which she has not yet fought wholly free. The major part of the blame for this may well be placed on the great private banks.

CHAPTER IV

Depression and " Réprise des Affaires "

In tracing the history of money, credit and banking in France during the war, we shall give attention to certain large topics, some of which can be treated with considerable detail. Among these are the following: (1) The economic depression that followed the outbreak of the war and the gradual resumption of industrial and commercial activity to which the French have given the name "*réprise des affaires.*" (2) The disturbances in the technique of industry, particularly in the matter of raw materials, labor force and coal, and in transportation, both by land and sea, which have grown out of the war. (3) The moratorium and the efforts to get rid of it. (4) The course of security prices on the French bourse and the main causes affecting them. (5) The rôle of the Banque de France during the war, including an account of its relations with the state, its aid to industry and commerce, its relations with other banks, its gold policy and the main changes in its balance sheet. (6) The effects of the war on the great private banks, the provincial banks and the savings banks. (7) Public finance, with special reference to taxes and public loans, and the reaction of public finance on banking and foreign exchange. (8) The foreign trade of France and the problem of foreign exchange rates and international payments. (9) The changes in the circulating medium in France: the disappearance of gold and silver coin, hoarding, substitutes for coin, the efforts to popularize the use of checks, the extension of the clearing house system. (10) The course of commodity prices in France and the main causes affecting them.

These topics are all interrelated and the order of treatment is more or less a matter of arbitrary choice. It will be convenient, however, to sketch certain general features in large outline before undertaking a detailed treatment of any of them.

There are two main ways of guiding and controlling production and consumption. One is the method of private enterprise, under which individuals and corporations, each seeking individual advantage, move under the stimulus of rising prices to those lines of industry where profits are greatest, or, when prices fall, curtail their production in the lines where profits are being cut. Rising prices tend also to curtail consumption in any line where there is shortage and falling prices encourage increased consumption. If prices in general are rising, but rising more rapidly in some lines than in others, the lines in which they are rising most rapidly will bid up the prices of supplies, labor, etc., and so force the lines where prices are rising less rapidly to curtail because of rising costs. This general peace time system has been analyzed in detail in our treatises on economics, and we feel that we understand it. State activity under this system need not involve any radical alteration in the system. The state may act on commercial principles, buying in the open market what it needs, paying going prices for what it buys and taking its chances with other buyers in the process. In a great war, the state may continue this policy, drawing labor and supplies to the production of what it needs, merely by offering so great a pecuniary inducement that other purchasers are forced to be content with less than they would otherwise have of the products of the country's industry. It was in this way that the North carried on the Civil War. It was in this way that the Spanish-American War was conducted by the federal government. In most wars in the last century down to the present great struggle, this peace time mechanism—private enterprise, economic freedom, industry motivated by free price offers—has been relied upon.

The other great system is the socialistic system, under which authoritative commands from the government are substituted for the lure of prices. Men produce goods because the government drafts their labor; men supply raw materials because the government commandeers their supplies—just as men go into the army, not because the government pays them to do so, but because the government conscripts them. Under this system there is need for a great deal more of conscious public planning than is the case under the system of private enterprise. Under the latter system the prices, summarizing the influence of many individual activities, give a clue whose guidance the individual can follow with a good deal of confidence. The prices are wiser than any individual who helps to make them. There need be nowhere in the social system any single brain which summarizes the whole situation. The economic process goes on, with a large degree of social unconsciousness, even though each individual be clearly conscious of those immediately relevant facts which affect his own personal activities. Under the socialistic system, however, there must be a social brain. It is as if the brain in the human body were supervising the beating of the heart, the flow of the blood, the digestive processes, the metabolic processes. Hitherto, since the development of modern industry, governments have rarely felt themselves strong enough or had an organization well enough developed to venture far in substituting conscious public control for the informal, socially unconscious, private control of industry. In this great war, however, the emergencies have been so great, the need for fundamental reorganization of industry has been so obvious and the ability of private enterprise to make the sudden readjustment has been so doubtful, that there has been a wide extension in all countries of the system of authoritative control.

Part of this has been in the direction of price fixing, which to be effective has also involved control of production and control of distribution of supplies, with, in many cases, actual rationing out of stocks. When prices are fixed, some form of control of consumption and production must go with it.[1] The present study will not deal, except in passing, with price fixing in any of the countries considered. But it must be mentioned as one of the interesting compromises between the system of free enterprise and the system of complete social control.

Practically no country has gone all the way in substituting authoritative control of industry for the price system. Germany has gone further than any other country.

[1] *Cf.* present writer's paper, "Value and Price Theory in Relation to Price Fixing and War Finance," in Papers and Proceedings, Supplement to the March, 1918, *American Economic Review.*

Among measures which have been used to greater or less extent by all of the European belligerents, and most of which have been applied in the United States, we may mention the following: moratoria, or informal substitutes for moratoria,[1] which practically means a temporary pooling of assets and liabilities of private enterprises, to give those most demoralized by the shock of war an opportunity to get their bearings and, if possible, avert bankruptcy; the supplying of credits by the state, or by banking houses acting together in a public capacity, to meet the same difficulty; the supplying of credits or the giving of unusual contracts which afford an unusual degree of safety to the *entrepreneur*, to those enterprises which are called on to provide vitally needed supplies for war purposes—often accompanied by the virtual commandeering of their plants; the public control of capital issues of corporations, including municipal corporations, with a view to limiting credits given to " non-essential " industries, to lessen their competition with the government or with essential industries in the markets for goods and labor; the drafting and regimenting of labor as part of the general system of drafting men for the army—a process rarely carried to its possible limits, and usually accomplished with as little interference with the economic interests of the laborer as possible; the control of transportation, which gives a powerful lever for checking non-essential production and encouraging essential production; the control of basic raw materials, especially coal, steel, copper, cement, etc., to make sure that they go where most needed for public purposes; price fixing, which has commonly gone with this control of basic raw materials, as well as with the control of food and other necessities of life; control of foreign trade, both in the matter of exports and imports; control of gold shipments, sometimes done through government agencies, as the Treasury and Federal Reserve Board in the United States, though more frequently through central banks, as in England and France; conscious public policy exercised in the same general

[1] In the United States, this was limited to the outbreak of the great war in 1914 and then confined to the stock market. There was no formal moratorium, but informal arrangements between the clearing house banks in New York and the stock exchange authorities met the situation.

way with reference to international exchange rates, involving cooperation of all the agencies concerned with gold shipments, imports and exports and public loans, as well as the diplomatic service, and great private banking houses concerned with international loans for private corporations. In this connection it is interesting to note that there have been some international duels fought in the neutral exchange markets, Germans seeking to depress sterling, franc, rouble and even dollar exchange; the English seeking—at times with decided success—to depress mark exchange. The full story of this may later be told and will make an interesting chapter in the history of the war. For the present the writer is able merely to mention it in general terms.

The contrast between Germany and France with reference to the extent to which public control has been substituted for private control will perhaps be the best means of exhibiting the distinctive features of France's economic situation. In the first place Germany, blockaded by the overpowering British navy, saw from the begining that she must make herself self-sufficing and that a radical transformation of her industries was therefore necessary. Control over both consumption and production was early instituted and increasingly strengthened. France, on the other hand, had access to the sea. During the early months of the war her strong creditor position enabled her to make purchases abroad very readily. There was the theory held in France that her capital accumulations invested abroad would enable her to live on her capital during the war.[1] Not only had she great foreign investments, but she also had great stores of " capital " in the form of hoarded billions of francs in bank notes. To be sure, industry was badly off for money, but this was merely because individuals were afraid to venture their funds in industry, not because " capital " was scarce.[2] The state, however, could get this capital on its own short term notes readily enough and make what purchases it needed.

[1] See the interesting article by Kurt Groba, "Frankreichs Wirtschaft, im März, 1917," Schmoller's *Jahrbuch für Gesetzgebung, Verwaltung und Wirtschaft, im Deutschen Reiche*, 41. Jahrgang, Zweites Heft (1917). See also London *Economist*, January 16, 1915, page 107.

[2] London *Economist*, January 16, 1915, page 107.

German writers [1] have made much of the contrast between Germany, the " labor state," and France, the " capitalist state," the former living by her daily toil, resting on the firm foundation of goods and services currently provided, and the latter seeking vainly to live on past accumulations. The contrast is better stated as that between the capitalist state and the *entrepreneur* state. There is not a little in the contrast. But it must be clear that France's greatest economic difficulties after all grew out of the seizure of her richest manufacturing sections by the German armies, and that her capitalist position, even based as largely as it was on the inferior foreign investments we have described, though it has proved inadequate as the basis of a long war, was her only salvation in the early months, when her own industry was so completely demoralized.

Free, then, from the immediate necessity of reorganizing industry at home, France allowed the general industrial situation to drift on old lines for a time and the earliest public efforts were given to the rehabilitation of credit, so that industry might be set going, rather than to a redirection of industry. Very early the phrase " *réprise des affaires* " began to be used,[2] and the ideal involved in this phrase seems to have been the restoration of peace time conditions in the midst of war. This was symbolized by revivals in ordinary trade, including the trade in luxuries, by the increase in railway gross receipts, by the growing shipping statistics, by the return of normal life to Paris. " Paris is itself again " and similar phrases were heard. France was slow in seeing that war could not be conducted on a peace time basis.

There was rational ground in part for the failure to stop the production of luxuries. France exported luxuries to pay for the importation of necessities. And this was seemingly well enough in the earlier period of the war. It could not then have been foreseen that the time would come when even the exhaustless resources of the United States would be strained, when the United States, an ally of France, would be curtailing both the domestic production and the importation of luxuries, when the

[1] *E.g.*, Groba, *loc. cit.*
[2] " La Tendence à une certaine Réprise des Affaires," *Economiste Français,* October 24, 1914, pages 435-436.

labor of virtually the whole world would be needed to repair the terrible wastes of the gigantic war. But this made serious trouble for France in time. With the industrial recovery and with the large earnings of women who had hitherto had their expenditures closely supervised by men, but who now enjoyed unheard earnings which they were free to spend in their own way, there came a great deal of luxurious expenditure in France —by no means confined to the laboring women—especially in 1916. Efforts on the part of the government to suppress luxury were checked in various ways. They were checked by the false economic philosophy of the *réprise des affaires,* which saw in growing business activity in itself a sufficient economic basis for the loans and taxes needed to support the war; and they were checked by difficulties which the government encountered when it undertook to limit the importation of luxuries. If France should restrict the importation of luxuries from other countries, then they would retaliate by restricting the export of French luxuries, on which France relied heavily to offset her ever growing adverse balance of trade.

Meanwhile, as 1916 wore on, the falseness of the business philosophy became increasingly clear. There was, despite business revival, a great shortage of labor, of goods, of coal, of iron and of other things. The balance of international payments turned against France in an ominous way and the franc was at a heavy discount in many neutral markets. The world's shipping, moreover, was increasingly inadequate for the great demands made on it, as the German U-boats made increasingly effective raids upon it. Ribot had tried an ineffective move to check imports of luxuries early in 1916. But the fear of retaliation checked his move, and it was not till the unrestricted U-boat campaign began in 1917 that effective steps were taken. Then England despite French protests checked the importation of French luxuries and France, on March 28, 1917, prohibited all private importations, except as specifically authorized by the state.[1]

Slowly and reluctantly, therefore, France came to the thorough

[1] Groba, *loc. cit.*

and consciously planned industrial reorganization which Germany put into effect at the very beginning. There was enough of governmental interference, as we have seen, at the very beginning, especially in connection with the moratorium. But the movement that followed was a reaction, an effort to get away from the moratorium, to get business free from the toils which the state had thrown around it. The third phase, forced on France, and perhaps not yet thoroughly accepted in France, involved a conscious and comprehensive acceptance of a new philosophy of war economics—the doctrine of goods and services instead of money and business activity; the doctrine of necessities as opposed to the doctrine of " making money circulate."

It will be of interest to trace with greater detail certain phases of the industrial depression and renaissance in France which we have sketched in broad outline. A good deal of statistical material is at hand with which the picture can be made more concrete.

The demoralization of French industry and trade could hardly have been greater in August, 1914. By the middle of that month the government was making inquiries with a view to starting industry again, but it was hampered by many difficulties. not the least being the moratorium. On October 24, 1914, the *Economiste Français*[1] reports that conditions are improving. Paris had been repeopled after the retreat of the Germans. Confidence was returning. Business in luxuries was dull, but was reviving in ordinary lines. Mail was more regular than it had been—there had been intentional delay in the mails for military reasons. Passenger trains and water transportation both on sea and on rivers were still irregular, but much improved.

But business revived very slowly. There was no ready money. The silk trade in Lyons, for example, one of the first industries for which statistics were made public, showed almost a complete prostration. In September, 1913, 765,000 kilogrammes of raw silk were handled there; in August, 1914, only 18,000; in September, 1914, only 60,000.[2] Raw silk was down 25 per cent in

[1] Pages 435-436.
[2] London *Economist*, November 14, 1914, page 883.

price. Through December business was very inactive. There was much unemployment from the very outbreak of the war. The government as quickly as possible organized relief work and a free distribution of food—which was complicated by refugees from northern France and Belgium.

In the coal industry, 192,000 people were employed in the first half of 1914. The figures for August, 1914, are 36,000; for September, 1914, 29,000. The average for the second half year of 1914 is 37,000. This industry, as the metal industry, was of course directly affected by the invasion. The invasion of the Nord and Est probably reduced capacity by 60 per cent. At one time the Germans held fully 80 per cent of the metal industry of France. In September, 1915, about three-fourths of the blast furnaces remained in the war zone.[1]

Railway reports were gloomy in April, 1915. French seaborne trade had declined so sharply at the outbreak of the war that owners of vessels had been glad to have them requisitioned. Tonnage at the port of Dunkirk was 1,000,000 during the first seven months of 1914 and only 200,000 during the same months of 1915. A similar tale appears for Calais and Boulogne, while Cherbourg, which had been a clearing port for great German liners, had 2,877,000 tons in these months of 1914, and only 83,000 tons in 1915. There was, however, substantial revival of shipping for certain purposes by April, 1915, and freights were up.[2]

The labor situation was confused. There was general unemployment in many trades through the latter months of 1914 and through much of 1915. At the same time there was marked labor shortage in certain places, notably agriculture. Scattering figures appeared in 1915, based on investigations by the Labor Department, showing the increase in number of employes in considerable numbers of establishments. Thus, of 32,000 establishments, normally employing 1,070,000 persons, half were shut down in August, 1914, and the group lost two-thirds of its employes. By October, 28 per cent more were open, and 35

---

[1] London *Economist*, September 11, 1915, pages 402-403.
[2] *Ibid.*, May 1, 1915, page 854; September 18, 1915, page 438.

per cent more persons were employed. January, 1915, showed
43 per cent more firms open than August, and 83 per cent more
persons employed. Moreover, in August those firms which continued open were at work only a few days in the week and a
few hours a day. By January they were working full time and
some of them overtime. This was especially marked of course
where government orders were involved, but was not confined to
such firms. The china and glass trade showed a 63 per cent gain
in employes. In January, 1915, all the industries covered in the
investigation were about 20 per cent below normal in personnel.[1]
Later figures, covering a partially different set of firms, 27,000
in number, normally employing 1,100,000 men, showed only
373,000 employed in August, 1914, and 710,000 employed in
April, 1915. Many of those employed at the latter date were
old men, women and boys. In the leather trade, however, the
number employed was only 2 per cent below normal in April,
1915.[2]

These figures are not particularly significant from the standpoint of determining the extent of unemployment. They might
indicate merely that much of the labor was in the army. There
are, however, unemployment figures which roughly coincide with
these figures. Thus, in September, 1914, it was estimated that
258,000 were destitute and out of work in Paris; by March,
1915, this had been reduced to 151,000; by December, 1915, to
80,000, most of whom were in the building trade and in the
manufacture of textiles and finer clothing. By October, 1916,
this had been reduced to 47,000. There was in December, 1915,
no unemployment among mechanics, miners, engineers, etc.
Relief had been made so easy that some were out of work from
choice. At the outset of the war, the monthly charge on the
Ministry of Labor for unemployment relief was 3,200,000
francs; by October, 1916, this had fallen to 800,000 francs.[3] In
the industrial suburbs of Paris, unemployment had dropped 94
per cent. Nearly half the unemployment relief centers in the
provinces had been suppressed.

[1] London *Economist*, March 6, 1915, page 488.
[2] *Ibid.*, June 19, 1915, page 1215.
[3] London *Economist*, January 29, 1916, page 179; October 21, 1916, page 680.

Meanwhile, scarcity of labor had been seriously felt at many points. Female labor was being largely utilized, especially in the munitions factories. By the middle of 1915 there was a recognition that many more men were needed in industry than at the front. In July, 1915, Albert Thomas, Minister of Munitions, proposed a plan for the industrial mobilization of labor along semi-military lines, to prevent strikes and lockouts. The shortage of agricultural labor was very great. New types of agricultural machinery were being introduced to meet the problem and certain troops were given fifteen days' leave to help with the harvest. By the end of 1915, the class of 1917 was being replaced in industry by women, "*réformés,*" men unfit for military duty, etc., while soldiers were being given temporary leave for agricultural work. Skilled workers were being combed out of the army for the more important special work which they could do behind the lines in industry. By January, 1916, despite the fact that 24 per cent of the labor force was mobilized, 81 per cent was at work, showing that 5 per cent of new labor had been obtained, chiefly women and colonial and foreign laborers and refugees. By November, 1917, the figure for labor had reached 98 per cent of normal, despite the mobilization of 24 per cent of the old laborers, indicating a gain of 22 per cent in the labor force. By February, 1918, the labor force actually at work was larger than the prewar normal.[1] To attain this result, however, there had been very heavy drains on the women and colonies. In the munitions plants by March, 1917, the proportion of French was only 46 per cent, the rest being foreigners or colonials, and of the French a large and growing proportion was women.[2]

The figures for railway gross receipts show a marked revival

[1] London *Economist,* October 14, 1916, page 650; November 24, 1917, page 840; February 23, 1918, page 344.

[2] Groba, *op. cit.,* page 373. Groba thought that the best service which America, just entering the war as he wrote, could perform for France would be to send over 200,000 skilled workmen! But France herself was not over-credulous at the outset as to our power to be of real military assistance. Apparently the first thought on the French bourse, after our break with Germany, was that now the drain on the gold reserve of the Banque de France would be checked! *Vide* London *Economist,* February 10, 1917, page 233.

of business after early 1915. The following figures are for the month of September for five leading roads (Etat, A.R., Ouest-Etat, P.L.M., Orleans, Midi) for 1913, 1914, 1916 and 1917:

1913	Fr. 128,250,000
1914	90,741,000
1916	132,996,000
1917	149,087,000

These figures, when broken up, show a decided gain in commercial revenues, as compared with income from military shipments, when 1916 and 1917 are compared with 1914.[1]

Another significant index of revival, on which the French themselves have laid great stress, is the decline in moratorium bills held by the Banque de France and the gain in new bills. The following table shows this:[2] .

1914	Unmatured bills	Moratorium bills
July 23	Fr. 1,541,000,000	
July 30	2,444,000,000	
October 1	2,071,000,000	Fr. 2,405,000,000
October 29	905,000,000	3,282,000,000
November 12	313,000,000	3,771,000,000
December 3	254,000,000	3,587,000,000
December 31	276,000,000	3,351,000,000
1915		
January 28	244,000,000	3,182,000,000
February 25	233,000,000	3,054,000,000
April 1	231,000,000	2,709,000,000
April 29	236,000,000	2,553,000,000
June 3	262,000,000	2,375,000,000
September 2	284,000,000	2,049,000,000
October 28	280,000,000	1,916,000,000
December 2	324,000,000	1,860,000,000
December 30	429,000,000	1,834,000,000
1916		
February 3	469,000,000	1,778,000,000
March 30	395,000,000	1,673,000,000
July 27	440,000,000	1,441,000,000
November 2	576,000,000	1,357,000,000
November 30	645,000,000	1,357,000,000
December 27	620,000,000	1,339,000,000
1917		
February 1	709,000,000	1,319,000,000

[1] London *Economist*, November, 1917, page 860.

[2] *Ibid.*, February 24, 1917, page 390 See also annual report of the Banque de France, January 25, 1917, pages 38-40.

Later figures for these items are:

1917	Unmatured bills	Moratorium bills
July 28 ....Fr.	559,000,000	Fr. 1,194,000,000
December 6	802,000,000	1,146,000,000
1918		
February 14	1,335,000,000	1,124,000,000
August 8	1,002,000,000	1,068,000,000

These figures, especially when taken in connection with data from the great private banks, which we shall later present, do indeed show recovery. But they do not show that bank credit has been extended to industry and trade in France in anything like the degree that it has in England and the United States. The great increase, as we shall see, in bank credit in France has been in the form of advances to the state by the Banque de France.

The figures are also of significance in connection with the gradual emancipation—not yet complete by any means in the summer of 1918—from the moratorium.

Other important developments on the industrial side in France during the war have been in the substitution of hydroelectric power for coal, particularly in the Pyrenees, in Savoy, in Dauphiné and in the Central Plateau. The annual report of the Banque de France of January 25, 1917, speaks enthusiastically of this development. It proves a much cheaper power than coal had been. German writers have minimized the extent of this and it has apparently not been sufficient to avert a real crisis, long continued, in coal.[1]

Certain phases of the philosophy of the *réprise des affaires* have a curious look to one wholly indoctrinated in the " philosophy of goods and services." Thus, France has been very much concerned about the vintage, and wine is the first agricultural product to return to normal after the outbreak of the war. Moreover, wine shipments on the railways were early larger than normal—due of course to the wine ration for the army. The French, perhaps wiser than we, regard wine not as a luxury,

[1] Annual report, Banque de France, January 25, 1917, page 5. London *Economist*, October 14, 1916, page 650. Schmoller's *Jahrbuch*, 41 Jahrgang, 1917, Zweites Heft, pages 360-361.

but as a necessity, and this fact when viewed from that standpoint need not appear strange. It is somewhat strange, however,
to find the French Ministry of Public Works appointing late in
1916 a " Conseil Superieur du Tourisme," preparing for the
rush of sightseers after the war to the battle fields! But plans
were made for enlarging existing hotels, and for wide advertising, and a committee appointed to provide the necessary capital.
The Minister of War was approached—somewhat prematurely—
on the subject of the admission of visitors to the war zone![1]

It is somewhat pathetic to think of the enthusiasm with which
the problem of repatriating the refugees in the zone abandoned
by Hindenburg's retreat was taken up in 1917 in the light of the
events of the summer of 1918.

There is something fine in the institution of a fair at Lyons,
where France could exhibit her new products which were making
her self-sufficient. The first of these fairs was held in 1916 and
had 1,340 exhibitors; the second, held in 1917, had 2,600
exhibitors.

Efforts of the government to promote French shipping, especially by granting credits[2] to builders and purchasers of new
ships, may be passed with a mention. The development of new
blast furnaces and the whole great movement for increased
munitions production, powerfully aided by the state, are matters
which our papers have often mentioned. In connection with the
granting of credits to encourage shipping, it is significant that
this seems to be merely one application of a general principle of
pooling the credit resources of the nation with a view to bringing
all industry to its feet. M. Klotz, Finance Minister, in December, 1917, speaking to a Committee of the Deputies, laid
down the general principle that the nation must be a unit in
meeting the burden of the war and must help to the utmost those
injured by invasion. He laid special stress on the granting of
necessary credits even to firms spared by the enemy, to encourage
production.[3] It appears probable that the policy of governmental

[1] London *Economist*, November 4, 1916, page 868.
[2] See *Journal Officiel*, May 12, 1917.
[3] London *Economist*, December 15, 1917, page 950. October 20, 1917, page
570.

credits to agriculture and industry has been carried further in France than in England and America because of the inability or unwillingness of the ordinary banks in France to extend such credits and that an appreciable part of the " advances to the state " by the Banque de France is due to this cause.

Throughout 1917 and 1918 the *réprise des affaires* has been under the depressing influence of the submarine and of the shortage of shipping, interfering with the export trade as well as with the import trade. It has been hampered by shortage of coal from the first. With normal business activity nearly restored, however, with credit functioning again, and with the government well organized enough to deal directly with industrial problems, substituting authoritative control for the price mechanism where necessary and supplying credits where ordinary business methods could not secure it, the slackening of the business *tempo* was not an unmixed evil. The check on the luxurious consumption which was so strongly marked in 1916 was at all events clear gain. Moreover, the check was not a serious one, so far as the mere activity of business was concerned. The real evils were in shortages of goods. The worst here may have been passed,[1] though the summer of 1918 has been a hard one. It will be convenient to review some phases of the shortage in commodities in connection with the subject of French prices, to which we now turn.

[1] See annual report of the Banque de France, January, 1918.

CHAPTER V

Prices of Commodities in France during the War

General index numbers, covering a wide range of commodities, have not so far as the writer can discover been worked out for France for the first two years of the war. Beginning with the third quarter of 1916 the *Bulletin de la Statistique Générale de la France* has published a quarterly index number, with a base in the prices of 1901-1910, which it compares with Sauerbeck's English prices (the *Statist's* index number). There is also an index number for fifteen commodities, worked out by the same authority, beginning with the first quarter of 1911 and running down through the first quarter of 1915. Between the first quarter of 1915 and the third quarter of 1916, however, there appears to be a complete gap, so far as general wholesale price indexes are concerned. Fragmentary information can be found, however, dealing with special classes of commodities, and certain generalization regarding " cost of living." Much information is contained in the French correspondence of the London *Economist* from time to time.

It may be well to make at this point a distinction between " general commodity prices " and " cost of living." The former is concerned with wholesale prices; the latter is concerned with retail prices and in addition such things as house rents, which vitally affect the family budget. When we speak of " cost of living," moreover, we often have in mind a particular class of the population and most commonly the laborers. Further, neither changes in " general prices " nor in " cost of living " are to be identified off hand with changes in " the value of money." Changes in prices or in cost of living may grow out of changes in the value of money, but they may also grow out of changes in the values of goods. It may happen, moreover, that both causes are operative. The present chapter is chiefly a record of facts—not a theory of causes.

The end of October, 1914, shows little rise in prices, except for certain commodities where there had developed an abnormal scarcity. Chief among these were coal and sugar, both of which came largely from territory occupied by the Germans. The coal supply of Belgium was of course shut off and the occupied territory supplied normally 26,000,000 metric tons, about two-thirds of the normal coal production of France.[1] Beet sugar again was concentrated in northern France and Belgium. Wine, especially cheap wine, was also short outside southern France because of transportation difficulties. These commodities rose in price. But the general list stayed down. Metal prices even fell. Bar copper went down from 200 francs per 100 kilos to 145 francs; tin from 485 francs to 365 francs. Only lead remained steady. These prices are significant of great industrial depression.[2] Raw silk went down 25 per cent in price.[3] The London *Economist* of December 5 reports food prices still low.[4] Beef fluctuates between 1.05 francs per half kilogramme against a May average of .92 franc. Mutton, 1.20 francs in May, was only from .85 franc to 1.05 francs in December. Wheat was slightly below its May price. Flour, however, was somewhat above its May average. The *Economist* of December 12 [5] reports a sharp fall in sugar, following substantial importations. The government bought large quantities of sugar in New York, Cuba and the East Indies. Sugar from Germany and Austria came in *via* Holland and Italy released sugar to France. The high price of sugar brought its own cure promptly.

France was greatly dependent on foreign sources for food and there was a general modification of the tariffs on necessary articles, despite protests from the protectionists. This helped the price situation. On March 23, 1915, the *Economist* reports that bread was cheaper in Paris than in London, because the French Government was selling flour below cost to the bakers,[6] and on

---

[1] Laughlin, *op. cit.*, pages 158-159. London *Economist*, October 31, 1914, page 803.
[2] London *Economist*, November 7, 1914, page 842.
[3] *Ibid.*, November 14, page 921.
[4] *Ibid.*, page 997.
[5] *Ibid.*, page 1033.
[6] *Ibid.*, page 535.

April 24 it states that wine had become cheap again through the marketing of the excellent 1914 vintage.[1] Real estate prices were threatened seriously by the protracted rent moratorium. The price of wheat was giving occasion for concern in May of 1915, and government control of supplies and prices was being put through.[2] The *Economist* of September 4 [3] reports a fairly satisfactory harvest, largely gathered in, with, however, food prices generally higher, except for poultry, potatoes and fruit, which were normal in quantity and price.

By the first quarter of 1915 it seems clear that no great rise in prices had occurred. The Service de Statistique Générale made investigations covering fifteen commodities, by quarters, from the first quarter of 1911 to the first quarter of 1915, inclusive. The index shows: [4]

    1911 (first quarter)..1,015
    1913 (first quarter)..1,018
    1915 (first quarter)..1,105

In the Nord, the rise was somewhat greater, the figures being:

    1911 (first quarter)..1,057
    1915 (first quarter)..1,159

Late in September, the government made admission that extravagant prices had been paid on government contracts because of haste.[5] In October a law was passed putting control of the grain trade definitely in government hands, with maximum prices for grain.[6]

The quantity and price of wine have been throughout the war a matter of great concern to the French. It is interesting to note that the tonnage of wine transported between November, 1914, and July, 1915, was 50 per cent greater than for the same months in the year preceding.[7] Coal, labor and raw materials were all high and scarce in the fall of 1915.[8] The *Economist* gives a

[1] London *Economist*, November 14, 1914, page 806.
[2] *Ibid.*, page 1122.
[3] *Ibid.*, page 368.
[4] These figures are taken from the London *Economist*, April 15, 1916, page 712, and cover only the thirteen most important commodities of the fifteen studied by the Service de Statistique Générale.
[5] London *Economist*, October 2, 1915, page 508.
[6] *Ibid.*, October 23, 1915, page 620.
[7] *Ibid.*, November 6, 1915, page 781.
[8] *Ibid.*, pages 736, 815.

general estimate of the rise of cost of living in its issue of November 27 [1] as about 30 per cent—50 per cent in some parts of France.

By early January, 1916, the sugar situation was really acute.[2] Official quotations of sugar were suppressed and the actual prices went high. Meat had become scarce at the butchers'. Butter, which had sold at 3.26 francs in October, 1913, sold at 4.35 in October, 1915. Cheese during the same period had doubled in price.

The official figures for exports and imports from January to May, 1916, show an adverse trade balance of 1,295,000 francs. These figures are based on 1914 prices. Imports, at 1914 prices, were 3,687,000, and exports 1,392,000. In connection with these figures, the *Economist* of July 29 [3] remarks that the adverse balance would be much greater if account were taken of the tremendous rise in prices of the preceding two years. In connection with similar figures, the *Economist* later undertakes to reestimate the extent of the adverse balance, giving data from which some indication of the extent of the rise might be computed though not with precision. Thus, for the first seven months of 1916 the figures show an adverse trade balance at 1914 prices of 3,419,000 francs; corrected figures would show exports of 2,990,000, and imports of 10,336,000, making the adverse balance 7,346,000. We reach more certain ground in the estimate of the Customs Department for the imports and exports of the first nine months of 1916, where it is stated that articles of import are 90 per cent higher in price than in 1914, and articles of export 50 per cent higher than in 1914.[4]

This gives us an average for the first three quarters of 1916 so far as articles of export and import are concerned. Exports during that period at 1914 prices were 2,516,000; imports 7,381,-000, or more than twice as great. But the imports are much understated, since not all government imports were declared at the customs house. If we weight imports by three, in construct-

[1] London *Economist*, November 6, 1915, page 900.
[2] *Ibid.*, January 15, 1916, page 99.
[3] *Ibid.*, page 189.
[4] *Ibid.*, October 28, 1916, page 823.

ing our average, and exports by one, we shall not be exaggerating imports. The average rise in prices of exports and imports on this basis then would be 80 per cent, as compared with 1914 prices, for the first three quarters of 1916. This takes no account of internal prices. It takes no account of many items needed in a good index number. It is not at all a satisfactory figure to compare with the figures of the *Bulletin de la Statistique Générale de la France,* which begin with the third quarter of 1916. But it may be worth something for this comparison.

The figures of the *Bulletin de la Statistique,* compared with the figures for English prices of the *Statist* (Sauerbeck's series), both reduced to a base of 1901-1910, are as follows: [1]

FRANCE

	1901-1910	1912	1913	1916	1917	1918
Entire period	100	118	116	...	...	...
1st quarter	...	...	...	...	258	370
2d quarter	...	...	...	...	297	384
3d quarter	...	...	...	215	315	...
4th quarter	...	...	...	229	339	...

UNITED KINGDOM

	1901-1910	1912	1913	1916	1917	1918
Entire period	100	116	116	...	...	...
1st quarter	...	...	...	...	223	255
2d quarter	...	...	...	...	240	260
3d quarter	...	...	...	181	240	...
4th quarter	...	...	...	203	249	...

There is a pretty close convergence of the estimates of the two French authorities. The rise over 1913 of the general wholesale index number of the *Bulletin de la Statistique* is about 85 per cent for the third quarter of 1916. The rise for wholesale prices of exports and imports estimated by the customs house authorities for the first three quarters of 1916 is about 80 per cent. Perhaps the figures given will suggest the following rough generalizations: prices of all kinds rose rapidly in France during 1916 and subsequently; prices of articles of import rose more rapidly and higher than other prices; prices of articles of export were lower than other prices.

In connection with the great rise in prices we have seen, it will be interesting to study some of the statistics regarding physical quantities of goods produced or imported, and to see something

[1] July, 1918, page 289. This is the latest number to which the writer has had access.

also of the extent to which economies in consumption have been made use of, voluntarily or otherwise, by the French public. We shall give some account of supplies in foods and in coal and shall refer briefly to consumption.

The following figures for cereal production in France are given out by the Minister of Agriculture:[1]

Year	Wheat Quintals	Millet Quintals	Rye Quintals	Barley Quintals	Oats Quintals
		(In thousands of francs)			
1912	90,991	1,554	12,382	11,014	51,541
1913	86,919	1,490	12,714	10,437	51,826
1914	76,936	1,353	11,147	9,758	46,206
1915	60,610	1,098	8,420	6,920	34,625
1916	55,767	1,079	8,471	8,331	40,223
1917	39,482	879	6,993	8,980	34,462

These figures are ominous. The wheat crop in 1917 was the most deficient in fifty years. The deficient oat crops of 1917 reflected itself by January, 1918, in an extensive slaughter of horses.[2] The whole drift of these figures would lead one to expect a diminution in the meat supply and in the numbers of live stock, which of course are dependent on cereal food. There has been a marked diminution, though it has not been so marked as the reduction in cereal production. The following figures will be of interest:[3]

	Horses	Mules	Bovines	Sheep	Pigs
December, 1913	3,222	188	14,787	16,131	7,035
July, 1917	2,282	150	12,443	10,586	4,200

The meat problem has been a grave one. The whole food problem has been increasingly grave. Increasing restrictions have been placed on restaurants and on the purchases of private families. Meatless days and meatless meals have been tried, milk has been wholly eliminated at times from the menus of public eating places, even when mixed with coffee, the number of courses has been limited—matters which American newspapers have found of interest and have discussed in considerable detail. The end of 1917 was an especially critical period in the matter of bread, in view of the wholly disappointing wheat crop in France and the submarine war. England came to the rescue as

[1] London *Economist*, October 6, 1917, page 496.
[2] *Ibid.*, January 19, 1918, page 83.
[3] *Ibid.*, October 13, 1917, page 535.

far as she could.   America with a short wheat crop had not the
ability to do as much as in previous years, despite the restrictions in America and the vigorous efforts of Mr. Hoover.   The
normal wheat consumption in France is 500 grammes per day
per person.   As a result of desperate efforts, it was possible by
January, 1918, to get the supplies in France back to a point where
300 grammes per day could be assured.   Switzerland, meanwhile,
had only 150 grammes per day, and England, between 225 and
250.   England was exceedingly generous to France.   The English recognized, however, that the habits of the French people
made bread a much more important part of their diet than was
the case in England.[1]   Food conditions continue very bad, even
chaotic, into the summer of 1918, and further restrictions are
being increasingly applied.

A similar story, though one of intensified degree, may be told
of coal.   French coal production was terribly cut at the outbreak
of the war, as Germany seized the best mines.   Throughout the
war, England has been helping her to the best of her ability.
The submarine war made this increasingly difficult.   French
domestic production, though cut heavily at the outset, has increased decidedly since the early days of the war.   As we have
seen, about two-thirds of the normal production was checked by
the German invasion.   Of the mines remaining in French hands
the production was further cut by the mobilization.   In August,
1915, there was still a labor shortage of 40 per cent in the
mines left under French control.   By the end of 1917, however,
the production of these same mines was 40 per cent above the
prewar normal.   With all that both France and England have
been able to accomplish, however, the coal supply of France
remained in 1917 and early 1918 about where it had been in
1916, nearly one-third below the amount normally consumed.
(The normal consumption is about 5,000,000 tons per month.
The 1916 consumption was 3,300,000 tons per month.)[2]

As has been stated before, 1916 was the period of greatest

[1] London *Economist*, November 17, 1917, page 806; December 8, 1917, page
915; February 2, 1918, page 159.   See *Journal Officiel*, December 5, 1917, for
details of the rationing plan.
[2] London *Economist*, May 5, 1917, page 776; May 27, 1916, page 1019;
September 22, 1917, page 424; September 8, 1917, page 357; June 23, 1917,
page 1154; annual reports of the Banque de France, for the war period.

luxury in France. Throughout, the peasants appear to have been thrifty. There are constant references to the hoarding of bank notes in France throughout the war as a matter involving billions of francs. Numerous other . classes, particularly the *rentiers,* those living on fixed incomes from investments, have been exceedingly economical. But in France, as in other countries (though it does not appear that the thing has gone as far in France as it did in Germany or as far as in the United States in 1916) those classes who have profited most by the war industries appear to have spent money freely in luxurious consumption. The laborers have done this, particularly the female laborers and the *entrepreneurs* who had war contracts or who shared in the prosperity growing out of these contracts. There was a great increase in the consumption of tobacco, especially in pipes, during 1916.[1] There was also a great increase in importations of American automobiles, other than those used for war.[2]

There was a good deal of talk about this in France and various efforts were made to enforce economy, as well as to shame the people into it. Some of the methods of coercion have all the legal indirectness of American constitutional law. Thus, there was a prohibition on the wearing of dress suits in state aided theaters.[3] Coal was economized by various measures, including early closing hours for restaurants, limitations on lighting, etc. The people did not take kindly to these measures and at times openly defied the restrictions on the use of gas in their own homes, when it was a matter of heat in the midst of a cold winter.[4] But by and large, there is not evidence enough at hand to justify the general charge of extravagance against the French people at any stage of the war, and barring the year 1916 they may even be credited with general frugality. Their troubles were real troubles, unavoidable troubles, in large degree, and their high prices were due far more to inevitable scarcity than to avoidable consumption.[5]

[1] London *Economist,* August 12, 1916, page 287.
[2] *Ibid.,* June 3, 1916, page 1065.
[3] *Ibid.,* November 25, 1916, page 998.
[4] *Ibid.,* February 3, 1917, page 187.
[5] The luxury taxes, which came into effect in the summer of 1918, produced much less than was anticipated. For July, 1918, the actual yield was ten million francs, against an estimated yield of thirty-two millions. The

The question of causation involved in these price changes need not detain us long here. We shall discuss the general theory of war time prices briefly in connection with American prices, where data are more abundant. The present monograph is chiefly concerned with history, rather than with theory, in any case. It is easy enough to find reasons connected with the abundance or scarcity of individual commodities which indicate the general direction in which their prices will have to move. There is a great scattering of prices, some rising greatly through extreme scarcity and others rising little if at all because abundant in supply. The latter category grows increasingly small as the war goes on and labor scarcity is felt in every field. Goods of almost all kinds in France grew scarce, there was a general rise in the values of goods and hence a general rise in commodity prices. To this general cause there must undoubtedly be added a further rise in prices due to the depreciation of the franc. The Banque de France early ceased to redeem its notes on demand and for four years they have been circulating under *cours forcé*. Prolonged suspension of specie payments has never failed in the history of money to lead bank notes to depreciate below their nominal coin equivalent.[1] It is not easy to measure the extent of the depreciation of the notes of the Banque de France. There is no free gold market in France, as was the case in New York during the greenback period in the United States. The foreign exchanges have become so dislocated that the rates on different countries tell different stories. We shall have occasion to consider the matter in connection with the subject of the foreign exchanges.

tax is an exceedingly unpopular tax, as so much of French business has normally been in the field of luxuries and amusements. Undoubtedly, however, the tax is checking luxurious expenditure. The tax on all meals costing over five francs is leading very many people to dine at home instead of at restaurants. How far social saving is involved in this—savings in terms of actual food, labor, fuel, etc., consumed and wasted—is not clear. Probably there is real saving. On other things, the saving is pretty clear. *Vide* London *Economist*, August 17, 1918, page 210.

[1] There is one case, that of Austrian paper money following 1866, where, after a prolonged period when the notes were depreciated below the value of the silver in which they were nominally redeemable, they finally appreciated above the value of the silver. But there are many complications here, and a discussion of this episode lies outside the scope of this paper. *Cf.* the discussion of this case in Professor Laughlin's *Principles of Money*, and the present writer's discussion of the principles involved in chapter 7 of his *Value of Money*.

There is a further possibility that gold itself may have depreciated during the war, which would add a third cause to the rise in French prices. This possibility should be entertained, since competent writers have suggested it, but we shall elsewhere offer reasons for regarding it as an error.

By the fourth quarter of 1917 French wholesale prices had risen, as compared with 1913, 192 per cent; English wholesale prices had risen only 114 per cent; wholesale prices in the United States, as shown by the Bureau of Labor Statistics index number, had risen only 81 per cent by December, 1917. The writer ventures the general thesis that at this period the rise in prices in the United States was wholly a matter of increased values of goods, currency depreciation being non-existent; that for Great Britain, the rise was chiefly a rise in goods, with currency depreciation slight; that for France, there was a still greater rise through scarcity in the values of goods, but that even so the element of currency depreciation was large.

A great many details for individual commodities and classes of commodities may be found in the *Bulletin de la Statistique Générale de la France,* especially after July, 1916. These details are for the most part unsummarized, except for the general index numbers given above. Such examination as the writer has had time to give to them will justify the general conclusion that the rises are in considerable measure correlated with variation in supplies, and that they are very uneven. Professor Laughlin has summarized certain of these figures, taken from the *Bulletin* of July, 1916 (pp. 306-312) in the following table: [1]

RISE OF PRICES FROM MIDDLE OF 1914 TO MIDDLE OF 1916

	Per cent
Freights	300-400
Chemicals	130
Fodder (Paris)	74
Vegetable oils (Paris)	116
Metals (Paris)	70
Cotton yarn (Rouen)	47
Grains (Paris)	64
Sugar, rice, etc. (Bordeaux)	217
Silk (Lyons)	36
Cotton, wool, leather, etc. (Havre)	67

[1] Laughlin, *op. cit.,* page 183, note.

Professor Charles Gide, writing in April, 1916, places the rise in French prices at 35 per cent, against a rise of 50 per cent in England and a rise of 100 per cent in Germany. Gide does not give his sources.[1]

[1] For Gide's discussion, see Kirkaldy: *Labour, Finance and the War*, London, 1916, pages 251-253.

CHAPTER VI

The Effects of the War on the Medium of Exchange in France: Coin, Bank Notes and Checks

At the outbreak of the war, gold money in France quickly disappeared from circulation. France had had a large circulation of gold coin and also a large volume of silver. The silver franc and five franc pieces, though no longer issued under free coinage, had unlimited legal tender privilege, not only in France, but also through the other countries of the Latin Monetary Union: Switzerland, Belgium, Italy and Greece, while the silver coins of these countries had the same privilege in France. How much gold was in circulation before the war is difficult to say. Widely varying estimates are given by French writers. Gide thinks that 6,000,000,000 francs in gold were in circulation.[1] This seems incredible. The Governor of the Banque de France estimated in 1908 that France had from 5,000,000,000 francs to 6,000,000,000 in gold, of which the Banque held about 3,200,000,000,[2] leaving only about 1,800,000,000 to 2,800,000,000 for general circulation. The gold holdings of the Banque increased substantially after 1908, and presumably also the gold in circulation. Edmond Théry[3] estimates the total gold money (coin and bullion) in France at 7,487,000,000 francs in 1912. Raphaël-Georges Lévy estimates the gold in France at the outbreak of the war at about seven billions, of which four billions were in the hands of the Banque, and three billions in the hands

[1] Gide, Charles: "Issues of Paper Money in France, and Prices," in Kirkaldy's volume on *Labour, Finance and the War*, published by authority of the British Association for the Advancement of Science, London, undated (date in preface, August, 1916), pages 251-252. It seems clear that Gide can not be talking about the total amount of gold money in France, including the holdings of the Banque de France, first, because the six billions is too small for that, and, second, because he states explicitly that he is estimating the money *in circulation*, in the effort to determine whether from a quantity theory viewpoint there is "inflation."

[2] Laughlin, *op. cit.*, page 171.

[3] London *Economist*, March 2, 1918, page 387.

of the people.[1] Lévy is undoubtedly one of the very best authorities on French money and banking. Giving no estimate for the amount of silver in circulation, Lévy points out that the Banque had about 700 million francs in silver at the beginning of the war, of which it had let half, or 350 millions, go into general circulation. This by the summer of 1915. Very early, silver as well as gold began to be hoarded by the people. *Die Bank*, a German financial journal of high standing, estimates that by the end of 1914 there were four billion francs of " hard money " hoarded in France, of which two and one-half billions were gold, and the rest, one and one-half billions, silver.[2] As to the general fact, namely that there was a great stock of gold in circulation in France when the war began, anyhow over two billions, and that it wholly disappeared from general circulation, there can be no doubt. The extent to which silver disappeared is a little less certain, but there seems little doubt that at present there is little silver in current circulation in France, despite a great deal of new coinage [3] by the government during the war, and despite the release by the Banque de France of a large part of the silver it had held in its reserve. (The Reichsbank early released all its silver in Germany, recognizing that a silver reserve was an anomaly from the standpoint of the gold standard.) [4]

The hoarding of silver may at first appear to indicate a very great depreciation of the bank notes indeed. To the strict " metallist " theory of money, which sees the sole source of the value of paper money in its prospect of redemption in full weight coin and which would explain the hoarding of coin in a period of restriction as merely due to the operation of Gresham's Law (that only the cheapest money continues to circulate, when there are several kinds, of unequal value, any of which may be used to pay debts, etc.), it would seem to follow from this phenomenon

[1] " French Money, Banking and Finance during the Great War," *Quarterly Journal of Economics*, November, 1915, pages 67-68.

[2] *Die Bank*, February, 1915, page 179.

[3] One hundred and fifty-four million francs in silver were issued in 1916—no gold coin at all was minted in that year. London *Economist*, August 11, 1917, page 209.

[4] Lévy, *loc. cit.* *Cf.* also Lévy's article in the *Economiste Français* of November 28, 1914, pages 543-544, on money in France, England and Germany.

that the bank notes fell in value below the value of the bullion content of the silver coins, which at this time were worth as bullion much less than their nominal gold equivalent. During the maintenance of the gold standard, the silver in France had been sustained at its nominal value by its legal relation with gold, but after the suspension of gold payments by the Banque, the silver coins were in no better plight than the bank notes from this standpoint, they had no more legal tender quality than the bank notes had, and if they were hoarded and disappeared from circulation, it must have been, from the standpoint of the strict "metallist" theory, because their bullion content made them more valuable than the bank notes, which would indicate that the depreciation of the bank notes was very great indeed.

Such a phenomenon did indeed occur in the northern States during the Civil War. In 1862, as soon as the depreciation of the greenbacks exceeded three or four per cent, it became profitable to take silver out of circulation and send it out of the country.[1] When the greenbacks reached their lower levels, even the copper coins tended to disappear. This was due not only to the depreciation of the greenbacks, but also to unusual demands for copper. This phenomenon, the disappearance of copper,[2] has also occurred to some extent in France.

The writer does not think that the hoarding of silver in France is adequately explained by the "metallist" theory, or

[1] At the mint ratio of 16:1, silver in the United States was undervalued, the world market ratio (dominated by the mint ratio in France) being a little above 15½ to 1. No silver dollars were thus in circulation at all. But silver half dollars, quarters and dimes were in circulation. By the act of 1853 their weight had been reduced seven per cent below the weight of silver dollars of equivalent amount (i.e., ten silver dimes weighed seven per cent less than one silver dollar). They thus remained in circulation, as ten dimes would have been worth only about ninety-seven cents in gold if the dimes were melted down, so long as the gold standard was maintained. (A silver dollar would have been worth about $1.04 in gold.) When, however, the greenbacks became worth less than ninety-seven cents in gold, ten dimes or four quarters or two half dollars in silver were worth more than a greenback dollar, and they disappeared under Gresham's Law. The paper fractional currency devised to replace the disappearing silver is one of the interesting monetary features of the Civil War period. For a detailed account of this episode, see W. C. Mitchell's *History of the Greenbacks.*

[2] London *Economist*, November 20, 1915, page 856. The explanation of this is not, apparently, to be found in the high value of copper, but in the desire of the peasant for "hard money," to which later reference will be made.

that the bank notes depreciated at the beginning of the war below the value of the bullion content of the silver coins. The "metallist" theory probably gives a virtually correct account of the greenback episode, though there are complications even there. The "metallist" theory can account for the disappearance of gold coin in France. But for the hoarding of the silver somewhat more is necessary.

And first let us note that bank notes also were hoarded to the extent of billions. Gide estimates that perhaps three billions of notes were hoarded in 1916.[1] The hoarding of notes in the earlier period may well have exceeded this substantially. The hoarding of silver, therefore, may be viewed merely as part of a general hoarding of money and need not represent a distrust of the notes.

That all kinds of money should be hoarded, gold, silver and bank notes, represents in large degree a phenomenon of a very different character from that involved in Gresham's Law, as commonly stated, though there is still an element of Gresham's Law in it. It represented in part distrust of *bank deposits.* in the *private banks* and a preference for money of any kind actually in hand over bank deposits.[2] This distrust, as we have seen, was justified in the early part of the war. The banks except for the Banque de France took advantage to the full of the moratorium and depositors were able to get only very limited amounts from them. Naturally, they were not willing to make further deposits with them and hoarded what money they had rather than redeposit it. But, further, money ceased to circulate freely, because in the time of danger and uncertainty people were afraid to spend freely. The future for individuals, whatever the future of the state and the Banque, looked very dark, and men who had resources preferred to keep them in hand. The hoarding represented the use of money as a "store of value," and as a "bearer of options"—men needed liquid

---

[1] Gide, *op. cit.*, page 252. This may not be meant by Gide as a real estimate, since he puts it in hypothetical form.

[2] I.e., in terms of Gresham's Law, the "cheap money" was deposit credit, and it tended to drive the "dear money" (gold, silver and bank notes) out of circulation. But this is only a minor element in the explanation, because of the great difficulties in using deposit credits at all.

resources to enable them to sleep at night. They needed something which was instantly convertible in the market into anything which they might happen to need—food, railway tickets if flight should be called for, or, if they chose, unusual bargains which others, harder pressed than they, might throw upon the market.

In ordinary times these functions are shared with money by many other things, especially deposit credits at the banks and securities with a ready market. But now there was no market for securities that could be depended on, and the banks were not attractive depositories. When the short term Treasury notes (*bons de la défense nationale*) of the French Government began to come out, this hoarded money was ready in adequate quantity, since the people had confidence that the state would really pay them and that they could market these Treasury notes, even if nothing else, at need.

The hoarding of silver was in no small part due to the fact that many of the hoarders had comparatively little in any case. Gold and bank notes were in denominations that were too large. The fact that some people hoarded silver, moreover, making a scarcity of silver in the daily routine of life, made others accumulate a reserve of small change in order to enable them to make daily purchases. After the people began to give up their gold to the Banque de France, their hoarding of silver increased.[1] Silver did not wholly disappear. It simply became exceedingly scarce and merchants were unwilling to break bills of large denomination for the same reason that merchants in America after banking hours often refuse to do so.

But there is a further point of significance. " Hard money " has a reality to the minds of most people in France which Americans perhaps do not share. Little trained in monetary theory, the French peasant and workman are nearer in feeling on this point to the attitude of the Hindu than to that of the American banker. Hard money, whether gold or silver, seems to them more truly money than paper does. That the silver had in considerable part a fiduciary character was not a matter of common

---

[1] London *Economist*, October 9, 1915, page 541.

knowledge in France. Indeed, it is not strictly a matter of legal theory in France. The silver is not redeemable by law in gold. Indeed the notes of the Banque are legally redeemable in silver or gold at the option of the Banque and the Banque does even in ordinary times sometimes protect its gold supply by proffering silver and charging a slight premium for paying gold instead. The value of silver is upheld by the value of gold in France in ordinary times. The two are tied together. But they are not tied together by the simple direct process of immediate redemption of the silver in gold. It is more a matter of indirection. In no small part it is the fact that a limited supply of silver is available for uses where gold would otherwise be required, which constitutes the linkage between the two metals. From the fact that small change is in some measure a necessity, from the fact that the silver coins are legal tender, from popular usage and social convention, from various indirect measures employed where necessary by the Banque, and from the fact that the silver, limited in amount, may be used where gold would otherwise be required, the silver coins have attained, and still retain, a value well above the value which they would have if melted down into bullion. The bullion value itself, moreover, has risen during the period of the war. The hoarding of silver, therefore, is not by itself significant of any great depreciation of the bank notes in France.

Various substitutes for coin in circulation were devised in France. The first extraordinary remedy was the issue of legal tender currency notes in small denominations. These had been prepared before the war—a forethought in which France was more fortunate than England—and were immediately sent out. These were in denominations of twenty francs and five francs. They are said to have been readily accepted by the people, although they were slow in reaching small towns.[1]

Bons de la défense nationale were issued in denominations of 100 francs, 500 francs and 1000 francs. The smaller denominations passed at once into circulation to some extent as part of the normal currency. Military requisitions were paid partly in these

---

[1] London *Economist*, August 15, 1914, page 321.

and partly in legal tender currency notes. The chambers of commerce in various parts of France issued early paper currency in denominations of fifty centimes and one franc, which took the place of small silver. These chamber of commerce notes were secured by notes of the Banque de France deposited with the Banque de France. They were supposed to circulate only locally and one had difficulties with them outside their neighborhood. Proposals were made in 1917 that these be replaced by notes of the same value to be issued by the Banque de France, the reasons for the proposals being that: (1) the monopoly of the Banque would thereby be preserved, and (2) the notes would thereby have a wide currency. The Minister of Finance objected to this. He preferred that the Banque should not issue small notes. He pointed out that the Banque had already given instructions to its branches to accept and call in such notes when current outside the home areas. These notes are cleared at the Banque in Paris and sent back to the area of their origin. The British army has also made arrangements through its Paymaster General to exchange such notes in the hands of British soldiers for notes locally current.[1]

In an earlier section we have discussed the view that checks have been little used in France and that the bank note has been the chief medium of exchange. This view we saw to be in large part erroneous. Checks have been used and are used in France for large transactions on a great scale. The masses of the people are not familiar with them, small tradesmen object to them, rents, taxes, and many other payments which would ordinarily be made in this country by check have been in France made by bank notes or coin, but the large transactions on the stock exchange, in wholesale trade, etc., have been handled by means of deposit credit, frequently employing checks, though, to a much greater extent than in America, making use of the bank transfer as a means of payment.

During the war an effort has been made by many agencies to increase the use of checks in payments in France. Reference has

---

[1] London *Economist*, January 16, 1915, page 107; September 2, 1916, page 405; December 15, 1917, page 950.

already been made to the proposal of Raphaël-Georges Lévy in
1914 shortly after the outbreak of the war that bank deposits
be mobolized by means of checks " good only through the clearing house " accompanied by the use of clearing house certificates
to be used in payments between the banks. Lévy has been interested in this matter throughout the war. There was an interesting symposium participated in by Lévy, Picot, Guyot and others
on the check and deposit system in May, 1916, of which an
account is given in the *Economiste Français* of May 29, 1916.
Arrangements were made permitting payment of taxes by check
under orders from Ribot, in 1916, when he was Minister of
Finance, and to some extent payments have been made by the
state by " crossed " checks. (Crossed checks are common enough
.in London. A check marked by two diagonal lines across the
face will be paid by the bank on which it is drawn only if
presented through some other bank. This is a safeguard against
fraudulent identifications.) The theory of the crossed check
in France appears to be that if the state pays by crossed checks
and these checks are deposited by their recipient, the transaction
constitutes a payment into the banks; whereas, if the state pays
by bank notes, which the recipient uses for general purposes, this
constitutes a payment out of the banks.[1]

The view seems to be that this will prevent " inflation." This
view is an illustration of a number of misconceptions which seem
to be current in France, regarding the difference between bank
note issue and the deposit and check system. It is a common-
place among American and English writers on money and banking that the difference between bank notes and deposits subject
to check, when the bank notes are issued under the " assets "
system, is largely a difference in form rather than in substance.
Notes and deposits alike constitute a medium of exchange. Notes
and deposits alike tend to grow out of the lending operations of
the banks. Notes and deposits alike, so long as instant redemption in gold is assured, tend automatically to expand and contract
with the needs of trade and finance, and deposits may expand

---

[1] London *Economist*, April 15, 1916, page 711. *Cf.* Bellom, Le Paiement
des dépenses d'Etat et des départments par des virements de banque.
Economiste Français, August, 1916.

quite as dangerously as notes when banks cease to meet their gold obligations and when they surrender their lending policy to the fiscal needs of the state. There is no magic in the check and deposit system. It is not a substitute for sound finance.

The Bank of France, through its director, M. Pallain, in 1916, issued a booklet containing pictures of check forms and a circular to all of its branches encouraging the use of checks. It suppressed the commission charge on letters of credit and issued crossed checks without charge except for the twenty centime stamp.[1]

The Orléans R. R. agreed late in 1916 to accept certain kinds of checks at the stations for freight charges for amounts over two thousand francs and it agreed that responsible customers might pay every ten days instead of daily so that the amounts might reach two thousand francs.[2]

Payments of interest, where the bondholder is willing, are being made by book transfers by the banks and with postal orders for small bondholders. The postal orders and postal checks have been developed in France during the war and about the end of 1917 a law was passed allowing current accounts at the post office with arrangements for checking and for transferring credits from one account to another by orders presented to the post office.[3]

This process has not gone on without friction. Deposits and checks were discredited in the autumn of 1914. Moreover, the French law regarding checks was very little developed at the outbreak of the war. It was necessary in the summer of 1916 to pass new legislation making it a criminal offense to issue checks when the drawer knows he has no funds or to withdraw funds after issuing checks. In August, 1916, *Le Temps* gravely discussed the question of stopping the payment on checks. There had been a court decision in March to the effect that this might be done. *Le Temps* contended that if this is permitted it will make all the agitation to extend checks useless and discredit the

---

[1] London *Economist*, May 6, 1916, page 821.
[2] *Ibid.*, December 30, 1916, page 1221.
[3] *Ibid.*, January 19, 1918, page 83. Bellom, Le chèque postale, *Journal des Economistes*, July, 1916.

instrument. *Le Temps* proposed to extend the law against withdrawing funds after giving a check to cover the case of stopping payment on checks, making stopping payment a fraud.[1]

There is sufficient evidence in this new legislation and in this naïve attitude of *Le Temps* that the check is not a familiar thing to the masses of people in France. More recently still the Banque de France has seemed to change its attitude toward extending the use of checks. In the summer of 1918 the Banque laid down the rule that checks will not be accepted in payment of dues to any department of the French Government unless presented on the day they are drawn. This would seem to be an ingenious device to make the use of checks impossible in payments to the government. The use of checks has also met a snag in the new tax on payments of all kinds. The tax amounts to two francs per thousand on receipts for money payments and is of course easily collected when checks are cashed or deposited at banks, since the check is a receipt. An evasion of this tax has been devised by creditors drawing checks on individual debtors instead of on the banks and using these checks as a means of paying their own debts—virtually a substitute of the old private draft or bill of exchange for the bank check. A bill was introduced in August, 1918, backed by the Ministers of Justice, Finance and Commerce, prohibiting the drawing of checks except on bankers, *Agents de Change* and official representatives of the French Treasury. This is designed to prevent this tax evasion.[2]

It is not clear, however, that this may not prove an effective blow at the widely used bill of exchange, which when drawn " on sight " is legally identical with a check drawn on a private individual.

Mention should also be made of the extension of the clearing house system during the war. Before the war, the Chambre de Compensation des Banquiers de Paris was an unimportant affair, most of the actual clearing operations being made by transfers on the books of the Banque de France. During the war, a new Caisse de Compensation was formed, to meet the needs of

[1] London *Economist*, August 11, 1917, page 209; September 1, 1917, page 322.

[2] *Ibid.*, August 17, 1918, page 210.

English and American banks, and in July, 1917, this was consolidated with the old organization in the new Chambre de Compensation, which includes all the important banking houses in Paris. Its operations are limited, however, and the overwhelming bulk of bank settlements continue to be made by transfers through the Banque de France.

CHAPTER VII

French Fiscal Methods during the War

The financial expedients of a state in war time may be listed under five main heads:

I. Taxes

II. Long time bond issues

III. Short time Treasury loans issued in anticipation of receipts from taxes and long time loans

IV. Direct advances to the state by a state bank of issue

V. The issue of government paper money

Between the last two methods, when specie payment is suspended by the state bank, the line is often difficult to draw. The issue of government paper money as a means of meeting the current expenses of the state is generally recognized as the least desirable form of financing; the last resource of financial weakness. This was a case with the greenback issues of the North during the Civil War, although in that case it represented financial inaptitude rather than real weakness, and was held within reasonable limits after a strong tax and loan policy was begun. It represented much less weakness than the advances by the state banks of Russia and Austria have meant during the present war.

During the present war the doctrine that the entire expenses of the state should be met by taxes has occasionally been stated. This is an extreme view which probably today has few if any responsible advocates. It is impossible to carry out. The theory underlying it is that the essential problem is a problem of goods and services; that the amount of goods and services available is fixed; that the problem is simply to divert goods and services from private to public use; and that the simplest way to accomplish this is for the state to take private incomes and spend them, thus reducing private demand by exactly the same amount that the demand of the state for goods and services increases. The difficulty in applying this plan grows out of the pre-existing fabric of debts and credits which would promptly be thrown into chaos by any such drastic reduction of private incomes as the taxes necessary to carry on a great war would involve. Universal bankruptcy would result from it. Instead of private demand falling off in proportion to the increase in the demands of the state, private demand would fall off very much more than state demand increased and the fiscal receipts of the state itself would be very much less than the taxing authorities might anticipate for the very simple reason that bankrupts can not pay taxes. The doctrine is further wrong in its assumption that the volume of goods and services is fixed. It is probable that physical volume of production in the United States, for example, has increased over twenty-five per cent [1] since 1914 under the stimulus of expanding credit and rising prices. Under ordinary conditions there is a large slack in industry. There is unemployment, there are idle plants. There is, moreover, a large industrial reserve in women and children and retired laborers, and most of the labor force can be induced to give more overtime work than it is accustomed to give in normal times. Rising prices and interest rates connected with an expanding volume of war time demand can, moreover, induce extra saving, especially by active businesses, and increase capital accumulations.

Further, the doctrine that only taxes should be used, ignores the temporal sequence of the cessation of private demand and the beginning of public demand for goods and services. If the state is to rely only on taxes it can not spend its income until it receives it and it can not receive it until the people have given it up. The friction of tax collection makes it certain that a considerable interval will intervene, during which industry slows down and becomes demoralized.

A recognition of these difficulties has led Professor O. M. W. Sprague, the leading American advocate of heavy taxation, to insist that the first reliance of the state should be on short time

---

[1] *Cf.* the present writer's discussion of this point in the " Annual Review " of *The Annalist*, January 6, 1919, pages 5-6 and 61.

loans, issued in anticipation of taxes, to be taken largely by the banks. The advantage of such short time financing is, first, that the state gets its money at once and so may take its time in passing tax laws and collecting taxes; and second, that an easy money market is created by the expanding bank credit connected with the larger loans which tends to prevent the collapse of credit and makes the shifting from peace time industrial pursuits to war time industry easier.

In practice, however, even a policy of taxation and short time loans has proved a counsel of perfection. The periodic paying off of short time loans by receipts derived wholly from taxation would still impose far too heavy a burden on the existing fabric of debts and credits, and long time loans in large volume have proved a fiscal necessity. If the long time loans are taken entirely by the people, individuals surrendering their current income to the state, the difference between loans and taxes is not great. But practically the people can not make such a complete surrender of their incomes and the difference between loans and taxes lies largely in the fact that a government bond is good collateral at a bank, while a tax receipt is not. The bondholder is thus in a better position to borrow at the bank funds which he needs to continue a certain part of his ordinary expenditure than is the tax payer. It is not true that taxes lead to no borrowings at the banks. In 1918 in the United States there was a great deal of borrowing, especially on the part of corporations, for paying the excess profits tax, and to a very considerable extent the bonds issued by the federal government have been taken up out of the current income of the people, reducing *pro tanto* popular expenditure and consumption. But in general the loan policy of the government leads to an increase in governmental expenditure without an exactly corresponding decrease in private expenditures, which tends to raise commodity prices. This increased expenditure at rising prices tends also, however, to increase aggregate production, and in this fact we have perhaps its greatest superiority over an all tax policy.

An important qualification must be made with reference to the doctrine that rising prices stimulate production. During 1915,

1916 and 1917 this was clearly true in the United States, as shown by figures for railroad gross receipts, bituminous coal production and other indicia, but by the middle of 1917 progress slowed down decidedly. The country had nearly reached its maximum capacity. Further stimulus of this kind would have its chief effect in pull and haul among industries competing for a relatively inelastic supply of labor and materials. No doubt there is still some slack, but no amount of further rise in prices or expansion of bank credit could duplicate the increase in production which the first three and a half years of the great war brought the United States. The desideratum would probably be an increasing substitution of taxes for loans as a country approximates its full industrial capacity and as the shift from peace time industry to war time industry becomes more completely accomplished.

Taxes in France

In France it was virtually impossible to adopt a strong tax policy at the outset of the war. As we have seen, France was in the midst of a severe crisis before the war. The budget had been delayed for several months by a bitter struggle over the income tax and the tax on securities, and the opposition of influential elements of the population, the *rentiers,* the financial press, banking houses and others to heavy taxes, was a matter of long standing tradition. There was, moreover, a theory in France that war should be financed by short loans and advances from the Banque (as had been the case in 1870) and that permanent fiscal measures of taxes and loans to retire the short time obligations should be put into effect only at the end of the war. Further, the invasion of the industrial and mining sections of France robbed France of her richest sources of current revenue. For a long time after the outbreak of the war the economic demoralization, in no small part caused by the moratorium, made a strong taxing policy impossible, and the political difficulties of taxation persisted for many months more. The French Ministry of Finance had always to reckon with the possibility of aggravating " defeatist " sentiment by vigorous fiscal measures.

By the end of 1914 the yield of existing taxes was 38⅞ per cent below normal. Monthly figures for many months thereafter show heavy deficits. September, 1916, was the first month in which the tax yield got above normal. The revenues for September, 1916, were 346,000,000 francs, 49,000,000 above normal in September, and 110,000,000 above September, 1915, but the first eight months of 1916 were still 189,000,000 below normal, although 494,000,000 above the first eight months of 1915. This turn of the tide, however, still represents a deficit in fact, because the aggregate of taxes, other than customs, was still below normal in this month and the customs receipts represented in large measure payments by the government in its capacity of importer to the government in its capacity of tax gatherer. It was not until June, 1917, that the tax yield, excluding customs, reached the prewar normal.[1]

Later in 1917 the total tax receipts declined somewhat as a consequence of the falling off of customs with a restriction on shipping, but receipts other than from customs have tended on the whole to increase pretty steadily. An income tax and an excess war profits tax went into effect during the year 1916 and additional tax legislation was passed in December, 1916. The income tax passed just before the war had remained in abeyance. New taxes on profits, on payments of over ten francs and on luxuries went into effect in 1918. The luxury taxes have proved very unpopular and their yield in July, 1918, was less than one-third of the yield anticipated, ten millions as against an estimate of thirty-two millions. Their main effect has been in checking luxury. The heavy tax on meals costing over five francs, for example, has led enormous numbers of people in Paris to dine at home instead of dining at restaurants. The total tax yield for July, 1918, was 472,000,000 francs. This is 26,000,000 francs below the estimate for that month, the chief deficit being in the tax on luxuries. It is 40,000,000 francs above the receipts of July, 1917, an increase of 9 per cent.

On the whole, the tax policy in France has been lamentably lacking in vigor. As compared with taxation in England or

[1] London *Economist,* October 21, 1916, page 686; July 21, 1917, page 86.

taxation in the United States, the showing is very poor.[1] For the first two years of the war a valid defense for it exists in the fact that nothing else was politically or economically possible. Beginning with the summer of 1916, however, it would seem that much heavier taxes could have been imposed.

Bons de la Défense Nationale

Apart from advances by the Banque de France the main reliance of the French Government at the outbreak of the war was short term Treasury bills, the so-called " bons de la défense nationale." These have been purchased steadily and cheerfully by the people. The great private banks have bought them, most of them placing them in the " portfolio " in their balance sheets. Their commercial discounts have declined heavily and they have bought a considerable amount of bons de la défense nationale instead. The Banque de France rediscounts them, or makes collateral loans against them. In England and the United States such short term obligations of the governments have been taken chiefly by the banks, although to some extent large tax payers have bought them in anticipation of tax payments and large corporate and individual purchasers of long time securities have bought them in anticipation of the long time issues. In general, in England, France and the United States, provision has been made for the government to accept these short time securities in payment of taxes or of subscriptions to the long time loans. The smallest denominations of these bons de la défense nationale, those for one hundred francs, passed to some extent into general circulation and all of them represented liquid assets which the people felt safe in taking in exchange for their hoarded gold or hoarded bank notes which they were holding for emergencies. The first issues were at 5 per cent for three and six months. By December, 1914, the rate on the three months' issues was reduced to 4 per cent. By early December over seven million francs of these had been sold. A later table will show something of the total amounts involved.

[1] Even Germany has done better.

The Long Time Loans

Early in 1915 provisions were made for the issue of long time "stock," but it was not until the fall of 1915 that long time financing on a large scale was undertaken. In November of that year, a great loan was floated. This was a 5 per cent issue and was marketed at eighty-eight. The receipts at this price were $2,648,600,000,[1] or nearly 13,250,000,000 francs.

There were about 3,000,000 subscribers. As a means of protecting the 3 per cent *rente,* whose price had sagged to sixty-three, sixty-four and sixty-five, the government allowed a certain part of the subscriptions to be paid in the *rente perpetuelle.* The main items received for the loan of November, 1915, were as follows:[2]

```
Cash .............................................Fr.  6,360,000,000
Bons de la Défense Nationale.................      2,228,000,000
Rente Perpetuelle ...........................      1,431,000,000
```

Some savings banks deposits receipts were also taken and some other minor items. The *rente* was taken at an arbitrary price of 66 as against the bourse price of 64.50 on November 23, but was accepted only for a part of each subscription and had to be accompanied by new money or national defense bonds. The loan was open only fifteen days and the large subscription was regarded as very gratifying. The position of the Treasury was greatly strengthened thereby.

The second loan came in November, 1916. This also was a perpetual *rente* at 5 per cent and it was issued at 88.65. The total subscription to this loan was somewhat less—about $2,-275,000,000 or about 11,360,000,000 francs.[3]

Of this loan 55 per cent was paid in cash, whereas of the previous loan only 47½ per cent had been paid in cash, the balance in each case being paid in various obligations

---

[1] E. L. Bogart: *Direct Costs of the Present War*, page 19, published by the Carnegie Endowment for International Peace.

[2] London *Economist*, January 22, 1916, page 141.

[3] Bogart, *op. cit.*, page 19; London *Economist*, November 25, 1916, page 998.

of the French Government. The next great loan was in November, 1917. This time a 4 per cent perpetual *rente* was issued at 68.60. The total subscription was 10,250,000,000 francs or about $2,051,000,000. As before, a substantial part of the loan was paid in other obligations. The government had asked for only 2,000,000,000 francs of fresh money, but in the actual payment about half of the total subscription was in fresh money.[1]

In October, 1918, preparations for a fourth great loan are under way. The bill was introduced by M. Klotz, Minister of Finance, on September 18. The loan is to be a 4 per cent tax free loan, unlimited in amount. It is to be issued at 70.80. Subscriptions will be taken between October 20 and November 24. One interesting feature is that Russian coupons will be accepted in payment up to 50 per cent of any given subscription.[2] The French Government, since the collapse of the Russian Government, has been paying the coupons on Russian state securities and this is merely part of its policy of protecting these obligations.

All of these loans have been essentially funding operations. The government has gone as far as safety permitted in the issue of national defense bonds and in direct borrowings from the Banque de France. It has then issued a long time loan with which it has somewhat reduced its debt to the Banque and with which it has retired a large part of the short time obligations.

It will be most convenient to treat the advances by the Banque de France to the government for war purposes in our chapter on the Banque de France. The tables which follow will show the proportion which such advances bear to the total revenue and receipts from loans of the French Government. It is interesting to note that following the first great loan in November, 1915, the state reduced its borrowings from the Banque from 7,500,000,000 to 5,000,000,000 francs, and that the note issue of the Banque declined about 250,000,000 at the same time.

---

[1] Bogart, *op. cit.*, page 20. London *Economist*, January 5, 1918, page 13.
[2] *New York Times*, September 19 and 27, 1918.

Following the loan of November, 1916, the advances to the
state in the Banque's balance sheet were reduced from 8,600,-
000,000 to 6,600,000 and notes were also somewhat reduced.
The effect of the loan in the fall of 1917 upon the Banque's
balance sheet was less clearly marked, but there was as a result
of that loan a substantial temporary retardation in the rate of
increase, both of advances to the state and notes. By August
29, 1918, advances to the state had reached 19,150,000,000,
while note issue had reached 29,434,000,000.   Since about
November, 1916, these two items have kept a close parallelism,
remaining just about 10,000,000 francs apart. The state pays
the Banque 1 per cent on these advances. The rate is to be
3 per cent after the war, 2 per cent of which, however,
is to be counted as a sinking fund for the ultimate extinction
of the principal of the debt.[1] There is theoretically a legal limit
to the state's borrowings from the Banque, but practically this
limit has been raised by successive steps whenever it has been
approached. Commonly, the legal limits on the advances to the
state and note issues have been raised at about the same time. Of
the total borrowings of the state something less than 20 per
cent had been borrowed from the Banque de France and the
Banque de l'Algérie by December 31, 1917, as will appear in the
tables below. At the outbreak of the war, however, the main
reliance was on the Banque de France. From August 1, 1914,
to December 31, the state borrowed twice as much from the
Banque as it was able to borrow from all other sources. From
January 1, 1915, to May 15 of that year, however, the tide
turned and the borrowings from other sources were about three
times as great as the borrowings from the Banque.[2] It is in no
sense true that the main reliance of the French Government
has been the Banque de France. During the first six months of
1918 the growth of the advances by the Banque to the state
was very rapid. It is probable that this had some connection
with the expenditures of the American Government in
France.

[1] London *Economist*, December 21, 1914, page 1112.
[2] *Ibid.*, June 5, 1915, page 1166.

The following tables, prepared by Professor E. L. Bogart,[1] are the most authoritative summary the writer can find of the main elements of French war financial history:

EXPENDITURES IN FRANCE, AUGUST 1, 1914–DECEMBER 31, 1917

(In millions of francs)

Period	Strictly Military Expenditures	Charges on Debt	Social Expenditures	Other Expenditures	Total
Aug. 1–Dec. 31, 1914..	5,867	60	494	167	6,589
Jan. 1–Dec. 31, 1915..	15,765	1,900	2,711	2,428	22,805
Jan. 1–Dec. 31, 1916..	23,673	3,267	3,291	2,402	32,633
Jan. 1–Dec. 31, 1917..	29,100	4,500	4,200	3,200	41,163
Total	74,405	9,727	10,696	8,197	103,190

RECEIPTS AND EXPENDITURES OF FRANCE
AUGUST 1, 1914–DECEMBER 31, 1917

(In millions of francs)

Period	Expenditures	Revenue Receipts	Loans
Aug. 1–Dec. 31, 1914.............	6,589	1,000	6,365
Jan. 1–Dec. 31, 1915............	22,805	3,884	19,856
Jan. 1–Dec. 31, 1916............	32,633	4,667	27,429
Jan. 1–Dec. 31, 1917............	41,163	4,730	35,230
Total	103,190	14,281	88,880

TOTAL BORROWINGS, AUGUST 1, 1914–DECEMBER 31, 1917

Treasury bills, etc....................................	Fr. 21,700,000,000
5% loan of 1915.....................................	13,243,000,000
5% loan of 1916.....................................	11,375,000,000
4% loan of 1917.....................................	10,256,000,000
National defense obligations.........................	840,000,000
Bills sold in England, etc............................	7,340,000,000
Loans in the United States..........................	3,000,000,000
Advance by United States Government	6,425,000,000
Advances from banks of France and Algeria.........	12,200,000,000
Additional borrowings, unclassified...................	2,500,000,000
Total	Fr. 88,879,000,000

This is an enormous war debt for a country whose total annual income before the war was estimated at 30,000,000,000 francs or $6,000,000,000. How can France ever pay it? The

---

[1] *Op. cit.,* pages 20-21. Professor Bogart's figures are given in dollars. The writer has reconverted them to francs, counting five francs to the dollar, in order to make them comparable with the other figures given in the discussion of France.

interest charge alone would make up a large fraction of the pre-war national income while a rapid reduction of the principal would seem to be an impossibility. We have here presented in the case of France a problem that all the belligerents and many of the neutrals are considering very solemnly today: "How can such debts be paid?" If the interest on the war debt had to be paid out of the national income as it existed before the war, the problem would be indeed a serious one, perhaps a hopeless one. But consider—the interest paid on the war debt, to the extent that it is received by French holders of the debt, is an *addition* to their incomes. What the government takes out of their pockets in taxes to pay the interest on its bonds it returns to their pockets in the interest that it pays them. Figures for the income of the people and figures for the budget of the state are thus swollen by what is after all merely a transfer of funds. Abstracting from foreign debts and abstracting from the fact that people who receive the interest on the war loans are not exactly identical with the people who pay the taxes, the transaction becomes merely a bookkeeping transaction. The burden of the war is after all borne during the period of the war. It can not be thrown on future generations. The future generations are of course poorer to the extent that the physical wealth of the country has been depleted. They are poorer to the extent that the labor force is depleted by deaths and sickness and wounds. They are poorer to the extent that the social organization has been demoralized; that family life has been interrupted; that the education of the children has been interfered with; to the extent that the children have been undernourished and become weaker men and women as a result. But the mere existence of a huge war debt owed by the state to its own people does not constitute in itself an additional burden upon the country as a whole.

It is not safe, of course, to abstract from debts held abroad. France has probably been changed from a creditor nation to a debtor nation as a result of the war, or at all events will so be changed if the war lasts another year and its borrowings from the United States continue at their present rate. The loans made by France during the war to her allies are much less than her borrowings in other countries unless it should develop that French advances to the United States Government in 1918 and 1919 turn the scale.

It is far from safe of course to abstract from the fact that the people who pay taxes are not identical with the people who receive interest or who receive payments of the principal of the loans. In the past it has often happened that a war debt has been a crushing burden on labor. The rich have lent money to the state and the poor have paid the taxes with which the loan was paid off. This need not be. With the growing political strength of labor; with the growth of income taxes, inheritance taxes and other forms of taxes aimed chiefly at the rich, it is more likely to be true that the flow of funds from the pocket of the tax payer through the Treasury to the pocket of the bondholder will tend to redistribute wealth in the interests of the poor, rather than the other way.

Nor need it be true that the taxes required to pay the interest on these loans and ultimately to amortize them will be a handicap to business men in competition with the business men of other countries where the tax burdens are lighter. Not all taxes are a burden to industry and trade. Some taxes effect prices, others do not. Some taxes check production, others do not. Taxes on incomes without reference to their source, taxes on inheritances without reference to their manner of accumulation and, within limits, taxes on land, need not check production or handicap trade. If France does not become insolvent during the war there is little reason to suppose that she will become insolvent after the war, and to the present writer there seems little or no indication of any real danger of insolvency either of the French Government or the French banks during the war. It may be added that even insolvency on the part of the state need not interfere with its continuance as a fighting power if only the state is strong enough to seize by direct methods the physical goods and services needed for the continued prosecution of the war. The Southern Confederacy was virtually bankrupt for two years or more before Appomattox. If vigorous taxes are applied, the problem is manageable.

CHAPTER VIII

The Banque de France during the War

At various points in the foregoing chapters reference has been made to the part played by the Banque de France in the financial drama of the war. It may be well at this point, however, to summarize some of these points and to deal with the matter somewhat systematically.

The Banque de France has played a great and heroic rôle. Such criticisms as may be justly made of its policy are also criticisms of the state and of long standing French financial tradition. The Banque has been both prudent and courageous. It has been above all patriotic. It has been statesmanlike, conceiving its task to be to lead in the financial and industrial readjustment which France has had to make. It has been obliged to carry an unexpected burden because of the weakness and timidity of the great private banks of France and because of the inability of the state to put through a taxing policy of sufficient vigor. But it has borne this burden and it continues to be a strong and solvent institution capable of bearing even heavier burdens if need be.

The gold policy of the Banque has been one which from the standpoint of English banking traditions is not courageous. Before the war the Banque had accumulated an enormous reserve, amounting on July 30, 1914, to 4,767,000,000 francs. Of this 700,000,000 was in legal tender silver and the rest, 4,067,000,000, was in gold. One wonders for what purpose this huge accumulation, amounting to more than half the total assets of the Banque and amounting to a very high percentage of its chief liability, its circulating notes, was made, if not to be used for keeping its notes convertible in an emergency. The Bank of England with very much less gold has conceived it to be its duty to go to the limit in meeting its gold obligations and although forced to exercise control over external shipments of gold has apparently never refused to meet lawful calls for gold over its counter. The Banque de France, however, following what seems to be not only the French but the general continental tradition, promptly suspended gold payments at the outbreak of the war and has since hoarded its gold jealously, though from time to time sending gold abroad, as a last resort and under special restrictions, to protect the foreign exchanges. Early in the war, however, the Banque released 350,000,000 francs of its silver and it has since released a little more. Its silver holdings in August, 1918, had been reduced from 700,000,000 to 319,-000,000 francs.

Early in the war, also, a movement was inaugurated, in which Raphaël-Georges Lévy took an active part, for bringing in the gold hoarded by the people to the Banque in exchange for the Banque's notes. Lévy estimated in 1915 that something like 3,000,000,000 francs of gold were in circulation among the people at the outbreak of the war. The response to the call for gold to strengthen the Banque's reserves was enthusiastic and a very large amount of gold was brought in. By August 10, 1915, 315,000,000 francs in gold had been brought in by the people and by September 28, 1915, the total had reached 800,000,000.[1]

By December 8, 1915, 1,204,000,000 francs had been brought in by the people. By December 18, 1916, the figure had grown to 1,948,000,000.[2]

The Banque, suspending gold payments within the country, has sent a good deal of gold abroad, but only when the exchange situation became acute. In May, 1915, 500,000,000 francs of gold was exported to England under an agreement by which 1,550,000,000 francs in credit was obtained in England and the United States to be used in protecting French exchange.[3] The Banque retained title to this gold, and continued to count it as part of its reserve. In the first quarter of 1916 more was sent out and throughout the war from time to time the Banque has released gold, no small part of which has come to the United

---

[1] London *Economist*, August 14, 1915; October 2, 1915, page 508.
[2] *Ibid.*, December 23, 1916, page 1176.
[3] *Ibid.*, May 15, 1915, page 937.

States. This gold is still counted, however, in large part at least, as part of reserve of the Banque, though separately mentioned in the statements of the Banque since June 8, 1916, as " gold held abroad." On June 8, 1916, the reserve stood: silver, 350,000,000; gold in vaults, 4,676,000,000; gold abroad, 69,000,000. On August 22, 1918, the Banque's reserves stood as follows: silver, 319,000,000; and gold, 5,435,000,000, of which 3,398,000,000 was held in the Banque's vaults and 2,037,000,000 was held abroad.

It is not clear that either the French Government or the Banque is disposed to give thorough going acceptance to the theory that gold should be hoarded in war time. Perhaps the theory itself is too vague a theory for public men to be enthusiastic about giving explicit statement to it. It rests in part upon the notion that a large gold reserve, even though it be hoarded, is a basis for popular confidence which helps to sustain the value of circulating notes and which increases the general credit of the state. This consideration is not without force. Confidence based on the existence of a large hoard of gold is to a considerable degree nonrational, but very many of the forces which make for value are nonrational. The notes of the Banque de France have a higher value than they would have if it were not for the Banque's reserve, even though a lower value than they would have if they were being redeemed on demand in gold. The decision to put an embargo on gold was one to which Ribot gave hesitant assent. Ribot concluded his statement upon this point with a panegyric on free trade.[1] He appears to be an adherent of the English doctrine with reference to the handling of gold reserves—the doctrine that gold reserves are to be used rather than hoarded; that they are accumulated in tranquil times precisely for the meeting of emergencies. He appeared also to feel that the emergency was so great that even the huge hoard which France had accumulated was inadequate and that it was better to conserve it than to use it ineffectively.

The annual report of the Banque de France at the beginning of 1916 discussed the matter also. The Governor states that it

[1] London *Economist*, July 17, 1915, page 98.

seems not wise to use the gold reserve freely to protect the foreign exchanges. He suggests, but does not state that the effect would be insufficient.

There may have also been in the minds of statesmen and financiers, not only in France but in Germany as well, the thought that the huge gold accumulations might serve for something more than a fetish for the people to look at and draw comfort from. They may have looked forward to a time when credit resources would be exhausted and when actual gold in hand would be the only means of obtaining goods from neutral countries, the time when the country with the largest gold accumulation would have the necessary supplies in the final week of the war. No doubt, too, all of the gold hoarding financiers have had an eye to the advantage of a huge gold accumulation in the after the war period as a means of aiding in a resumption of the gold standard.

The most striking developments in the balance sheet of the Banque are in two items: "advances to the state for war" and "notes in circulation," with, as an item of growing importance after April, 1915, "Treasury bonds in respect of advances to foreign governments." Notes in circulation on February 5, 1914, were 6,029,000,000 francs. By August 29, 1918, they had reached the huge total of 29,434,000,000. "Advances to the state for war" were, of course, zero on February 5, 1914, but by August 29, 1918, they had reached 19,150,000,000. There is a striking parallel between these two items. They have steadily moved together and since November 2, 1916, they have been just about 10,000,000,000 francs apart pretty uniformly. The loans to the government for advances to foreign governments started with a modest 100,000,000 francs on April 15, 1915, and had reached 3,463,000,000 by August 29, 1918. Counting these two items, "advances to the state" and "Treasury bonds in respect of advances to foreign governments," the state was indebted to the Banque for war purposes to the extent of 22,050,000,000 francs on August 29, 1918 (or counting five francs to the dollar) to the extent of $4,050,000,000. This is by far the greatest part of the total assets of the Banque which stood on the day in question at 34,477,000,000 francs or nearly $7,000,000,000.

To many writers this great expansion of the notes of the Banque de France and this huge figure for advances by the Banque to the state have seemed portentous of shipwreck for French finances and have seemed to represent a degree of " inflation " far in excess of anything discernible in England or the United States.   To the writer the situation does not seem to be hopeless.   The actual debt of the state to the Banque is slightly greater than the amount of our Third Liberty Loan. It is less than the total of the two great war loans in 1915 and 1916 in France by about 1,000,000,000 francs.   Funding operations after the war, whereby the debt of the state to the Banque will be changed for a debt of the state to the people in the form of a long time *rente*, with a corresponding reduction of the Banque's note issue, will not be easy, but will be perfectly possible.   This would be better, from the standpoint of the soundness of French banking, than the slower plan of a sinking fund of 2 per cent a year, which was planned in the fall of 1914, at a time when the advances to the state were not expected to exceed six billion francs.[1]   The state pays the Banque only 1 per cent on these advances.   It was expected that after the war this would be made 3 per cent, of which 2 per cent should serve to reduce the principal.   But unless speedier methods are adopted, even though more expensive methods, the note issues of the Banque will remain so large that resumption of specie payments may be difficult.

The notion, however, that bank credit in France is dangerously expanded must be considered in the light of the facts developed in our earlier discussion of the French system as it existed before the war.   France, as compared with England or the United States, was to a large extent on a hard money basis. The proportion of gold reserve to extensions of bank credit, or even to notes, current accounts and deposits for all French banks, was vastly larger than the same proportion in England or the United States.   During the war practically the only expansion

[1] London *Economist*, December 26, 1914, page 1112.

in France has been in the form of notes, as we have in part seen in the section dealing with the outbreak of the war, and as will be made clearer in the section on private banks in France. Every private bank whose accounts the writer has examined, with the exception of the comparatively unimportant Banque Nationale de Crédit, shows a decided falling off in its credit extensions through most of the war period. The total volume of deposit credit subject to check by others than banks in France is probably less in 1918 than it was before the war, and the volume of bank acceptances is enormously less. The current accounts (deposits subject to check or draft) of the Banque de France itself have expanded. They were only 713,000,000 francs on February 5, 1914, and they rose to 2,328,000,000 by January 28, 1915, reached 3,610,000,000 on June 6, 1918, and fell to 3,477,000,000 on August 29, 1918. These current accounts of the Banque de France, however, represent in part accounts taken away from the private banks by distrustful depositors, and in part represent the hoarded reserves of the private banks which early in the war rediscounted heavily with the Banque de France and subsequently largely refrained from lending out the funds thus procured. No small part of the increased note issue of the Banque de France has thus been hoarded, either by the private banks or by the people.

It would be hard, by the way, to give a more complete refutation to the theory that bank loans and deposits bear a definite relation to bank reserves than the history of France during the great war—and for that matter the history of England and the United States—affords. The Banque de France has expanded its note issue and deposits courageously without reference to its reserves, to meet the emergencies of the situation. The other banks in general, counting as their reserve largely bank notes and deposits with the Banque de France, have very greatly increased their reserve percentages.

The figures for the Banque's new commercial discounts and for its premoratorium bills have already been treated in the chapter on " Depression and *Réprise des Affaires.*" The Banque took over an enormous volume of premoratorium bills from the other banks at the outbreak of the war and these bills have largely been paid off, declining from a maximum of 3,771,000,000 on November 12, 1914, to 1,068,000,000 francs on August 8, 1918. The unmatured bills or commercial discounts have risen from a low of 244,000,000 on January 28, 1915, to a high of 1,335,000,000 on February 14, 1918, declining again to 1,002,000,000 on August 8, 1918.

The Banque was perhaps not quite as courageous as the Bank of England in rediscounting for the private banks, but, bearing in mind the timidity of the institutions with which it had to deal, it gave them certainly all the accommodations to which they were entitled. There was some complaint in the fall of 1914 that the Banque was hesitant about new commercial credits, but on the whole its policy seems to have been vigorous enough. The large issue of new bank notes by the Banque de France was the one effective stimulant which revived French industry and commerce from their syncope. But stimulants are not indefinitely effective.

The note issue of the Banque de France has always been virtually free. The Banque represents the primitive type of bank of issue. When specie payment was suspended in 1848, however, a legal limit was placed upon the issues, and since the suspension of 1870 this practice has remained. The legal limit has always been raised, however, well in advance of any pressure of actual issue of notes and apparently the main reason for retaining any legal limit at all has been the desire on the part of the legislature to bargain with the Banque in connection with other matters. At the outbreak of the war the legal limit was raised from 6,800,000,000 to 12,000,000,000 francs and it has subsequently been raised by successive steps as follows:[1]

May, 1915, to	Fr. 15,000,000,000
Mar., 1916, to	18,000,000,000
Feb., 1917, to	21,000,000,000
Sept., 1917, to	24,000,000,000
Feb. 1918, to	27,000,000,000
May, 1918, to	30,000,000,000

The note issue of the Banque de l'Algérie has been raised during the war from 300,000,000 to 700,000,000 francs.[2]

[1] London *Economist*, February 16, 1918, page 246; *Bulletin de Statistique et de Législation Comparée*, May, 1918, page 853.
[2] *Bulletin de Statistique et de Législation Comparée*, 1918, page 887.

The maximum of advances of the Banque to the state on the 1 per cent interest basis was raised to 21,000,000,000 francs in June, 1918.[1]

Since early in 1917 the question of the renewal of the exclusive privilege of the Banque de France to issue notes in France has been under discussion and the debate over this question has been bitter and prolonged. In late October, 1917, an agreement was signed between the Governor of the Banque and the Finance Minister renewing the Banque's privilege of twenty-five years, but the chambers were very slow in ratifying this agreement. In the course of this debate many interesting discussions of various phases of French money and banking took place. The policy of the private banks already discussed was harshly criticised by defenders of the Banque de France itself, particularly their policy of discouraging issues of French industrial securities and of selling to the French investors many tens of billions of second rate foreign bonds. The main controversy over the renewal was between the socialists who wished to make of the Banque a state institution and the economic liberals or individualists who prefer the system of private enterprise and who believe that the credit of the Banque is safer if it is left free from state control. In . the course of the controversy the old argument has been revived that if the Banque de France remains a private institution its credit would survive even a repudiation by the state of its debts —an argument hardly valid in the face of the present fact that advances to the state constitute nearly 20,000,000,000 of the state's 35,000,000,000 of assets, while Treasury bonds taken by the Banque in connection with loans by the government to its allies constitute three or four billions more. On July 30, 1918, the Chamber of Deputies voted to adopt the measure for the renewal of the privileges of the Banque de France for twenty-five years.[2] The vote was 231 to 72.

The accompanying table shows the most significant changes in the balance sheet of the Banque de France during the period of the war.

[1] London *Economist*, June 15, 1918, page 1010

[2] New York *Morning Sun*, July 31, 1918. See also London *Economist*, March 31, 1917, page 586; November 3, 1917, page 732; July 13, 1918, page 42. *New York Times*, July 12, 1918.

SELECTED ITEMS FROM BALANCE SHEET OF BANQUE DE FRANCE, 1914 TO 1918

(In millions of francs)

	1914			1915					1916				1917				1918		
	Feb. 5	June 4	July 30	Jan. 28	April 15	June 17	Sept. 2	Nov. 4	Feb. 3	June 2	Sept. 7	Nov. 2	Feb. 1	June 7	Sept. 6	Nov. 2	Feb. 7	June 6	Aug. 20
Total assets	7,381	7,607	8,787	13,648	14,673	15,135	16,257	17,393	16,853	18,453	19,572	18,812	20,569	23,204	24,383	25,616	27,511	32,821	34,477
Cash in hand	4,199	4,410	4,767	4,600	4,605	4,295	4,693	177	5,373	5,092	5,155	5,318	5,410	5,536	5,574	5,581	5,614	5,662	5,756
Discounts in Paris	580	562	1,364	103	68	76	82	99	192	155	153	255	325	196	225	304	874	909	448
Foreign bills	14	9	9	4	2	2	1	2	1	2	2	3	6	1	2	2	16	9	4
Discounts in branches	944	1,161	1,081	137	160	180	200	224	276	285	232	318	378	296	333	430	457	481	452
Moratorium bills	....	....	....	....	2,655	2,304	2,045	1,906	1,778	1,514	1,399	1,371	1,319	1,216	1,168	1,154	1,126	1,081	1,065
Advances to state for war	....	....	....	3,900	5,100	5,900	6,400	7,100	5,400	7,600	8,500	6,600	8,200	10,600	11,300	12,150	12,500	17,500	19,150
Treasury bonds in respect of advances to foreign governments	....	....	....	....	100	215	480	550	750	1,035	11,355	1,580	1,935	2,505	2,875	3,090	3,275	3,420	3,463
Notes in circulation	6,029	6,131	6,683	10,474	11,501	12,044	13,060	14,079	14,034	15,531	16,509	16,128	17,514	19,680	20,857	22,018	23,740	28,012	29,434
Current accounts: Paris	624	643	819	1,617	1,629	1,658	1,775	1,789	1,226	1,327	1,253	961	1,474	1,609	1,567	1,517	1,578	2,220	1,882
Branches	89	122	129	711	695	557	724	732	684	779	869	782	866	1,032	1,097	1,162	1,003	1,390	1,595

CHAPTER IX

Private Banks and Savings Banks in France during the War

In earlier sections we have described in detail the character
and operations of the great French private banks. We have
seen that to a large extent their deposits represent actual savings
by their depositors instead of being the consequence of loans
made by the banks, and that in very considerable measure their
business has consisted of selling foreign securities of their
depositors, instead of promoting the industry and commerce of
France. We have seen the poor quality of many of these securities and have seen the disastrous results that came from this
policy, both in the period immediately preceding the war and in
the period that followed its outbreak. Overwhelmed by a disastrous break in the prices of the securities in which they had been
dealing and of which they probably held large amounts, the
great private banks felt themselves helpless when the war broke
out, largely ceased lending operations, rediscounted heavily with
the Banque de France and hoarded the proceeds of their rediscounting operations. The first reports of virtually all the private
banks after the outbreak of the war showed large declines in their
balance sheets. It was still possible for most of them to show
nominal profits and to pay dividends, but this is probably to be
explained by the fact that in the period preceding the war they
had accumulated large reserves of one kind or another which did
not always figure in their balance sheets. The Comptoir
d'Escompte, which had had a profit of 18,000,000 francs on its
1913 operations, showed profit of 11,000,000 francs on its 1914
operations. The Crédit Lyonnais had had profits in 1913 of
41,050,000 francs. Its 1914 profits were 14,000,000 francs. Its
1913 dividend was sixty-five francs. Its 1914 dividend was
twenty-five francs.

At the outbreak of the war virtually all the private banks took
advantage of the moratorium on deposits. On January 1, 1915,

however, the Comptoir d'Escompte, the Société Générale and the Crédit Lyonnais ceased to avail themselves of the moratorium law.[1]

It has not been easy to get any indication of the extent of the losses which French banks have incurred in view of the seizure of their branches in belligerent countries. Thus the Banque de Paris et des Pays-Bas in a recent report states that it has been unable to get any information from its main branch in Belgium.

Reference to the chart on stock prices on the Paris bourse in our chapter on the bourse will show the course of shares of five great private banks. They have declined very substantially during the war period, in striking contrast to the shares of the Banque de France shown on the same chart, which have risen very substantially. It is probable that provincial banks have gained substantially in prestige as compared with the great private banks during the war period.[2] Virtually all the French banks have been forced to close some of their branches through lack of personnel.

The following tables show the main changes during the war period in assets and liabilities of the Crédit Lyonnais, Comptoir d'Escompte and Société Générale:

CRÉDIT LYONNAIS [3]
(In millions of francs)

ASSETS	1914 Jan. 31	1915 Nov. 30	1916 Dec. 31	1917 Dec. 31	1918 May 8
Cash in vaults and in the banks	202	820	689	618	806
Portfolio	1,567				
Portfolio and national defense bonds		991	1,191	1,671	1,558
Advances on collateral and reports	329	229	228	198	192
Current accounts	743	432	406	450	433
Total assets	2,897	2,563	2,653	3,040	3,100
LIABILITIES					
Deposits	974	699	705	883	964
Current acocunts	1,259	1,206	1,246	1,497	1,465
Acceptances	144	18	20	21	18

[1] *Wall Street Journal News Bulletin*, Wednesday, December 30, 1914.
[2] London *Economist*, August 11, 1917, page 209.
[3] All these tables are made from the balance sheets published by the institutions in question.

COMPTOIR D'ESCOMPTE
(In millions of francs)

ASSETS	1913 Jan. 31	1914 Dec. 31	1915 Sept. 30	1916 Dec. 31	1917 Dec. 31	1918 Mar. 31
Cash in vaults and in the banks	137	386	406	278	360	334
Portfolio	966	355				
Portfolio and national defense bonds	●		598	916	1,338	1,349
Advances on securities	235	224	172	139	154	154
Current accounts	148	179	131	125	158	155
Total assets	1,826	1,347	1,491	1,755	2,265	2,240

LIABILITIES						
Deposits and current accounts	1,307	1,041	1,123	1,330	1,868	1,831
Acceptances	182	32	36	56	48	41

SOCIÉTÉ GÉNÉRALE
(In millions of francs)

ASSETS	1913 Dec. 31	1914 Dec. 31	1915 Dec. 31	1916 Dec. 31	1917 Feb. 28	1918 Apr. 30
Cash in vaults and in the banks	173	102	120	84	87	260
Portfolio	890	277	263			
Items for collection	81	22	20			
Portfolio, items for collection and national defense bonds				406	435	793
Advances on collateral and reports	448	375	288	260	278	265
Current accounts	561	608	522	479	507	557
Total assets	2,612	1,822	1,675	1,676	1,759	2,336

LIABILITIES						
Deposits	673	457	417	452	477	613
Current accounts	1,118	624	573	655	720	1,137
Acceptances	176	102	45	13	10	25

It is interesting to note that for all of these institutions the ratio of cash on hand and in the banks to credits extended or to deposit and current account liabilities has risen very greatly. It is notable that all of them have changed their form of statements so that " portfolio " is combined with " national defense bonds," making comparison with the prewar period impossible as to the extent of their commercial advances, even assuming that " portfolio " has in the past represented exclusively commercial credits.

Noteworthy too is the extreme drop in acceptances. It is very clear that no one of these institutions is performing anything like its prewar services for commerce. A similar story is told for most of the smaller institutions. An illustrative case would be the Banque Française pour le Commerce et l'Industrie, established in 1901 with a capital of 60,000,000 francs:

Assets:	July 31, 1913	July 31, 1917
Cash in vaults and in banks	Fr. 32,000,000	Fr. 34,000,000
Portfolio	105,000,000	40,000,000
Reports and advances on securities	83,000,000	27,000,000
National defense bonds		73,000,000
Current accounts	16,000,000	23,000,000
Total assets	327,000,000	250,000,000
Liabilities:		
Current accounts	191,000,000	158,000,000
Acceptances and bills payable	55,000,000	12,000,000

A notable and pleasing exception to the general drift of the figures of the French private banks is presented by the Banque Nationale de Crédit. This institution was established in 1913, taking over the Comptoir d'Escompte de Mulhouse. It had 144 branches and agencies in 1916, centering in Paris. It started out as a commercial bank. It did not issue loans before the war, though it has since aided extensively in floating the war loans. Of the banks of the second order this is now perhaps the first in size. Its good showing is probably due to the fact that it had not been involved in the disastrous loan flotations of the prewar period. It has done much better than the great credit houses in the matter of providing new credits. Its balance sheet shows the following changes during the war:

	Dec. 31, 1913	Dec. 31, 1915	Dec. 31, 1916	Dec. 31, 1917
Assets:	Francs	Francs	Francs	Francs
Cash on hand and in Banque de France	10,000,000	13,000,000	28,000,000	59,000,000
Other banks and bankers	24,000,000	28,000,000	31,000,000	38,000,000
Portfolio	75,000,000	79,000,000	117,000,000	169,000,000
Current accounts	40,000,000	55,000,000	61,000,000	78,000,000
Advances on securities	36,000,000	44,000,000	54,000,000	71,000,000
National defense bonds		52,000,000	92,000,000	244,000,000
Total assets	345,000,000	386,000,000	502,000,000	827,000,000
Liabilities:				
Deposits and current accounts	142,000,000	214,000,000	322,000,000	581,000,000
Acceptances	67,000,000	24,000,000	29,000,000	22,000,000

In only one respect do these bank figures resemble those of the other private banks considered and that is in the decline of acceptances. Bank acceptances, so prominent in France before the war, have evidently become a matter of minor importance.

It is interesting to note that this bank has kept separate in the figures its portfolio and the national defense bonds (as is the case with the Banque Française pour le Commerce et l'Industrie, the other smaller bank whose accounts we have examined). For the Banque Nationale de Crédit, the national defense bonds are now the most important asset and their growth has been enormous since they first appeared in its balance sheet. But the portfolio also shows a great increase. It is probable that this bank has been a beneficiary of the popular distrust of the great credit houses.

The writer finds no reason to suppose that the major private banks in France are in danger of insolvency. Their general policy before the war of selling securities to the people has been disastrous for France and the depression and panic preceding the war made it impossible for them to escape substantial losses to themselves despite their efforts " to stand from under." But on the whole they have probably shifted most of the losses. The people rather than the great private banks have borne the main burden of the appalling decline in the second rate and third rate foreign securities purchased through these banks. How great these losses have been we will consider in our chapter on the French bourse. At the present time it seems probable that all the private banks in France are in a very sound position and the main criticism which we shall pass upon their war time policy relates not to its safety but to its selfishness. They have not done their duty, by and large, to the commerce and industry of France. But this we have seen in an earlier chapter.

The French savings banks presented an alarming problem at the outbreak of the war—as indeed, in less degree, has been true of savings banks in England and the United States. The great difficulty grew out of the tendency of depositors to withdraw their deposits to meet the war emergencies and rising commodity prices at the same time that the securities held by these institutions were declining heavily in price on the bourse. Whatever the causes involved, the clear tendency in France, the United States and Great Britain has been for commodity prices to rise and for securities of a fixed yield to decline. The figures for deposits and withdrawals of the French savings banks are substantially represented in the figures of the operations of the Caisse des Dépôts et Consignations with the *caisses d'épargne ordinaires*. The former is a great state institution which receives trust funds from the courts, the deposits of the friendly societies and the deposits of the ordinary savings banks, with some other minor items. The latter, the ordinary savings banks, are institutions scattered all over the country which receive savings deposits from individuals and turn them over to the great central institution for investment. They are legally bound to do this. When their depositors call on them for funds they call on the central institutions. The total liabilities of the Caisse des Dépôts et Consignations on December 31, 1913, were 5,620,000,-000 francs, of which over four billions were due to the savings banks.[1] These funds before the war had been chiefly invested in the 3 per cent *rente,* at an average price above 85. During the war the price of the 3 per cent *rente* has declined from 84 or 85 to about 60, which, with the decline of other investments, no doubt has left the Caisse des Dépôts et Consignations technically insolvent. However, technical insolvency is not a serious matter for this institution, assuming that the state itself remains solvent, since there is a tacit understanding that the state will protect the institution. In the great loan of 1915, for example, the state took indirect steps to protect savings deposits by accepting them for subscriptions to the loan. At the outbreak of the war excess of withdrawals over deposits was large. Thus for the period January 1 to July 20, 1914, deposits exceeded withdrawals by about 21,000,000 francs. For the period July 20 to December 20, 1914, withdrawals exceeded deposits by 134,000,000 francs despite heavy restrictions under the moratorium on withdrawals.[2]

[1] See balance sheet in *Quarterly Journal of Economics,* November, 1915, page 75.
[2] See weekly figures in *Economiste Français.*

In June, 1915, it was still necessary to limit withdrawals to fifty francs per book per fortnight, and withdrawals still substantially exceeded deposits. In May, 1917, deposits and withdrawals were substantially equal, deposits being 16,563,000 francs and withdrawals, 16,697,000 francs. The week of October 11 to October 20, 1917, showed deposits of 7,215,000 francs and withdrawals of only 1,796,000 francs. The excess of deposits over withdrawals from January 1 to October 10, 1917, was 150,422,000, showing that the tide had turned definitely and that the savings banks were safe. It is not necessary that these institutions should be able to liquidate their assets in order to remain in a sound position. The emergency past, the most significant part of their operations lies in the field of income accounts rather than of capital accounts. With the state behind them they are safe.

Criticism of their policy of investing chiefly in the *rente* may be made.[1] Lysis says that the savings banks have been used by the state to protect the *rente* against attacks on the part of the great banks. This may be true. It is probably true in any case that the extensive purchases of the *rente* by the Caisse des Dépôts et Consignations has given the *rente* an artificial price in the prewar period and has made the earnings of the savings deposits consequently less than they would have been. The state is thus under great moral obligations to this institution.

In 1916 a new law raised the maximum deposits at the savings banks from 1,500 to 3,000 francs and the maximum deposits in friendly societies from 15,000 to 25,000 francs.[2]

. The position of the Crédit Foncier would in many respects be like the position of the savings banks since its main assets are mortgages on real estate—fixed investments which tend to depreciate as interest rates rise. The position would tend to be stronger to the extent that it had a large margin in the value of the real estate. On the other hand, its position would tend to be weaker in that a large amount of its loans were made in the territory occupied by the Germans. A large amount of its in-

---

[1] *Op. cit.*, page 208.
[2] London *Economist*, August 12, 1916, page 287.

come from the mortgages in occupied territory has been of course shut off.[1] On the whole, however, the Crédit Foncier has seemed to weather the storm. Its profits in 1916 were 12,594,000 francs and its dividend 25 francs. In 1917 its profits were 15,805,000 francs and its dividend 30 francs.[2] Early in 1917 the Crédit Foncier issued a new block of securities nominally amounting to 600,000,000 francs; actually issued at 285 per 300 franc bond. The interest was $5\frac{1}{2}$ per cent and the term seventy years. The issue was made more attractive by the prospect of valuable prizes: six in number, one of 500,000 francs and five of 250,000 francs, to be awarded one at a time at six periodical drawings. There was great popular interest in this issue.[3]

Early in 1917 some new credit institutions for small traders and manufacturers were established, mutual guarantee societies similar to the agricultural syndicates in certain respects.[4] There has been increasing recognition in France during the war of the need for credit for manufacturers and agriculturists, and we have already seen that the state itself has made extensive advances to various necessary enterprises.[5]

[1] London *Economist,* January 2, 1915, page 17.
[2] *Journal des Economistes,* May 15, 1918, pages 223-224.
[3] London *Economist.* March 10, 1917, page 472.
[4] *Ibid.,* March 24, 1917, page 554.
[5] In connection with the great loan of 1916, Albert Thomas stated that part of the loan was going into real capital, plants which would be useful after the war. *Ibid.,* October 28, 1916, page 822.

CHAPTER X

The Moratorium in France

In an earlier chapter dealing with the outbreak of the war we have seen how rigorous a moratorium was established in France and have seen something of the difficulties occasioned thereby. A distinguished French financial authority expresses the opinion that in the absence of a moratorium on the bourse the general moratorium would have been unnecessary. Tying up the bourse made the position of the banks very difficult in view of the large amount of loans they had on stock exchange securities. This compelled the banks in his opinion to have recourse to a moratorium on deposits and thus made it necessary for the general public to have a relief from the pressure of creditors. The weakness of the bourse was thus the crux of the whole matter.

The magnitude of the loans involved in the bourse settlement immediately preceding the outbreak of the war was about as follows:

```
On the Parquet....................Fr. 600,000,000
On the Coulisse (curb)  ........      150,000,000 to 200,000,000
```

with an additional 800,000,000 francs on extra-bourse collateral loans confined to the banks and credit houses, presumably also " *reports* " or " *contangoes* " supposed to be liquidated at the same time that the bourse settlement was made. The Parquet was in even worse position than the Coulisse, since many of the Coulisse securities were still negotiable at London and Petrograd.[1]

It is interesting to contrast the position of Paris and London, where the fortnightly stock exchange settlement prevails, with that of New York, where daily settlements are made. The daily settlement in New York gives rise to a much greater volume of

[1] London *Economist*, November 14, 1914, page 883; November 21, 1914, page 921; Laughlin, *op. cit.*, pages 157-158.

bank clearings, of shifting of loans and of checks between
brokers and brokers or between bankers and brokers. There are
times when it may be characterized almost as a nuisance in the
sheer physical magnitude of the mechanical operations which
bank clerks, stock exchange clearing house clerks, and brokers
have to go through with, but it has the supreme merit of giving
a clean slate at the end of each day. The problems in New York
following the closing of the stock exchange at the outbreak of
the war were much simpler as a result of the daily settlement than
were the problems of Paris and London, where the fortnightly
accumulation of operations hung over. It is of course not true
that the advantage in favor of the New York method is 14 to 1.
The actual magnitude of loans on the Paris bourse would in any
case have been great, but daily settlements would have had the
advantage in the first place of discovering the weak points earlier
and would moreover have substantially reduced the magnitude of
the loans hanging over.

Early in November, 1914, cautious plans were made and
agreed to by the Banque de France for the relief of the Parquet,
the official bourse. The plan involved an advance by the Banque
of 40 per cent of the reports or loans on securities for the fortnightly settlement, to be made on deposit of the securities with
the Banque, at 5 per cent. The Banque requires three names on
all loans made by it and these loans had only two names, that
of the lender and that of the borrower. To give the third name
required, it was arranged that the Parquet itself, the Syndicat
des Agents de Change, should guarantee these loans made by
the Banque. Forty per cent of the interest should go to the
Banque and 60 per cent to the original lenders.[1] Comparatively
little use seems to have been made of this arrangement owing to
difficulties made by the Syndicat itself, and Ribot resisted pressure to have the Banque de France liquidate the bourse on other
terms.[2] The Coulisse later in November tried to get relief from
the Banque by a similar plan, proposing to organize a limited
liability company with a capital of 44,000,000 francs (one-

[1] London *Economist,* November 14, 1914, page 883; November 21, 1914,
page 921.
[2] *Ibid.,* December 19, 1914, page 1069; July 24, 1915, page 133.

quarter paid in), which should supply the third signature for reports. Nothing seems to have come of this.

By July, 1915, the difficulties had become greater through the decline of the *rente*, which had dropped to 69.95, and of the Russian 5's of 1906, which were down to 86.75. Interest of course continued to accumulate. But there had been a great deal of private and voluntary liquidation on the bourse. Of the 600,000,000 francs on the Parquet, all but 180,000,000 had been settled. By August only 25 per cent of the Coulisse *reports* remained unsettled. In August a plan was arranged by the Parquet for the issue of 75,000,000 francs of 20–50 year points at 6 per cent to be issued at 980 francs per thousand, to be tax exempt, guaranteed by the members of the bourse as a whole, with the interest secured by a levy on their commissions,[1] to provide funds for the settlement. This high rate of interest on a loan of such length is striking evidence of the weakened credit of the bourse.

In October, 1915,[2] the bourse settlement, which had hung over from the outbreak of the war, finally went through with very little trouble and the bourse moratorium lapsed.

The general moratorium lasted much longer. On October 27, 1914, Ribot announced a modification [3] in the moratorium. For the general moratorium, a distinction was made between those called to the colors and those remaining at home. For the first class the moratorium continued absolute; for the second class a modified régime was set up to December 31. During November they could not be pressed by legal process, but after December 1 the question of whether the debtor was maliciously taking advantage of the moratorium could be raised by the civil tribunals. The decree also made a modification in the bank moratorium. The decree of August 9 had limited sums withdrawn by depositors to 250 francs plus 5 per cent of the surplus; on

[1] *Ibid.*, July 3, 1915, page 16; July 24, 1915, page 133; August 28, 1915, page 327.

[2] Professor Laughlin, *op. cit.*, page 169, dates this apparently as October, 1914, which would seem to be an error. *Cf.* London *Economist*, October 9, 1915, page 541.

[3] *Economiste Français*, October 31, 1914; London *Economist*, November 7, 1914, page 842.

August 29, this was raised to 250 francs plus 20 per cent of the surplus; on September 27, to 250 francs plus 25 per cent of the surplus. By Ribot's new statement, it was raised to 1,000 francs plus 40 per cent for November, and 1,000 francs plus 50 per cent for December.

This decree represented, of course, a very considerable though cautious modification of the moratorium, but it led to a frightened reaction. A new decree issued November 24 continued the moratorium in full rigor to the end of December, suspending the previous modification relating to nonmobilized debtors.[1] One difficulty arose from the fact that the distinction between those mobilized and those not with the colors was hard to draw, since a man might himself be with the army while his firm continued in business.

Certain of the great banks, however, ceased to take advantage of the moratorium on deposits on the first of January, 1915, as we have seen in our chapter on the private banks. But the general moratorium continued with many renewals and partial modifications for a long, long time. In the last statement of the Banque de France of August, 1918, there still appear over a billion francs of the premoratorium bills, a substantial reduction from the nearly four billion francs of the fall of 1914, to be sure, but still a large holdover.

The moratorium on rents has remained a vexed question into 1918. A measure was passed by the Chamber of Deputies in June, 1917, dealing with the matter, but the Senate refused to concur, and in March, 1918, the Chamber was still debating the question.[2] The exact status of the moratorium at the present time is not clear. A very large body of prewar debts have been voluntarily liquidated. Modifications of the moratorium which have put much discretion in the hands of the civil tribunals have led to further liquidations. No doubt many premoratorium debts can never be paid as the debtors are dead or ruined. There will probably remain, however, at the end of the war a substantial number of unpaid debts which will then be liquidated.

[1] London *Economist*, December 5, 1914, page 997.
[2] *Ibid.*, June 28, 1917, page 119; March 2, 1918, page 387.

In our section dealing with the outbreak of the war, the opinion was expressed that at every stage the moratorium legislation went too far, that, even granting the necessity of extraordinary remedies, no such rigid restrictions were called for. Certain it is that the moratorium hung as a millstone about the neck of France, hampering her recovery for a long time. The one doubt that must be expressed as to the validity of this verdict hinges on the weakness of the private banks; had they been strong enough and courageous enough they could have made such rigorous measures unnecessary. With their ability to rediscount on the Banque de France and to receive from the Banque its notes circulating under the *cours forcé*, it is not easy to see why they could not have expanded their credits to any necessary extent to enable solvent debtors to meet their obligations. But with the weak, selfish and timid course which the great private banks took, it may be that a moratorium was unavoidable. It is not to be forgotten in contrasting France with Great Britain and the United States in this matter, that virtually the whole man power of France was suddenly mobilized, that her whole industry and commerce were thrown violently out of gear by the necessities of the case, that her richest provinces were seized and that her capital city itself was in imminent danger.

CHAPTER XI

The French Bourse during the War

In our chapter on "France at the outbreak of the war," attention was centered on the bourse. The list of securities dealt in there had been weakened by prewar speculation and depression. We have seen how largely they consisted of second rate issues of foreign governments, Russians, Bulgarians, Brazilians, Argentine securities, Mexican securities and the like. When to this weakness was added the frightened selling on the bourses of Vienna, Berlin and other centers, followed by the wild panic when war was clearly in sight, it is not surprising that the whole fabric collapsed. We saw something of the extent of the decline of representative securities and the extent of the recovery by December 7, 1914, when the bourse was reopened for cash trading only. A preceding chapter has given an account of the bourse moratorium and of the lapsing of that moratorium in October, 1915.

The main story of the bourse in the four years following the outbreak of the war is best told in the accompanying charts. Attention may be called to the divergence between the prices of shares of the Banque de France and of the other French banks. The five banks treated in the curve for the other French banks are:

Banque de Paris et des Pays-Bas
Comptoir d'Escompte
Crédit Foncier
Crédit Industriel (liberée)
Crédit Lyonnais

There has been a steady rise in the shares of the Banque de France from the last quarter of 1915 and a decided decline in the shares of the other banks. The reasons for this have been fully stated in our previous discussions of these institutions.

The two railway shares chosen are the Midi and the Lyons,

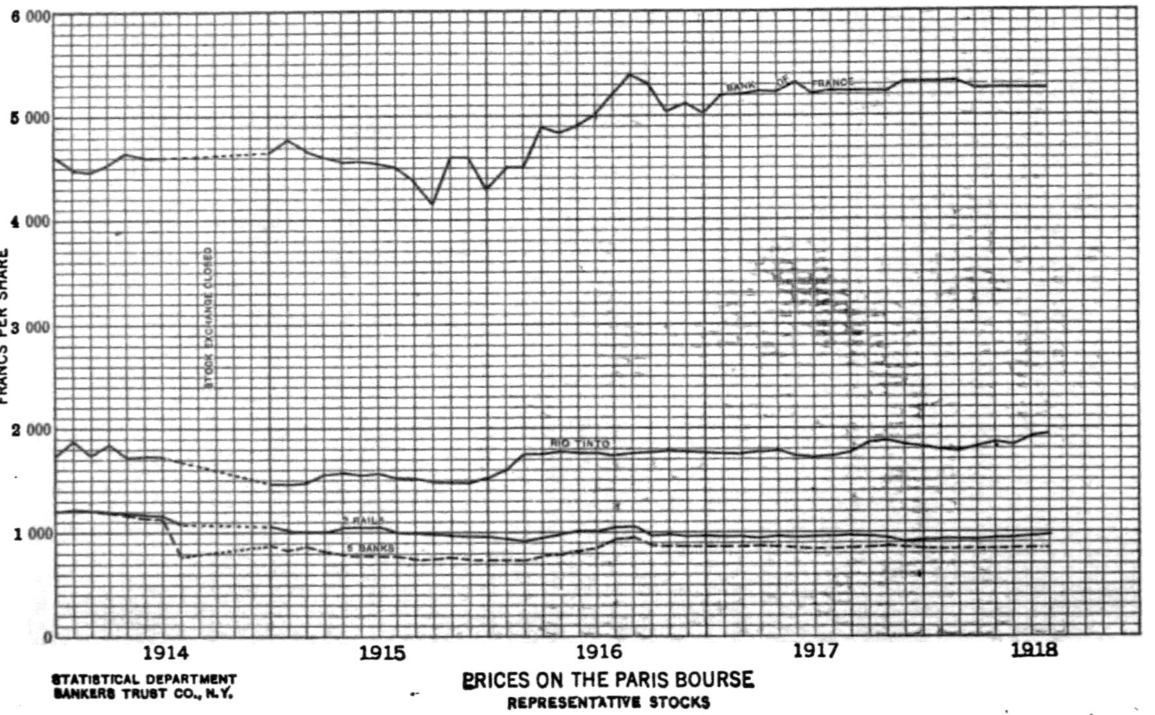
FRANCS PER SHARE
6 000
5 000
4 000
3 000
2 000
1 000
0
BANK OF FRANCE
RIO TINTO
5 RAILS
6 BANKS
STOCK EXCHANGE CLOSED
1914
1915
1916
1917
1918
PRICES ON THE PARIS BOURSE
REPRESENTATIVE STOCKS
STATISTICAL DEPARTMENT
BANKERS TRUST CO., N.Y.

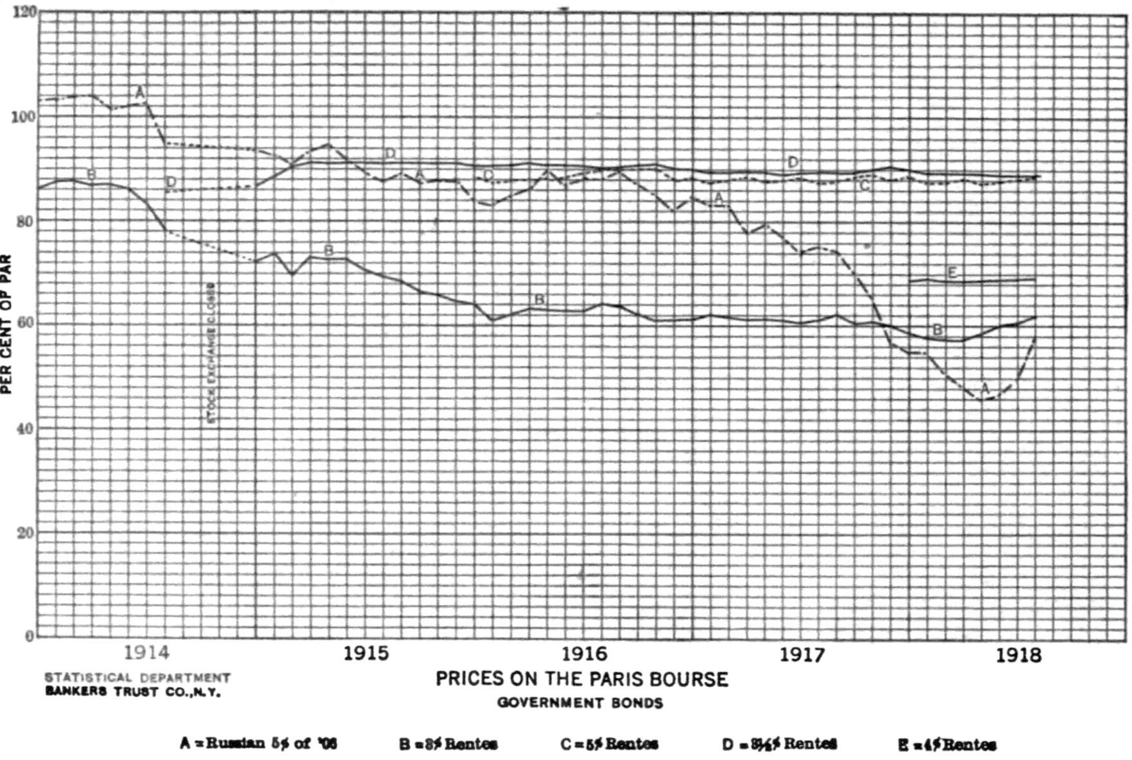
PER CENT OF PAR
120
100
80
60
40
20
0
1914
1915
1916
1917
1918
STOCK EXCHANGE CLOSED
A
B
C
D
E
STATISTICAL DEPARTMENT
BANKERS TRUST CO.,N.Y.
PRICES ON THE PARIS BOURSE
GOVERNMENT BONDS
A = Russian 5% of '06
B = 3% Rentes
C = 5% Rentes
D = 3½% Rentes
E = 4% Rentes

neither of which has been seriously affected directly by the German invasion. On the whole, the rails show less decline than the private banks.

Rio Tinto, a famous Spanish copper, dealt in on the London exchange as well as on the Paris bourse, is fairly representative of securities favorably affected, so far as earnings are concerned, by the war. Its moderate rise is significant of the general tendency of all securities to yield a higher return for given prices.

The two curves which are significant of the greatest losses to French investors are the 3 per cent *rente,* which has declined from 84 to about 60, though holding fairly steady since the beginning of 1916, and the Russian 5's of 1906, which have declined from over 100 to a low of 46, with a recent limited upturn. The decline in the price of the *rente* represents primarily not loss of confidence in the French Government, but scarcity of capital and a general rise in interest rates. The decline in the Russian security, however, is chiefly due, as our curve shows, to the collapse of Russia in 1917 and 1918. Many other Russian securities would show a much heavier decline, particularly Russian industrials, rails and banks. It is interesting to note that just prior to the Russian revolution, Russian securities were very strong. There had been an industrial revival in Russia and there was much confidence in France in the Russian situation.[1] Nor did the revolution itself immediately lead to depression in the price of Russian securities. The Russian revolution was exceedingly popular in France. Ribot, succeeding Briand as Premier in March, 1917, spoke very encouragingly of the Russian situation.[2] The general course of Russians held fairly well for some weeks, but by November, 1917, the collapse was pretty complete. The ruble was worth only 75 centimes (about 15 cents) against a mint par of over 50 cents, and Russian securities generally were shot to pieces. By January, 1918, it was clear that disaster threatened many small investors in Russian funds and steps were being taken by the French and British Governments to protect them. Vidal, a well

---

[1] London *Economist,* March 17, 1917, page 512.
[2] *Ibid.,* March 31, 1917, page 586.

known authority on French securities, gave out a reassuring statement on the inability of a great state to remain bankrupt. Lloyd George made the British Government responsible for the Russian Treasury bonds and commercial bills discounted under the commercial treaty of 1915 between the Bank of England and the Finance Ministry of Russia.[1] There was still a belief that the Bolsheviki would be unable to carry out their plans, however. Edmond Théry, well known as a writer of French finance, gave out a statement in January, 1918, with reference to the Russian situation, which tended somewhat to restore confidence. His figures served to show that the railway revenues in Russia, amounting to 321 million rubles, constituted 80 per cent of the interest on the Russian state debt by the close of 1912. He thought that not over 12,000,000,000 francs of Russian securities of all kinds were held in France at the outbreak of the war, though other estimates[2] have run as high as 20,000,000,000. About three-fourths of this 12,000,000,000 had been used, he said, in purchasing existing railways, in creating new lines, in developing industry and agriculture and in consolidating old loans. From 1902 to 1912 there had been rapid economic developments in Russia, shown by the following percentage increases for various commodities:[3]

	Per cent		Per cent
Wheat	30	Iron and steel	100
Barley	63	Imports	95
Oats	21	Exports	76
Potatoes	32	Ordinary budget receipts	40
Coal	77	Railway receipts	80

The French Government has not assumed full responsibility for the Russian securities, but it has paid the coupons, " *transitoirement et provisoirement*," [4] recognizing specially its responsibility for loans floated since the outbreak of the war and recognizing that a great deal of the French capital invested in Russia was invested by patriots who foresaw the war and felt that they were strengthening an ally who would protect France against the enemy. Most of the bonds are in the hands of comparatively

[1] *Ibid.,* January 26, 1918, page 118.
[2] *Ibid.,* May 2, 1918, page 915.
[3] *Ibid.,* February 2, 1918, page 159.
[4] *Journal des Economistes,* May 15, 1918, page 280.

poor people. The Russian loan of January, 1914, had been expressly sanctioned by the Finance Ministry on the ground that it was to be used for strategic railways. The total burden of interest on Russian securities would be about a billion francs a year, not easy for the French state to bear.[1] In connection with the new French war loan of October, 1918, provision is made for the acceptance of Russian coupons up to 50 per cent of a subscription.[2]

Our curves do not show the course of French war stocks because of the difficulty in getting quotations. There have been war booms in munition shares, among them Hotchkiss and Creusot. There have been vigorous booms in oil stocks, coppers, chemicals, rubbers and other securities.

An examination of the curves for French securities from 1917 on will show comparatively slight influence of the entrance of America into the war. The main immediate effect of American entrance into the war was an improvement in French exchange on foreign countries, particularly the United States, Great Britain and Switzerland. On the whole, the bourse has not been violently affected by political events since the reopening after the first outbreak of the war. There was heavy pressure on bad Italian and Russian news in the fall of 1917. The prolonged battle of Verdun, however, in the summer of 1916 left the bourse strong at the end of one hundred days. To a very considerable extent, the French bourse has been under control and violent breaks have been averted.

[1] London *Economist*, May 2, 1918, page 915.
[2] *New York Times*, September 19, 1918.

CHAPTER XII

French Foreign Trade and Foreign Exchange

In a large way we have already outlined [1] the course of the foreign trade relations of France during the war. From the beginning of the war, France has bought increasingly from foreign countries more than she has exported, and there has been a continuous piling up of an adverse balance of trade. Even before the war, the physical balance of trade was " adverse " to France, but this, as we have seen, was merely symptomatic of her creditor position. A rich country with large foreign investments can afford to import more than she exports, just as an individual capitalist can afford to consume more than he produces by his current labor.

In the first six months of the war, France was a creditor to all countries and a debtor to none. In the early two or three months of the war, checks on New York and on London were at a heavy discount in the French markets, owing to the interruption of the shipments of gold and the inability of American and English banks to meet their obligations easily in Paris. But during these six months France began to buy largely abroad and at the end of the six months she had become debtor on current items, so that the foreign exchange rates all turned against her with the exception of those on Italy and Russia. The climax on sterling and dollars was reached on April 13, 1916, when a check on London was worth 28.93 francs per pound (as against a mint par of 25.22) and dollar exchange (cable) was worth 6.07 francs per dollar (as against a mint par of 5.18). This represented a discount of over 12 per cent on the franc in terms of American dollars.

[1] Chapter on " Depression and ' *Réprise des Affaires.*' "

On April 14, 1916, there was an agreement made between the French and English Governments dealing with foreign exchange. The Banque de France through the Treasury was enabled to take control of the situation and it steadily improved. The chief factors have been large credits in Great Britain, the export of gold by the Banque de France to the Bank of England, the pledge of neutral securities as a basis for loans, growing confidence in Allied victories and large loan flotations in America, and finally after the entrance of the United States into the war, direct loans by the American Government to the French Government. The following table [1] of exchange rates in Paris on various points for three dates in 1916 will be of interest:

	Rate, Jan. 1	Highest Rate		Rate, Sept. 30
		Date	Rate	
London	27.80	Apr. 13	28.93	27.84
Holland	2.59	Jan. 11	2.66½	2.39
Italy	.89	May 2	.95	.90½
New York	5.86	Apr. 13	6.07	5.84½
Russia	1.74	Sept. 1	1.97½	1.87
Sweden	1.63	May 11	1.85½	1.66
Switzerland	1.11½	Apr. 11	1.17	1.10

An exact summing up of the debits and credits in France's balance of international indebtedness is not possible on the basis of data accessible to the present writer, but certain significant figures can be given which will outline the main elements in the picture. The adverse trade balance, large in 1915, became very great indeed in 1916. The first eleven months of 1916 show an adverse trade balance of 12,942,000,000 francs when allowance is made for rising prices. The official figures as commonly given out have been based on the prices of 1914, with, after the first year of the war, a correction for price changes.[2] The first eleven months, therefore, show an adverse trade balance well in excess of the great loan of 1916 (11,360,000,000 francs). These figures, however, do not indicate the full extent of the adverse trade balance, since many of the imports on government account were not included in them.

As we have earlier seen, France had difficulties in restricting

<hr>

[1] London *Economist*, October 14, 1916, page 650.
[2] *Ibid.*, January 6, 1917, page 14.

her imports. Relying on foreign trade to supply her with the necessities of the war instead of seeking early to make herself self-sufficient in those matters, she had had a revival of the production and export of luxuries with which to pay for the import of necessities. This policy, seemingly wise at its inception, when the volume of the world's shipping seemed adequate, presented increasing difficulties as the submarines grew more deadly and as the available shipping of the world became scarce. It led to a further complication in that France was hampered in her efforts to check the importation of luxuries. If she restricted the importation of luxuries from other countries, they would retaliate by restricting the export of French luxuries, which would hamper France in her efforts to pay for the things she needed. But in March, 1917, following England's restriction of imports of luxuries from France, the French Government took vigorous control of foreign trade and allowed no imports except by the state save on special authority.

In these figures for an eleven month period, we have indicated something of the magnitude of the problem which France had to face in making foreign payment. In part this has been done through direct borrowings from allies. From the governments of England, the United States and Japan and from private investors in the United States and Japan, France has borrowed as follows,[1] down to September 7, 1918:

England	Fr.	9,781,665,000
United States		10,325,000,000
Japan		390,000,000
American investors (seven principal issues)		2,652,500,000
Japanese investors		193,440,000
Total	Fr.	23,342,605,000

The seven principal issues referred to, taken by American investors, are as follows:

American Foreign Securities	Fr.	472,500,000
The Anglo-French Loan (half)		1,250,000,000
The French Republic Loan		500,000,000
City of Paris Loan		250,000,000
City of Bordeaux Loan		60,000,000
City of Lyons Loan		60,000,000
City of Marseilles Loan		60,000,000
Total	Fr.	2,652,500,000

[1] The writer is indebted for these figures to the Statistical Department of the National Bank of Commerce in New York.

To this 23,342,605,000 francs must be added large sums placed with English investors both through private agencies and directly by the French Government in connection with the great loans, and various smaller loans in Norway, Spain and other countries, chiefly short term credits to protect the exchanges. There have been other similar credits of short maturity, now largely repaid, placed in the United States, and to some extent Americans have invested directly in the war loans in Paris.

In partial offset of these debts, France had loaned her allies, Russia, Italy, Belgium, Serbia and Roumania, by December 31, 1917, 6,364,294,100 francs, and has provided in her budget for additional loans to allies of 56,632,100 francs by the end of the fiscal year 1918.[1] Our chapter on the Banque de France has dealt with the gold policy and foreign exchange policy of that institution. Certain of the loans placed in the United States have been based on American securities owned by French investors mobilized to serve as collateral. The extent of this has not been great. France had a comparatively small amount of American securities. In very large degree indeed the foreign securities held in France were not of a sort which she could dispose of in other markets. There has been during the past four years little enthusiasm among investors outside of France for Russian, Bulgarian, Brazilian, Turkish or Mexican securities. As early as June, 1915, the French Government through the great credit houses began to corral American railroad securities, making favorable terms to French investors in these issues. The result was a rise in the French bourse of American securities and a cordial response on the part of French investors to the requests of the government and the banks. But the total amount involved was small. A billion francs would probably cover all the American railway securities listed on the French bourse.[2]

Interesting episodes in the French exchange market have been the collapse of rubles, which in November, 1917, fell as low as 75 centimes per ruble (about 15 cents as against a par of over 50 cents), and the weakness of Italian exchange, which reached

---

[1] *Economic World,* March 23, 1918, page 410.
[2] London *Economist,* June 12, 1915, page 1205; June 25, 1915, page 1299.

its low point at about the same time. The problem of Russian exchange has been a serious concern for France from the beginning. In February, 1915, the finance ministers of Great Britain, France and Russia met in Paris for the purpose of uniting the financial resources of the Triple Entente, chiefly to protect Russian exchange which was then weakened by the failure to get wheat through the Dardanelles. In June, 1916, following other violent fluctuations in pesetas, a credit was secured in Spain of 20,000,000 francs monthly for six months. About the same time, England and France negotiated small loans in Norway. A rise in Brazilians in London in May, 1916, gave France some opportunity to protect her exchange by selling the securities in the London market, but the ability of the London market to absorb securities from other countries has not been great enough to aid substantially in the enormous exchange problem which France has had to face.[1]

In February, 1916, a loan for $30,000,000 (150,000,000 francs) was placed in America for the Schneider-Creusot munitions firm through twenty syndicate bankers in the United States. The French bankers supporting the loan were the Union Parisienne, Rothschild, the Crédit Lyonnais, the Comptoir d'Escompte, the Crédit Industriel and the Banque de Paris et des Pays-Bas. But this is a minor rill in a great river.

There has been increasing government control of foreign exchange operations, particularly since the middle of 1917. Distinguished French financial representatives have come to America more than once through the war and since our entry into the war. The French High Commission in Washington and the Agence Financière in New York have played a large rôle in securing and in disbursing French credits in the United States. Throughout the war the firm of J. P. Morgan & Co. has been closely associated with the British and French Governments.

During the summer of 1918 there has been a different problem in the financial relations of the United States and France in that

[1] London *Economist*, May 27, 1916, page 1021: "French Correspondence," March 25, 1916.

the American armies in France have made large expenditures in that country which have necessitated the securing of American credits in France. The details of this operation can not at present be stated. It is probable, however, that the rapid expansion in notes of the Banque de France during 1918 had some connection with this problem.[1]

One factor which at certain periods in the war has had no small influence on the standing of French exchange in neutral markets in Europe has been the efforts of the German Government to purchase French, Russian or American bank notes as well as securities held in France of certain Russian and Balkan industrial corporations. The explanation is not wholly clear. Apparently it has been easier for Germany to make payments in the Ukraine with notes of the Allies than to use her own notes for the purpose. The desire of the Germans to secure the stocks of Russian and Balkan corporations has apparently been due to the desire to get control of these corporations. Steps have been taken by the French Government to check the export of such moneys and securities.[2]

As stated above, the greatest discount on the franc in New York was something over 12 per cent in April, 1916. This had dropped to about 11 per cent by March, 1917, and with our break of diplomatic relations with Germany it dropped still further to a trifle over 8 per cent. The low since then was in September, 1917, when a 10 per cent discount was reached. In August, 1918, the discount on French money in New York was about 9 per cent.

From September, 1914, to March, 1915, the franc and pound sterling moved closely together in New York, but the decline in francs in 1915 in New York was much greater than that of the pound sterling. With March, 1917, however, the franc made an advance while the pound sterling remained unchanged. In a large way, it may be said that the franc and the pound sterling have shared similar fortunes in New York with the franc trailing substantially in the rear. On the whole, the slight discount throughout this period of gigantic expenditure is a striking

[1] London *Economist*, July 13, 1918, page 42.
[2] *Ibid.*

tribute both to the prestige of the French financial system and to the loyalty of Lombard Street. France has perforce leaned heavily on England in dealing with the exchange problem. Since March, 1917, of course, it has been almost wholly American credits which have sustained both the pound and the franc.

PART II

THE UNITED STATES

CHAPTER XIII

New York at the Outbreak of the War

The outbreak of the war found the United States with a very safe credit position. Trade was dull, merchants and bankers were moving under shortened sail, no great new enterprises had recently been undertaken and the general situation was thoroughly solvent. There had been indeed no real boom since the panic of 1907. Ordinarily following a panic and a period of depression such as that of 1907-1908, there comes a revival of business with progressive tempo, culminating in a period of active prosperity. The "business cycle," as we know it, is an alternation of prosperity, crisis, depression and prosperity again. But following the panic of 1907 there had been a steady drag. The year 1909 had been an active year and 1910 had continued activity with some reduction in the tempo, but 1911, as shown both by figures for prices and for physical volume of production (indicated by railroad gross receipts) had shown a setback. In 1912, there was a substantial rise in wholesale prices followed by a substantial setback in 1913, with a moderate continuance through both these years of physical productivity, as indicated by railroad gross receipts. But there had been nothing following 1907 that could be called a real boom.[1]

In retrospect, it is possible to offer an explanation of this, though some shrewd observers, as Mr. A. D. Noyes, had seen the explanation before the outbreak of the war. For a good many years before 1914 Europe had seen the war coming. The Banque de France as early as 1899 began its policy of accumulating gold, primarily as a war chest. Between 1899 and 1910 the Banque de France increased its gold reserves by 75 per cent, but increased its discounts and advances during the same period by only 5 per cent. In general, for several years before the war,

---

[1] *Vide* the present writer's *Value of Money*, page 278, for the statistics referred to.

European investors were becoming more cautious in their purchase of American securities and the United States were increasingly obliged to provide their own capital for industrial developments. As a debtor country accustomed to borrowing largely from foreign capitalists, we felt a drag when foreign investments in our securities declined. If Europe would not lend, we could not so readily expand. During the two years preceding the war particularly, France had been unable to make foreign investments as before. The investments which she had been making in the years preceding 1912 had been to a large degree, as we have seen, in Russians, Bulgarians, Argentine securities, Mexican securities and the like, and French investment in American securities had very largely ceased. With slight expansion, therefore, we were well prepared to meet the shock of the war— in striking contrast with France or with Brazil.

In one respect, however, the coming of the war found us unfortunately placed. We were subject to heavy calls from Europe for gold. There had been a drain on New York's gold for some time before. Beginning with 1912 Germany had been accumulating gold in unusual amounts and France and Russia began early in 1914 a rapid accumulation of gold.

Moreover, from March, 1914, to August, 1914, imports to the United States had substantially exceeded exports for every month—something unprecedented for many years before the war. An excess of imports over exports had not occurred for more than a month at a time for a number of years preceding March, 1914.[1] Europe was depressed and had reduced its buying. Our imports were not unusually large, but our exports were unusually small.

July is normally in any case the time of lowest exports from the United States, while our exports usually grow very large shortly thereafter, culminating in October, November or December in very heavy shipments of grain and other agricultural products. It has been a long standing practice of American bankers to tide over the period of low exports in July by draw-

---

[1] See L. C. Sorell: "Dislocations in the Foreign Trade of the United States Resulting from the War," *Journal of Political Economy*, January, 1916, page 28 (chart).

ing finance time bills on London in payment for imports which they liquidate later by documentary bills [1] drawn on London, connected with our heavy autumn exports. During July, 1914, the usual volume of these short term finance bills had been drawn and there was a large volume of current indebtedness by New York to London as a result.

As we have seen, New York bore the brunt of the heavy selling by frightened European investors of securities at the outbreak of the war. These securities, sold for cash in the New York market, gave rise to an enormous volume of demand indebtedness on the part of New York brokers to their European clients and enormously increased the demand for sight exchange on London.

At the same time the shock of the war had demoralized the London foreign exchange market and had interrupted the relations between New York and London bankers which would ordinarily make possible the creation of a new supply of finance bills on London with which to make these payments. Ordinarily, New York bankers, if they are willing to pay the interest rates demanded, have large leeway in drawing time finance bills on their London correspondents, which, accepted by these correspondents, may be discounted in the London market and provide cash funds against which New York bankers may draw. But the credit of the London acceptance houses was heavily shaken by the war and the business of accepting and discounting in London was practically stopped for a time. The only way, therefore, by which New York banks could increase their supply of sterling exchange was by the actual shipment of gold, and this became impossible after England declared war on Germany and the seas became unsafe for shipping. Under these conditions, exchange rates on London soared to unprecedented heights. Five, six and even seven dollars a pound were paid in certain cases. These high rates are not representative of an organized market, but merely of the virtual absence of available credits in

---

[1] "Documentary bills" are bills drawn by shippers of goods, accompanied by documents evidencing the fact and value of the shipments, as bills of lading, insurance policies, consular invoices, etc. "Finance bills" are drawn by bankers on bankers.

London and of the necessities of urgent purchasers anxious to honor their obligations in London.

In this unprecedented situation, the New York stock exchange was forced to close. In all its long history this institution has been closed but once before, in the panic of 1873, and then only for a period of ten days. It closed July 31, 1914, for an indefinite period and virtually all the other stock exchanges of the United States followed its lead. It was not until November 28, 1914, that it was reopened at all, and then only for bond trading for cash or " regular way " (*i.e.,* on the daily settlement basis) and at minimum prices fixed by a committee of the stock exchange. On Saturday, December 12, a restricted list of stocks, excluding those in which there was danger of heavy international selling, was admitted for cash or " regular way " trading again, with minimum prices fixed by a committee. All stocks were admitted on December 15, 1914, but minimum prices prevailed for a number of weeks following. All restrictions on prices were finally removed on April 1, 1915.

The stock exchange was in a fairly strong position in July, 1914. Prices had declined since early in the year, and the high prices of 1914 were not high as compared with earlier years. Various uncertainties as to the future of business had led, moreover, to a large short interest which constituted a protection when further selling should come, as the shorts would take advantage of further declines to " take profits." There had been a reduced volume of speculation for a number of years. The last preceding year of real stock exchange activity had been 1909, when 214,-000,000 shares were sold. The following table shows a steady decline in share sales from that year:

	Shares
1909	214,000,000
1910	164,000,000
1911	127,000,000
1912	131,000,000
1913	83,000,000
1914	47,000,000 [1]

Even 1909 had not been a year of extraordinary stock exchange activity. In 1906, 284,000,000 shares had been sold; in

[1] Exchange closed for over three months.

1905, 263,000,000; in 1901, 266,000,000. A number of other years had approached 1909 in magnitude. One must go back to 1897 to find a year in which share sales were as low as 1913.

The volume of stock collateral loans on June 30, 1914, in New York City banks was substantially larger than it had been in 1913, if figures for collateral loans of national banks may be taken as representative. The following table will show this:[1]

September 1, 1910	$517,000,000
June 7, 1911	520,000,000
June 14, 1912	550,000,000
June 4, 1913	506,000,000
June 30, 1914	627,000,000

The quiet selling that had been going on on the part of European investors for some months before the outbreak of the war had evidently led to some expansion of bank collateral loans. None the less, this volume of collateral loans was not alarmingly great, and both the banks and the stock market were in good position to meet any ordinary emergency. New York had at all events one advantage over London and Paris, in that the daily settlement prevailing in New York made it possible to test the solvency of brokers every day and there was no fortnight's accumulation of weakness when the shock came.

But the emergency that came was one that could not be met. In certain securities held in large quantities by European investors the selling was terrific and the declines in prices were startling. Among these were:

	High, 1914	July 30, 1914	Decline
Atchison	100⅜	89½	10⅞
Baltimore and Ohio	98⅜	72	26⅜
Brooklyn Rapid Transit	94½	79	15½
Canadian Pacific	220½	156⅛	64⅜
Chesapeake and Ohio	68	41½	26½
St. Paul	107⅛	85	22⅛
U. S. Steel	67¼	50½	16¾

[1] *Comptroller's Report*, 1914, Vol. 2, page 736. The collateral loans of national banks in New York City are not fully typical of total stock and bond collateral loans. First, obviously because they do *not* include the State banks, trust companies or private banks, and, second, because they *do* include certain loans on "other collateral security," including warehouse receipts, chattel mortgages, etc. On the whole, however, these other elements are of comparatively minor importance in New York and it is probable that the stock and bond collateral loans of the trust companies and State banks tend to expand and contract under the same conditions that those of the national banks do. It is interesting to note that the figure for 1913 is lower than the figure for 1904 (538,000,000). *Vide Value of Money*, page 511.

The general averages also showed startling declines. Twenty-five typical railway stocks had an average price of 78.18 at the end of June, 1914. They declined to 66.78 for their closing price in July. Twenty-five typical industrial stocks which had a closing price of 58.19 in June 1914, dropped to 48.76 by the end of July. The combined average of these rails and industrials dropped from 68.18 at the end of June to 57.77 by the end of July. The decline in bond prices was less dramatic. Forty representative bonds had as an average closing price at the end of June 86.56, and their price when the stock exchange closed was 82.73.[1]

The actual volume of sales made in July was not extraordinarily large as compared with many other periods. On Tuesday, July 28, when a great break came in the list, 1,020,000 shares were sold. The stock exchange has on several occasions exceeded two million shares, with much less change in prices. The significant points in connection with this selling, however, are first, that it was selling by investors rather than by speculators, and, second, that it was selling by foreigners rather than by domestic sellers. A moderate amount of selling by investors may make a much greater difference in the course of security prices than enormous sales by speculators, since the speculators selling short remain a potential buying power in the market and since the short seller provides loan funds to the bull, from whom he borrows the stocks which he must deliver. The investor, however, who sells withdraws funds from the loan market. The case is intensified when the seller is a foreign investor, because the foreigner not merely withdraws funds from the loan market, but tends also to withdraw gold from the reserves of the banks, restricting, temporarily, their ability to expand loans to protect the market.[2] With New York's gold supply already subject to calls from Europe for the other reasons already mentioned, this

---

[1] The securities chosen for the figures are those used by the New York Times *Annalist*.

[2] This is much less true in London or Paris than it was in New York before 1917, since New York was subject to legal reserve requirements. The amendments to the Federal Reserve Act in 1917 have virtually done away with legal reserve requirements, as we shall see in the chapter, *infra*, on the federal reserve system.

further cause for a drain placed the banks in a difficult position when it came to providing funds to sustain the market.

The closing of the stock exchange was necessary. Had it remained open another day, the break in prices would have been disastrous. The margins protecting collateral loans at the banks would have been hopelessly wiped out and bank resources technically impaired. Both in the interests of the banks and of brokers and brokers' customers, it was imperative that the exchange be closed, and inasmuch as danger to the banks, brokers and the brokers' customers would have involved the whole credit system of the country, it was essentially in the interests of the country that the exchange be closed.

The question has been raised as to whether it might not have been advantageously closed a day or two earlier. It is the view of Professor O. M. W. Sprague and Mr. H. G. S. Noble, President of the stock exchange, that it is fortunate that the exchange stayed open as long as it did. Stock prices went low, but not so low that the banks could not stand the strain. The market was pretty thoroughly liquidated. A reopening of the exchange was thus made much easier than would have been the case had stocks remained at a higher level with many sellers anxious to liquidate while the exchange was closed.[1] The control over selling outside the exchange during the period while the exchange was closed would, moreover, have been much less effective had not the market been thoroughly liquidated. As Mr. Noble makes clear in his interesting paper, the closing of the stock exchange was accompanied by a rigorous control over auction rooms, the curb and all other outside markets, and the volume of security selling was held within very narrow limits indeed during the period the stock exchange remained closed.

Apart from the closing of the stock exchange other emergency measures were called for. As has always happened in crises, the New York banks were subject to domestic drains on their

[1] O. M. W. Sprague: "Crisis of 1914 in the United States," *American Economic Review*, September, 1915; H. G. S. Noble: "The New York Stock Exchange in the Crisis of 1914," Garden City, N. Y., *Country Life Press*, 1915. These two papers are classics of permanent value. The writer is much indebted to both for his interpretation of the situation in New York at the outbreak of the war.

cash reserves in addition to the calls from Europe for gold. During the week ending July 31, the clearing house banks and trust companies in New York lost $56,000,000 in cash reserve, of which $20,000,000 represented withdrawals by American and Canadian banks.[1] Resort was had to the use of clearing house certificates, as had been the case in previous crises. The clearing house certificate is an instrument issued by the clearing house to the banks upon collateral deposited by the bank with the clearing house. It represents a pooling of the credit of all the banks and is good in payments between banks at the clearing house. The bank whose cash reserves are low is thus enabled to protect itself against drains at the clearing house. The clearing house certificate, however, is good only in payments between banks which are members of the same clearing house. It is of no use to a New York bank subject to drain from the outside.

Previous crises have meant that the New York banks have suspended cash payments, but in 1914 there was a further remedy available. The Aldrich-Vreeland Act of 1908 had been designed to enable national banks to issue notes freely in a crisis. This act was to have expired by limitation on July 1, 1914, but the Federal Reserve Act of 1913 fortunately extended it for another year to provide against emergencies pending the inauguration of the federal reserve system, and amended it by reducing the tax on notes issued under the Aldrich-Vreeland Act from 5 per cent to 3 per cent during the first three months of issue, thereafter increasing it by ½ per cent a month to a maximum of 6 per cent, where the original act had provided for increases of 1 per cent a month to a maximum of 10 per cent. Certain other restrictions in the original Aldrich-Vreeland Act had been removed. No use had been made of the Aldrich-Vreeland Act prior to this emergency. The very term " emergency currency " had been an obstacle. Banks had feared that it would be a confession of weakness should they make use of the act. But at the outbreak of the war speedy resort was had to it and the new notes were issued in large volume. Indistinguishable in form from ordinary national bank notes (except that they were new and clean),

---

[1] Sprague, *op. cit.*, page 517.

they were accepted readily by the people. Banks paying them out were enabled to retain their gold and "lawful money" as reserve. In all, 2,197 of the 7,600 national banks became members of the currency associations which issued these notes. The total amount of the Aldrich-Vreeland notes approved for circulation was $386,446,215 and the maximum outstanding was $386,616,990 on October 24, 1914. Redemption of this currency began as early as October, 1917. By December 26, redemption had amounted to $217,000,000 and on July 1, 1915, all but $200,000 of the authorized issue had been retired.[1] This emergency currency made it wholly unnecessary for the banks to suspend cash payments and the panic was safely passed without suspension.

The crisis of 1914 is unique in our history in that it was wholly due to external causes. As we have seen, the internal situation was thoroughly solvent. Writing in the summer of 1915, Professor Sprague was able to date the end of the crisis in the United States at November, 1914, except for the cotton growing southern States. Cotton was indeed hard hit. The current crop was 16,000,000 bales, a record crop. Demoralized by the prospective loss of the European market, cotton broke in price at the same time stocks did, at the end of July, and the cotton exchange closed when the stock exchange closed, the closing price being 10.50 cents per pound. The cotton exchange reopened in November, 1916, with quotations at 7.50 cents a pound, while cotton was being sold in the south at 5 to 6 cents a pound. The emergency was real, and under the leadership of the Federal Reserve Board, banks in northern States subscribed a fund of $100,000,000, while southern banks provided $35,000,000 as a fund for cotton loans. Very little use was made of this fund, however. A decided increase in the foreign demand for cotton which came early in January, 1915, from Europe brought cotton up to 9 cents by the end of January, and 10 cents by the end of February. From that time on, there has been no serious depression through lack of demand at reasonable prices in any of the major industries of the United States.

[1] *Journal of the American Bankers' Association,* May, 1916, page 1039.

The general situation regarding commercial credit in the United States has been on the whole surprisingly satisfactory during the war. The outbreak of the war led to a substantial increase in failures, as was to be expected—22,000 in 1915 as against 16,000 in 1913. The number of failures has markedly declined in 1916 and 1917, while for the first nine months of 1918 the figures are even lower. The following figures are taken from *Dun's Review* of January 5, 1918:

Year	Number of Failures	Amount of Liabilities	Average Liabilities
1906	10,682	$119,201,515	$11,159
1907	11,725	197,385,225	16,834
1908	15,690	222,315,684	14,169
1909	12,924	154,603,465	11,963
1910	12,652	201,757,097	15,947
1911	13,441	191,061,665	14,215
1912	15,452	203,117,391	13.145
1913	16,037	272,672,288	17,003
1914	18,280	357,908,859	19,579
1915	22,156	302,286,148	13,644
1916	16,993	196,212,256	11,547
1917	13,855	183,441,371	13,168

	Number of Failures	Assets	Liabilities
First 9 mos. of 1918	8,069	$75,142,781	$122,975,024

CHAPTER XIV

Gold, Foreign Trade and Foreign Exchange

We have seen that New York had been subject to heavy drains of gold for some time before the war. The excess of exports over imports of gold in 1913 was over $28,000,000; to the end of June, 1914, it was $84,000,000; and for the whole of 1914, $165,000,000. One factor which complicated the situation in the crisis of 1914 was the fact that New York City had short term obligations maturing to the amount of $100,000,000, of which $80,000,000 were held in England and France. With London exchange almost unattainable, the city's obligations were in danger of dishonor. To protect the credit of the city, a syndicate, in which all but four of the 130 banks and trust companies of New York participated, agreed to supply gold or exchange as might be necessary. As a further means of protecting the country's reputation for honoring gold obligations, a gold pool of $100,000,000 was organized under the guidance of the Federal Reserve Board involving the clearing house banks of all the reserve cities. Shipments of gold to the depository of the Bank of England at Ottawa by this pool proved sufficient to ease the situation greatly and to bring sterling exchange down to a reasonable figure.

But it was less these emergency measures than it was the tremendous volume of foreign demand for American products for war purposes which brought relief from the critical situation. In October the United States lost $44,000,000 of gold; in November they lost $7,000,000; in December, the tide turned and the United States gained about $4,000,000 net excess of imports over exports of gold. The explanation is of course the very heavy shipments of commodities on European account. From December, 1914, to May, 1917, the United States gained

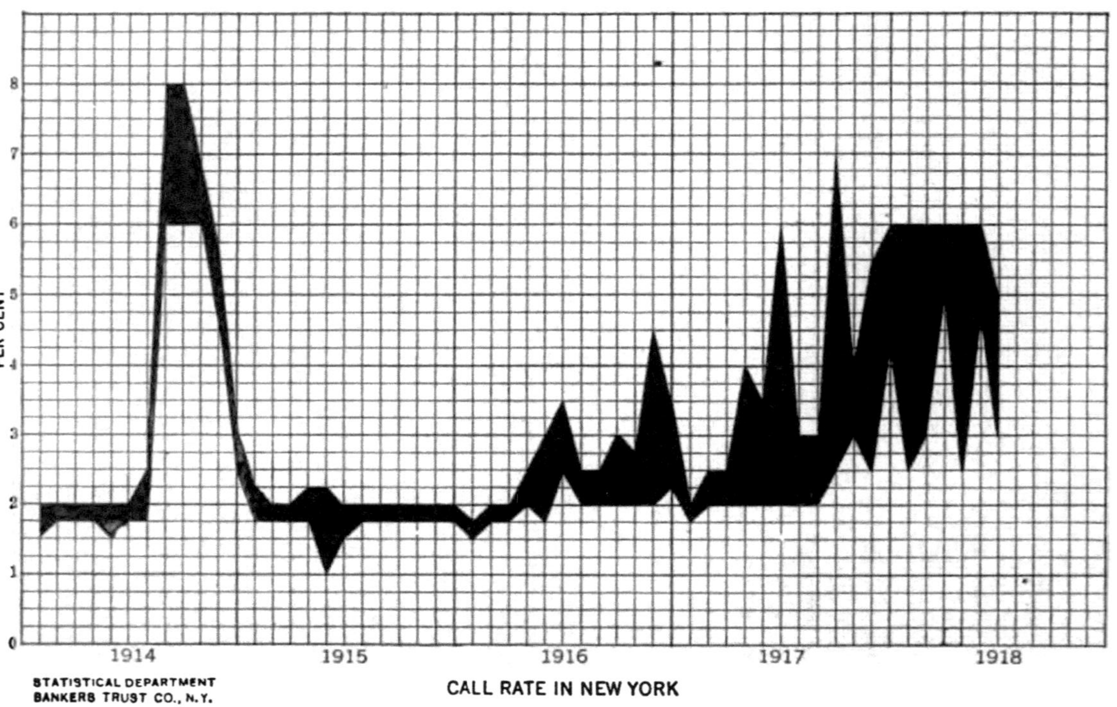
PER CENT
8
7
6
5
4
3
2
1
0
1914
1915
1916
1917
1918
STATISTICAL DEPARTMENT
BANKERS TRUST CO., N.Y.
CALL RATE IN NEW YORK

gold at a rate never dreamed of before. In 1915 the excess of imports over exports of gold was over $420,000,000; in 1916 over $520,000,000 and in 1917 over $180,000,000, a net gain for the three years, 1915-1917 inclusive, of $1,111,000,000 in gold, and a gain of more than a billion from the outbreak of the war.

On April 1, 1917, the general stock of gold coin, including bullion in the Treasury, was estimated at $3,089,000,000. The United States have lost gold somewhat since that time, the figures standing on April 1, 1918, at $3,043,000,000—a figure which has been changed little since, owing to the rigorous control of gold shipments under the Federal Reserve Board's gold policy, later to be discussed.

The most significant consequence of this huge flood of gold is to be found in the money rates in the New York market, illustrated by the accompanying chart for call rates. During the period when the stock exchange was closed and when the drain on New York for gold was heaviest, the call rates went up to 8 per cent, though favored customers were charged only 6 per cent. These rates were of course not, strictly speaking, call rates. Since the stock market was closed and the banks could not sell the collateral on which the loans were made, it was impossible to call the loans. They were in fact undated time loans. With the turn of the tide of gold in December, however, and with the reopening of the stock exchange, the rates dropped rapidly and for over a year from January, 1915, to May, 1916, New York enjoyed a period of the easiest money rates ever known in the history of the Street. The " high " on call rates at the " money post " of the stock exchange was 2¼ per cent, the " low " was 1 per cent, and the general range was from 1¾ to 2 per cent. It was not until the heavy financial operations of the government in the summer of 1917 that call money got as high as 5 per cent again. This easy money undoubtedly facilitated greatly the industrial recovery which followed, accelerated the volume of production and enormously accelerated the volume of exchanges, made easier the financial transactions required in the starting of new enterprises to meet the war demands and was a potent factor in the marvelous mobilization of the industrial resources of America.[1]

Foreign demand, directed first toward grains and munitions in the fall of 1914, gradually spread over a wide range of American products; while domestic demand from the industries made prosperous by European demand quickened every field of American industry. The story of the industrial recovery and expansion of the United States will best be told in the following table indicative of physical volume of production in which the physical production in 1910 is counted as 100 per cent:

	Per cent
1910	100.0
1911	99.0
1912	106.9
1913	112.5
1914	104.5
1915	110.0
1916	129.0
1917	131.3 [2]
1918	124.8

The rising volume of production was accompanied by and indeed largely caused by rising prices (the explanation of which we shall take up in a later section) and the combination of rising physical volume of production and rising prices led to a wholly extraordinary increase in the income of the people of the United States, as indicated by the following table:

1910	$30,500,000,000
1911	29,600,000,000
1912	33,800,000,000
1913	34,800,000,000
1914	32,600,000,000
1915	35,400,000,000
1916	49,200,000,000
1917	68,600,000,000
1918	73,400,000,000

The comparative importance of foreign and domestic trade as

[1] But it is possible to question this. London was losing gold heavily during this same period, and yet London discount rates were kept low on the whole. See charts, *infra*, appendix. London, however, was not on a strict gold basis.

[2] This index of physical volume of production is based on railroad gross receipts for the years 1910 to 1916, inclusive. For 1917 and 1918, a different method is employed. For the method of this computation, see the present writer's *Value of Money*, appendix to chapter 13, and *Annalist*, January 6, 1919, pages 5-6 and 61.

this rapid expansion went on is indicated by the following table showing the ratio of foreign to domestic trade:[1]

	Per cent
1910	9.9
1911	11.4
1912	11.6
1913	11.5
1914	11.7
1915	11.4
1916	17.9
1917	13.7
1918	13.4

The apparent decline in the ratio of foreign to domestic trade in 1917 and 1918 does not mean that the volume of physical exports was comparatively reduced in these years. An enormous volume of exports was sent on account of the American Government itself to France which did not get into the export figures.

The heavy foreign purchases in the United States led to increasing difficulties in making payments. It was impossible for the belligerent countries to pay for the goods we sent them with goods produced by them exported to us. The balance of trade grew ever greater. From July 1, 1914, to July 31, 1918, the total excess of our merchandise exports over imports was $10,-110,000,000, virtually all of which represented a debt of the European belligerents, as our increasing exports to various neutrals were largely offset by exports from those neutrals either to us or to Europe. Part of the consequence of this heavy trade balance we have already seen in the enormous shipments of gold which we received. An early consequence of it was a decline in the exchange rates of the leading belligerents in the New York foreign exchange market, as shown by the chart opposite page 158. The decline in the pound sterling in the summer of 1915 to something like $4.50 per pound, though less dramatic than the decline in many other rates, was still the subject of perhaps most comment in view of the importance of sterling exchange. A detailed account of the exchange rates in New York for the various countries during the war would be fascinating, but lies beyond the scope of the present discussion. We shall content

[1] The basis of this estimate is contained in the same sources.

ourselves with an effort to estimate the main factors involved in protecting the exchanges in New York and in paying for the great excess of American exports and with comment upon some of the more interesting episodes in the history of these rates. The charts themselves will supply further details. In an address before the national convention of the American Institute of Banking in Denver, in September, 1918, Mr. John E. Rovensky, Vice President of the National Bank of Commerce in New York, undertook to cast a balance showing how we have been paid for our exports, as follows:

Here it may be interesting to analyze how our huge favorable trade balance was financed; in other words, what did we receive in exchange for the commodities we exported?

The merchandise trade balance plus the silver export balance amounted to a little over ten billion dollars. In return for this we received gold to the extent of about one billion dollars; we had returned to us about two billion dollars of our own securities that had .been held abroad; and we arranged to loan our allies and other foreign countries about 7½ billion dollars. This makes a total of about 10½ billion dollars. The difference between this figure and the export balances mentioned above amounts to a quarter billion dollars. This amount is probably represented by loans that have been made to allies and others and have not yet been used, increase in cash balances of foreign banks in the United States, merchandise paid for and not yet exported, etc.

TABLE SHOWING NET FOREIGN TRADE BALANCES AND
METHOD OF FINANCING SAME SINCE JULY 1, 1914

(In millions of dollars)

Excess of merchandise exports over imports, July 1, 1914–July 31, 1918	10,110	
Excess of silver exports over imports, July 1, 1914–July 31, 1918	195	
Total		10,305
Excess of gold imports over exports, July 1, 1914–July 31, 1918	1,043	
United States securities repurchased January 31, 1915, to January 31, 1917	1,743	
United States repurchased since January 31, 1917 (estimated)	250	
Loans by United States Government to Allied countries up to August 1, 1918, less unavailed balances of loans and less $60,000,000 credit by Argentina	6,029	
Loans by individuals to foreign countries to August 31, 1918.	1,500	10,565
Balance		260

A different estimate by Mr. O. P. Austin, statistician of the
National City Bank of New York, would place the securities
brought back from Europe to America at between $3,000,000,000
and $4,000,000,000.[1]

The following tables prepared by the statistical department of
the National Bank of Commerce in New York are believed to be
as accurate a statement as it is now possible to make of the loans
placed in the United States by foreign governments during the
war, either with the United States Government directly or with
American investors.

CREDITS EXTENDED BY THE UNITED STATES
(To September 26, 1918)

Great Britain	$3,745,000,000
France	2,065,000,000
Italy	860,000,000
Russia	325,000,000
Belgium	157,020,000
Greece	15,790,000
Cuba	15,000,000
Siberia	12,000,000
Liberia	5,000,000
Roumania	6,666,666
Total	•$7,206,476,666

FOREIGN GOVERNMENT SECURITIES IN THE HANDS
OF AMERICAN INVESTORS

United Kingdom of Great Britain and Ireland	$300,000,000
United Kingdom of Great Britain and Ireland	250,000,000
Dominion of Canada	75,000,000
Dominion of Canada	100,000,000
Anglo-French loan	500,000,000
American Foreign Securities Co.	94,500,000
French Republic	100,000,000
City of Paris	50,000,000
City of Bordeaux	12,000,000
City of Lyons	12,000,000
City of Marseilles	12,000,000
Italian Government	25,000,000
Imperial Russian Government	25,000,000
Government of Switzerland	5,000,000
Kingdom of Norway	5,000,000
Government of Argentina	25,000,000
Republic of China	5,000,000
Total	$1,595,500,000

The chart for exchange rates in New York on belligerent
countries shows virtually all rates adverse to New York at the

[1] *Economic World*, August 17, 1918, page 223.

outbreak of the war turning favorable to New York in all cases by March, 1915. With the exception of the rate on Yokohama, none of the rates on belligerent countries have been above par since that date. The course of French exchange we have discussed in a previous chapter. The course of London exchange is fairly simply explained. Following the turn of the tide in December, 1914, London exchange sagged heavily through the summer of 1915, when gold shipments to New York and a loan placed in New York brought it back to about 2 per cent below par. This discount was supposed to be not greater than the expense of shipping gold from London to New York when war time insurance rates and other expenses were taken into account. Sterling exchange with the exception of a slight break in November, 1916, has been kept "pegged" at this point. The operations have been largely conducted by J. P. Morgan & Co., through whom gold has been brought to the New York market and through whom purchases of sterling exchange have been made in enormous volume. Through much of 1916 and down to the entrance of the United States into the war in 1917, J. P. Morgan & Co. were purchasing in the New York market sterling exchange to an average of $10,000,000 a day. With the entrance of the United States into the war and the extension of credit by the American Government to the British Goverment, sterling has been in part protected by different measures.

The course of the neutral exchange rates in New York has been strikingly different. Interruptions by the British navy of shipments of gold to those neutral states so situated that the gold might go on to Berlin, notably Sweden, led early, as our chart opposite shows, to a premium on neutral exchange in New York. The situation was intensified after the entry of the United States into the war, and particularly after the Federal Reserve Board policy of restricting gold shipments was put into effect.[1] Rates on various points, Valparaiso, Madrid and the northern neutrals, grew very adverse.

[1] Really the policy of the Treasury, in which there is no reason to suppose that the Federal Reserve Board concurred. The Board acted merely as the agent of the Treasury in the matter. For a discussion of this policy, see chapter xv, *infra,* on the Federal Reserve Board.

The case of Spanish exchange is particularly interesting. So far as our direct trade relations with Spain are concerned, the balance of trade is favorable to us. We export to Spain more than we import from her. But the British and French Governments were making heavy purchases in Spain for their armies in France and later the American Government also made such purchases for its army—a procedure particularly desirable inasmuch as the goods crossing the Pyrenees were not exposed to danger from the U-boats. Spanish bankers thus became possessed of large amounts of sterling and franc exchange which they sold increasingly in New York, as they could there find the best market for it, in view of the credits which were being used there to protect sterling and French exchange. As a result, Spanish bankers became possessed of an ever increasing amount of dollar exchange in Madrid, and the price of dollar exchange was correspondingly depressed. The natural method of meeting this difficulty would be, of course, to ship gold to Spain. This, however, was not permitted by the Federal Reserve Board and during the summer of 1918 the premium on Spanish exchange (pesetas) exceeded 50 per cent, declining sharply late in the summer, when the defeat of the German armies in France was assured.

A similar tale might be told of South American exchange.[1]

The story, however, of the exchange rates on Madrid and Stockholm is not complete. In both these countries a further complication entered; namely, the suspension of the free coinage of gold and the cessation of the purchase by the Bank of Spain and the Bank of Sweden of gold for bank notes at a fixed rate. In both Sweden and Spain, as a consequence of this restriction of free coinage of gold and free issue of bank notes, the *money* of the countries rose to a value exceeding that of its nominal gold bullion equivalent.[2] Shipment of gold bullion to Spain, therefore, was not sufficient to bring Madrid exchange in New York

[1] See Circular No. 38 of the Latin American Division of the U. S. Bureau of Foreign and Domestic Commerce on "The Chilean Trade Balance and Foreign Exchange," released for publication June 21, 1918

[2] This has been taken by certain adherents of the quantity theory of money as a proof of the quantity theory. The present writer does not so regard it. See the present writer's *Value of Money*, chaps. 7 and 22.

to par, as shown by the fact that there was a premium of 5 per cent on Spanish exchange in September, 1916, at a time when it was still possible to ship gold to Spain. It is interesting to note, however, that French gold coin has currency rights in Spain. Spain has never been a full member of the Latin Monetary Union, but by convention between Spain and France, connected with the organization of the Latin Monetary Union, French gold coin has currency rights in Spain. The most effective method of using gold there to protect dollar exchange at Madrid would be to send gold bullion to France and secure in exchange French minted gold, which could be taken to Spain. This operation indeed would not require the actual shipment of gold to France since the Banque de France would in all probability consent to accepting gold deposited in America " earmarked " for its use.

By various indirect measures other than shipments of gold, including the efforts to negotiate loans in neutral markets, the authorities in charge of our foreign exchange have endeavored to rectify these adverse neutral rates. By October, 1918, the rates had improved very markedly. The present writer ventures to express the opinion, however, that the improvement in dollar, sterling and franc exchange in the neutral markets has been chiefly due to the efforts of Generals Foch, Haig and Pershing, rather than to the financial measures of those who have sought to substitute indirect measures for the direct shipment of gold.

An interesting episode in the foreign exchange relations during the war has been the rise in the price of silver and the rise in the price of exchange on the countries with the silver standard, notably China. Exchange rates on India, which has not been supposed to be on a silver standard, but rather on the gold exchange standard, have also been affected, since the silver rupee, redeemable in gold or gold exchange, has, by virtue of its silver content, become worth more than the gold in which it is supposed to be redeemed, and so has become an independent standard.

The accompanying chart reproduced here from the *Federal Reserve Bulletin* of September 1, 1918, exhibits developments in the London price of silver and the exchange rates on Shanghai, Hongkong and Bombay. The average price of silver in 1913 in London (60.458 cents per ounce, British standard 0.925 fine) [1] is taken as 100 per cent, and the movements in the London price of silver, indicated in our chart, are percentage changes from that basic price. The explanation of the rise in the price of silver involves several factors: (1) the diminution in Mexican production due to unsettled conditions in Mexico; (2) increased coinage of silver by certain of the European belligerents to replace silver which had been hoarded, which has been true, as we have seen, to a considerable extent in France; (3) the favorable trade balances of the far eastern countries, notably China and India, which were settled in part by unusual silver shipments. Other minor factors entered.

The shipment of silver instead of gold in settling foreign balances was viewed as a desirable circumstance by the federal reserve authorities, and to increase the silver available for foreign shipment, an act was passed by Congress, signed by the President, April 23, 1918, which authorized the retirement of silver certificates which constituted the major part of the small paper money of the United States, and the melting down of the silver dollars held behind these certificates. The banks were asked to send in silver certificates when deposited with them and a substantial volume of the Treasury silver was thus released. By November 21, 1918, more than 150,000,000 silver dollars had been taken from the Treasury vaults and had been melted into bullion for export to India and other countries, reducing the Treasury fund of silver securing silver certificates from $490,000,000 to $338,000,000. [2]

To meet the shortage in one and two dollar bills thus created, the act also provided that the federal reserve banks should issue federal reserve bank notes (not federal reserve notes) in denominations of one and two dollars. These federal reserve bank notes are issued under the general provisions of the old National Bank Act, and are secured by United States bonds and other approved

---

[1] *Federal Reserve Bulletin*, September 1, 1918, page 837.
[2] New York *Evening Post*, November 21, 1918.

securities. A large volume of these new federal reserve bank notes has appeared in circulation. The act further provides that the government shall later repurchase silver and restore the silver certificates to circulation.

Even before the act providing for the retirement of silver dollars and silver certificates, there had been a shortage of hand to hand money in denominations of one and two dollars, which had been met in part by transforming the old greenbacks (United States notes) of larger denominations into one and two dollar bills.[1]

[1] *Vide* E. E. Agger: "Our Large Change," *Quarterly Journal of Economics*, 1917.

CHAPTER XV

The Federal Reserve System during the War

The task undertaken in this study has been to set forth the effects of the war upon money, credit and banking, rather than to write a comprehensive history of developments in money, credit and banking during the war. A large volume would be required to treat adequately the extraordinary developments in the United States during the war, in view of the inauguration of our federal reserve system.

But it has been possible to trace the main movements in money, credit and banking, growing out of the war down to March, 1917, when the United States broke with Germany, with comparatively little reference to the federal reserve system.

The federal reserve system had not been set going when the great war broke out at the end of July, 1914. The Federal Reserve Board was not organized till August 12, 1914, and the federal reserve banks were not opened for business till November 16, 1914. It was the Aldrich-Vreeland notes, and the close cooperation of existing banks, clearing houses, stock exchanges and the Treasury, which met the first shock of. the war. The flood of gold which came to us beginning with December, 1914, made, as shown by our curve for call rates in New York,[1] the easiest money market in the history of Wall Street, and made it largely unnecessary, before April, 1917, for the banks generally to have recourse to rediscounting at the federal reserve banks.[2] Certain of the country federal reserve banks, as those at Dallas, Kansas City and Atlanta, began to rediscount substantially soon after they began business, particularly as the rise in agricultural prices and the revival of agricultural prosperity made increasing demands on the loan funds of the member banks in these districts.

[1] Page 154.
[2] Another factor was the reduction in legal reserve requirements, under the Federal Reserve Act.

But the federal reserve banks in the great financial centers were not rediscounting enough to enable them to pay dividends through practically the whole period prior to the entrance of the United States into the war.

The existence of the system, of course, lent confidence to bankers and business men throughout the country and the knowledge that it was available if emergency should come undoubtedly hastened the industrial revival. But the great and distinguished services of the federal reserve banks have come since March, 1917.

One great service for which the federal reserve system has been designed has been of course to constitute a reserve of lending power for the other banks. The system has been designed so that as other banks reach the limit of their own ability to lend on sound security they can turn over to the federal reserve banks parts of their loans and discounts and receive from them new funds which they can lend. At the beginning of 1917, the federal reserve banks had earning assets of $221,896,000, including rediscounted paper purchased from member banks, bills of exchange bought in the open market, various government securities, State and municipal warrants and the like. Their chief asset, however, was the non-earning asset, gold. Foreseeing war from the beginning of 1917, the federal reserve banks sought to strengthen their position by reducing their earning assets, and when the war broke out their earning assets amounted to only $167,994,000. With decks cleared for action, they were prepared to begin rediscounting on an enormous scale as the burden of war finance should compel the other banks to have recourse to the federal reserve system.[1]

The growth in virtually all the items of the balance sheet of the federal reserve system since the United States entered the war has been very great indeed, and reflects services of inestimable importance to the country. With this growth of resources and liabilities has come also an extraordinary increase in earnings, which has wiped out all arrears in dividends and placed

[1] *Federal Reserve Bulletin*, May 1, 1917, page 335.

the federal reserve system, as jocosely suggested by a distinguished financial writer, in the class of the " profiteers."

The following table [1] shows the growth of the system:

PRINCIPAL RESOURCE AND LIABILITY ITEMS OF THE FEDERAL RESERVE SYSTEM ON SELECTED DATES

(In thousands of dollars)

	Nov. 26 1915	Dec. 22 1916	Oct. 25 1918
RESOURCES			
Total gold reserves..................	[a] 492,063	[a] 728,445	[a] 2,045,132
Total cash reserves..................	[a] 529,375	[a] 734,470	[a] 2,098,169
Bills discounted:			
Secured by government war obligations			1,092,417
All other	32,794	32,297	453,747
Bills bought in open market........	16,179	124,633	398,623
U. S. Government long term securities	12,919	43,504	28,251
U. S. Government short term securities		11,167	322,060
Total earning assets................	89,200	222,158	2,295,122
Total resources	637,261	1,009,852	[b] 5,270,785
LIABILITIES			
Capital paid in and surplus.........	54,846	55,765	80,324
Government deposits	15,000	29,472	78,218
Member banks' reserve deposits.....	[c] 397,952	[c] 648,787	1,683,499
Other deposits, including foreign government credits			[d] 117,001
Federal reserve notes in actual circulation	165,304	275,046	2,507,912

[a] Includes amounts of gold and other lawful money deposited with federal reserve agents against federal reserve notes issued.

[b] Includes clearing house exchanges and other uncollected items formerly deducted from member bank deposits.

[c] Net amount due to member banks.

[d] Exclusive of deferred credits on account of uncollected checks and other cash items.

One very important item in the expansion of the resources and liabilities of the federal reserve banks since the United States entered the war, and an item which represents a great growth in

[1] I am indebted to Dr. M. Jacobson, statistician of the Federal Reserve Board, for this table. Changes in accounting methods since the inauguration of the system, partly due to changes in the law, make it difficult to compare off hand the earlier and later statements.

strength for the system, is to be found in the increase in gold on the assets side, matched by the growth of federal reserve notes and member bank deposits on the liability side. The total stock of gold coin (including bullion in the Treasury) in the United States on April 1, 1917, was estimated at $3,088,905,000, a figure which has not been substantially altered since, as both exports and imports of gold have since been comparatively slight. Of this, the United States Treasury held $203,868,000, the federal reserve system held $938,046,000, and gold " in circulation," supposed to be largely held by banks, was placed at $1,946,991,000.[1] Between April 1, 1917, and April 1, 1918, roughly a billion dollars of the gold held by other banks and in general circulation was turned over to the federal reserve banks, raising their gold holdings from $938,046,000 to $1,813,924,000. By September 20, 1918, the total gold holdings of the federal reserve banks had risen to $2,023,558,000. Over two-thirds, therefore, of the free gold of the country is now concentrated in the hands of the federal reserve banks. The policy of accumulating gold is expected to continue, and a member of the Federal Reserve Board recently expressed the opinion that the gold holdings of the system might be expected to reach $2,500,000,000 before the end of the process is reached.[2]

It is probable that the estimate for the total stock of gold in the country is too high. It is doubtful if there remained on April 1, 1918, approximately a billion dollars of gold in circulation or in the hands of other banks. It is probable that the estimates for the gold held in the country before the war have been too high, that there has been an underestimate of the annual consumption of gold in the arts and that the original figure with which the Director of the Mint started his computation was too high. Competent students have suggested to the present writer that the overestimate in the total stock of gold may be as great

[1] Much of this was in gold certificates, " yellowbacks," of large denominations, held by the banks as a convenient means of interbank settlements, or in smaller denominations for general circulation. The actual gold was to a large extent in the United States Treasury.

[2] Further concentration of gold will be facilitated by the proposed issue of federal reserve notes in large denominations, which will make it easier for member banks to dispense with their large denomination gold certificates.

as from two to five hundred million, though these figures are largely guess work. If this view be true, however, then the proportion of gold held by the federal reserve banks is substantially greater than two-thirds of the total stock. It represents an accumulation which should make us impregnable against any foreign drain on our gold, and which, barring a panic introduced by an injudicious policy on the part of the federal reserve banks themselves, should forever banish doubt as to the ability of the banks of the United States to pay all gold obligations on demand.

This policy of collecting gold was greatly facilitated by the amendments to the Federal Reserve Act in the summer of 1917, which reduced the reserve percentages required of member banks and which allowed them to count as their legal reserve only deposits with the federal reserve banks, so that gold or lawful money held in their own vaults no longer counted as legal reserve. This made it possible for the member banks to turn over all their gold to the federal reserve banks, receiving in return either deposit credits or federal reserve notes, depending upon their own preference and their customers' needs.[1]

It may be observed in passing that this fundamental change in the law relating to cash reserve was accepted almost without question, whereas the more moderate proposal to make federal reserve notes available as legal reserve for member banks had led to a violent outcry by those who feared " inflation " only a short time before. Practically, there is little difference between the two proposals. It is, if anything, easier to get a deposit credit with a federal reserve bank than to get new federal reserve notes from a federal reserve bank. Federal reserve notes, and deposits with the federal reserve banks are in economic nature virtually identical. In the present writer's view, it is perfectly legitimate that either should be used as reserve by member banks. In the present writer's view, the whole system of legal reserve requirements is ridiculous in any case. In the provision that deposits with the federal reserve bank constitute the only legal reserves of

---

[1] Another amendment in 1917 simplified the process of exchanging gold for federal reserve notes and made it possible to count the gold in the system as reserve for either notes or deposits, interchangeably.

member banks, we have an achievement in the direction of sound banking of the first magnitude—we have virtually an abandonment of the legal reserve requirements, since it is almost always possible for member banks to get additional " legal reserve " by rediscounting paper. Their real reserves become, therefore, their portfolios rather than their cash on hand, bringing them into line with the policy which European bankers had long since taken for granted.

Unnoticed by the great mass of the people, the federal reserve banks have introduced a smoothness and simplicity in handling huge financial transactions that would have been incredible under the old system. In the summer of 1918, the federal government collected around $4,000,000,000 in taxes in a few weeks. In connection with the First Liberty Loan, $2,000,000,000 were paid into the federal Treasury in a short time. With each of the succeeding liberty loans, larger amounts have been handled in short periods, funds collected from all over the United States, transferred to the credit of the government and disbursed largely in other parts of the country from those which originally contributed them. Financial transactions of this magnitude would have led under the old system to drains falling particularly on the New York banks, which would have forced them instantly to suspend cash payments. Had the subtreasury system remained in full vigor, under which all payments to the federal government were taken from the banks and placed bodily in the vaults of the government itself, the mechanism would have broken down with the First Liberty Loan. Under the federal reserve system, however, these huge financial transactions have been largely accomplished by bookkeeping entries. Various officers of the federal reserve banks, and very specially the central office of the Federal Reserve Board at Washington, have developed a marvelous *finesse* in balancing debits and credits. This has involved a study in advance of the probable demands to be made on banks in various localities, the effort to route collection items through them in such a way as to give them funds which would break the shock of the heavy withdrawals, providing in advance to rediscount paper for them, and suggesting to the

Treasury the best places where government deposits might be made to offset heavy drafts. It has also involved the policy of rediscounting on the part of one federal reserve bank for another in such a way as to keep their gold reserve ratios approximately equal.

The Treasury policy of preceding the great loans and heavy tax payments by the marketing of short term Treasury certificates, maturing on the dates when tax payments or payments on the liberty loans were due, and receivable by the Treasury for such payments, has in itself been a factor of first magnitude in reducing financial friction. But under the old system, these Treasury certificates themselves would have strained the machinery severely.

Shortly after the inauguration of the federal reserve system, the Federal Reserve Board required the federal reserve banks to create a gold settlement fund in Washington, on the analogy of the gold fund on deposit in the New York clearing house, designed to lessen the necessity of the physical transfers of gold from one federal reserve bank to another in connection with interregional settlements . This gold fund, originally $12,000,-000, $1,000,000 from each bank, has subsequently been added to very greatly.

On July 1, 1918, daily settlements between the federal reserve banks were inaugurated, reducing, in general, the amount of gold that has to be transferred from one to another at any given date, and making it possible for the Federal Reserve Board at Washington to keep in constant touch with the reserve situation of each bank and to keep reserve percentages equalized by constant rediscounting. Daily settlements do not necessarily mean daily shipments of gold to and from Washington. "Suspense accounts" kept by the various federal reserve banks with the gold settlement fund, obviate this.

It would be hard to give too much praise to the efficiency and initiative of the men who have worked out this wonderful system of substituting book transfers for the large cash shipments which the old system, despite its great economies, involved. War finance on our present scale could hardly have been carried on by the old machinery. It is a supreme vindication of the federal reserve system.

Another important part of the work of the federal reserve system has been in the control of credits, both in reducing credits to non-essential industries, and in securing credits for essential industries. This has taken place largely in an informal way through advice and suggestions to member banks. Thus in the summer of 1917, the Federal Reserve Board sent out a letter saying that cattle feeders, paying high rates of interest, were finding their interest charges running from 35 to 40 per cent of their total expenses, and urging the member banks to extend them credits more liberally and at lower rates. At various times and with increasing vigor and definiteness, the Federal Reserve Board has urged upon the member banks the policy of restricting credits to non-essential industries. Various federal reserve banks have gone far in explicit advice and guidance of member banks in this matter. In a more authoritative way the Capital Issues Committee of the Federal Reserve Board has sought to limit the issues of new securities by non-essential industries, turning over this work recently to the newly formed War Finance Corporation.

In one respect the Federal Reserve Board and the federal reserve banks have failed to use a powerful means of restricting non-essential credits. They have kept their rediscount rates low, lower than the facts of the money market warranted, and lower than has been consistent with a vigorous control over the credit situation. In this, as will appear later, they have probably not had a free hand, but have submitted their policy to the policy of the Treasury.

Another important policy in which the Federal Reserve Board has been nominally responsible, has been in the control over foreign gold shipments, and in the regulation of foreign exchange rates.[1] The policy has been one of restricting gold shipments, virtually prohibiting them, with few and minor exceptions.

[1] The Federal Reserve Board has really been acting as the agent of the Secretary of the Treasury in this matter. There is no evidence that the board approved the policy at the time of its inception.

Those who have carried out the detailed application of the gold policy have been loath to discuss the matter in detail, and have been unwilling that much should be said in public discussion of it, fearing that their international operations, involving delicate negotiations with foreign banks and even with foreign governments, might be interfered with by discussion of their plans and purposes. It is not easy, therefore, to state with justice or with vigor the theory which has animated them. The policy has involved not merely the restriction of gold shipments to foreign countries, but it has also involved a restriction of gold payments within the country,[1] and a limitation upon the gold available for manufacturing jewelers, dentists and others. The present writer finds it impossible to sympathize with this policy or to defend it.

The essential elements involved in the gold standard are: (a) the free interconvertibility of bullion into coin, (b) the free interconvertibility of coin into bullion and (c) the instant redemption on demand of paper and other subsidiary money in gold coin. Whatever may be said of the policy of restricting gold shipments abroad, it is difficult to make a case for the failure to preserve the gold standard in its full integrity at home. The voluntary surrender by banks and people of gold to the central gold reserves is desirable, and the effort of the Federal Reserve Board to accomplish this—following the policy of the Reichsbank and of the Banque de France—is praiseworthy. But the whole point involved in such a policy is to increase the certainty that the federal reserve system can meet its gold obligations on demand.

There is no sure basis for the value of paper money except instant redemption in standard money on demand. It is true that other factors [2]—the loyalty of the people and of the banks, the confidence of the people in the credit and success of the government, the mere existence of a huge gold reserve with the knowledge that the power to redeem *exists—may* sustain the value of the paper at par. Value is after all psychological. It appears

---

[1] This feature of the policy is informal, and has involved the cooperation of many agencies, including virtually all the banks of the country.
[2] *Vide* the writer's *Value of Money*, chap. 7.

that paper money in the United States has been so far maintained at par in most places during the past year, but such a basis for the value of paper money is insecure. Overnight changes in the attitude of the people or banks might upset it; a dramatic event, calling attention in a conspicuous way to the fact of inconvertibility, might upset it, leading to just such a depreciation as was witnessed in federal demand notes or in the State bank notes of the North, following January 1, 1862.

Assuming that the value of our paper money at home is not affected by such a policy, there can be no question at all that our credit abroad is affected. The foreign exchange rates alone should make that clear. But further, and looking to the future, had the United States maintained the record of paying gold to all legitimate creditors without question throughout the war, had New York remained the one free gold market in the world, New York would have needed in the future to carry much less gold in reserve than she will need for years to come. The institution or the community that maintains the reputation of honoring its obligations at all times is rarely called upon to honor them unnecessarily. London, with vastly less in the way of gold resources than the United States have had, preserves her reputation in this matter far better than we. Having gold, she paid it out. London has probably a small amount of gold at the present time. The Bank of England's gold reserves, as shown in published figures, are larger than before the war, but to a very considerable extent the actual reserves are probably to be found in South Africa or in Canada in depositories established by the Bank of England. But by the courageous use of such gold as she has had, London has preserved her credit to an astonishing degree.

A little more than two decades ago, President Cleveland faced a situation in which his gold reserves—little more than $20,000,000—promised to be exhausted in forty-eight hours. He continued, however, the policy of paying out gold on demand, and by his courage saved the gold standard. New gold was secured within the forty-eight hours, the reserves were replenished, and the country was saved from another period of demoralization growing out of fluctuating irredeemable paper money or the adoption of the silver standard. It is not a picture to inspire enthusiasm when one sees our federal reserve system, entrenched safely behind over $2,000,000,000 of gold, showing less of courage than President Cleveland manifested with his scant $20,000,000.

Surely the history of money has made sufficiently clear the dangers and evils of irredeemable paper, the fundamental disorganization and demoralization that such paper can occasion, to make argument with reference to the essential importance of the preservation of the gold standard unnecessary.

On the part of some of the defenders of the policy of restricting gold payments within the country and of restricting gold shipments abroad, there appears to be a wholly irrational fear that the end of the war will bring so great a drain upon the gold resources of the country, as foreign countries call upon us for gold, that we can not meet it unless we now hoard our gold. This fear seems baseless. The outside world will owe hundreds of millions a year in interest and dividend payments alone to the United States. The probability is rather that we will be left with more gold on hand than it is economical for us to keep. In any case, the main reason for having gold either now' or after the war is to be in a position to meet the demands of those who have the legal right to obtain gold from us.

The argument has been presented that by retaining $3,000,-000,000 of gold we will be placed in a position of such great strength that we can finance the world, displacing London as the international center. It is not improbable that London bankers who have seen this statement have smiled quietly. They do not *need* $3,000,000,000 to finance the trade of the world! Before the war, Great Britain financed the trade of the world with half a billion dollars in gold and with much less than that in the actual reserves of her banks. The banker who can do business with a half billion in gold can undercut in the competition of the world's money market the banker who requires three billions. An excess of gold is a dead asset, a burden rather than an aid in competition in international finance. America has great financial strength, but is surely showing a lack of financial *finesse* and courage, so far as the gold policy is concerned.[1]

In connection with these strictures on what we have called " the Federal Reserve Board's gold policy," it is just to repeat that the policy appears to be that of the Treasury rather than that of the board—that the board appears to have surrendered its monetary policy to the fiscal policy of the Treasury.[2] The central purpose of the Treasury in this connection appears to be to float liberty bonds at a low rate of interest. For this purpose an easy money market is regarded as necessary. The Treasury policy reacts on the policy of the Federal Reserve Board at two vital points: (1) Rediscount rates must be kept low, thus making the control of credits to non-essential industries harder. (2) Gold must not be allowed to get away lest money rates be forced up to stop the outflow of gold.

Viewed as a policy of protecting the credit of the United States Government, this course seems grotesque. Surely, the money of the United States is more sacred than the liberty bonds! Surely it is more important to maintain the *demand* obligations at par than to protect the current price of the *time* obligations! Surely, the credit of the government is more dependent on the punctual fulfilment of its contract obligations than on the day by day standing of its long time securities in the market!

Viewed as a measure for saving money for the government it is exceedingly questionable. The saving of ½ per cent or more in interest can be much more than offset by two vital factors: (1) If through the easy money market, non-essential industries can get credits which they would not get if discount rates were higher, then their competition for labor and supplies will raise the prices which the government must pay for the things it buys, increasing the amounts which the government must borrow. (2) More fundamental, if as a consequence of

---

[1] For a variety of opinions on this general problem, see *Hearings before the Senate Committee on Banking and Currency*, on the proposed " Federal Reserve Foreign Bank," summer of 1918; and also an address by Mr. F. I. Kent, reproduced in *Congressional Record*, May 1, 1918, pages 6358-6363.

[2] So far as the foreign exchange policy is concerned the Federal Reserve Board is really merely the agent of the Treasury, exercising delegated authority.

the failure to redeem the money of the government in gold, the paper money itself should depreciate, that again would lead to higher prices, to larger expenses for the government, to say nothing of great demoralization in the whole business and financial fabric.

Finally, it is probable that liberty bonds will be sold at whatever rate of interest the government proposes in any case. By and large, the American people are not taking liberty bonds as investments; they are taking them through loyalty as a means of winning the war. The difference of a fraction of 1 per cent or even of 1 per cent, in the interest rate would probably make slight difference in the amount of liberty bonds sold, and the loyalty of the people and of the banks is less strained if they are asked to take liberty bonds at an interest rate below the prevailing market rates for capital than when they are expected to protect the value of the paper money of the United States in the absence of gold redemption.

Following the amendments to the Federal Reserve Act in the summer of 1917, which removed certain of the objections which State banks and trust companies had had to entering the system, the President of the United States issued an appeal on October 13, 1917, to the State banks and trust companies to enter the system as a war time measure, that they might contribute their strength to the system and that they might secure for themselves and their patrons the protection which the system afforded. The response has been distinctly gratifying. The great State banks and trust companies of New York City entered rapidly and readily. By June 1, 1918, 486 State institutions with combined capital and surplus of $621,000,000 and with total resources of approximately $6,000,000,000, had entered the system.[1] The great majority of State institutions still remain outside, but many of the largest institutions, whose addition to the system would add most to its strength, have joined.

There have been various minor developments of the federal reserve system, important in themselves, but not so immediately connected with war policy, of which only brief mention can be

[1] *Federal Reserve Bulletin*, June, 1918, page 509.

made. The various federal reserve banks have established branches and agencies at home and abroad. The Banque de France and the Bank of England have become agencies of the federal reserve bank of New York. The Philippine National Bank has become the agency for the federal reserve bank of San Francisco; the San Francisco federal reserve bank has established branches at Seattle, Spokane, Portland and Washington; the St. Louis federal reserve bank has established an agency at Memphis, primarily for the purpose of keeping cotton warehouse certificates, used as collateral, where they could be quickly got at by the borrowers.[1]

The federal reserve system has inaugurated a check collection system. It has put through a campaign for acceptances which has led to substantial modifications in banking practices in the United States. The Federal Reserve Board, in connection with its admirable *Federal Reserve Bulletin,* has undertaken far reaching statistical plans which involve the development of scientific statistics which will be of use in business forecasting.

But it is outside the scope of our program to write a history of the federal reserve system. We are concerned with an outline sketch of the effects of the war upon it, and of its rôle in meeting the problems of the war.

[1] *Federal Reserve Bulletin,* March 1, 1917, page 168.

CHAPTER XVI

Public Finance and Bank Credit

The entrance of the United States into the war brought at
once a very great increase in expenditures by the federal government, particularly when advances to the Allies are included. The
following table [1] prepared by Professor Bogart gives the expenditures of the United States through the months of 1917, excluding advances to Allies. · The first three months, when expenditures were on a peace footing, are also given by way of contrast.
The entrance of the United States into the war was on April 6,
1917:

	Monthly	Daily
January	$79,910,714	$2,577,765
February	75,844,498	2,708,406
March	72,773,903	2,347,545
April	81,599,598	2,719,986
May	114,102,810	3,680,736
June	134,304,040	4,776,801
July	208,299,031	6,719,323
August	277,438,000	8,949,613
September	349,013,305	11,337,768
October	465,045,360	14,904,690
November	512,952,035	17,098,401
December	611,297,425	19,719,272
Total	$2,982,580,719	

Professor Bogart gives also a table covering three fiscal years
showing the objects of expenditures, as follows:

Purpose	1915-16	1916-17	[a] 1917-18
Civil establishment	$380,911,373	$425,565,747	$1,995,886,359
Military establishment	132,185,275	409,789,321	8,964,443,485
Naval establishment	155,029,426	257,166,437	1,609,178,036
Rivers and harbors	32,450,301	30,487,560	38,295,750
Panama Canal	17,503,728	13,112,130	23,739,099
Public debt	22,910,313	24,742,129	93,454,000
Miscellaneous	1,016,310	34,028,110	344,120
Total	$742,006,726	$1,194,891,434	$12,725,340,849
Purchase of obligations of foreign govern- ments		885,000,000	[b] 3,351,400,000
Total		$2,079,891,434	$16,076,740,849

[a] Appropriations.   [b] Actual for period July 1–December 31, 1917.

[1] E. L. Bogart: *Direct Costs of the Present War*, page 2.

The rapid developments in the plans of the American Government, coupled with the unexpected intensity and magnitude of American participation in the war in the summer of 1918, has led to a substantial growth in the expenditures of the government, and the total appropriations authorized for the fiscal year 1918-1919 run far above $30,000,000,000. The loans made by the United States Government to its allies down to September 26, 1918, total $7,206,476,666, distributed as follows:

Great Britain	$3,745,000,000
France	2,065,000,000
Italy	860,000,000
Russia	325,000,000
Belgium	157,020,000
Greece	15,790,000
Cuba	15,000,000
Siberia	12,000,000
Liberia	5,000,000
Roumania	6,666,666
Total	$7,206,476,666

The fiscal policy of the Treasury in raising funds for these staggering expenditures has been on the whole an admirable one.[1] Advantage has been taken of the mistakes of other belligerents, and a very judicious balancing of short term financing, taxes and long term bonds has been devised.

Professor Bogart's table [2] for the revenues of the United States for three fiscal years is as follows:

Source	1915-16	1916-17	1917-18
Customs	$213,185,845	$225,962,393	$220,000,000
Internal revenue:			
Ordinary	303,486,474	354,387,426	973,000,000
Emergency	84,278,302	95,297,554	
Corporation income tax	56,993,658	179,572,888	535,000,000
Individual income tax..	67,943,595	180,108,340	666,000,000
Excess profits tax......			1,226,000,000
Sales of public land.......	1,887,662	1,892,893	1,800,000
Miscellaneous	52,012,529	80,952,632	265,000,000
Total	$779,788,065	$1,118,174,126	$3,886,800,000
Less normal revenues......		779,788,065	779,788,065
War revenues		$338,386,061	$3,107,011,935

[1] The adverse criticisms have already been indicated. They relate to the reactions of the Treasury policy on the gold policy and discount policy of the Federal Reserve Board.

[2] *Op. cit.*, page 4.

This table was prepared before the actual revenues were collected in 1918. Approximately correct for customs and approximately correct also for actual receipts for internal revenues, as shown in the report of the Treasury Department of September 14, 1918 (when collections of $3,694,703,334 were recorded), it probably underestimates by a very substantial amount the total internal revenues when evasions and delinquents and underestimates by tax payers are all straightened out. In a single day, the authorities of the Treasury concerned with revising the tax returns picked up an extra hundred millions from a single industry. Good authorities have expressed the opinion that the total revenues from taxes and customs for the fiscal year 1917-1918 will reach $4,500,000,000. For the fiscal year 1918-1919, new legislation is pending which is expected to bring the tax receipts up to $8,000,000,000.

Such taxes, wholly apart from the further drains on the income of the people through the enormous loans, would have been deemed incredible by students of taxation a few years ago. The total income of the country, including all interest, wages, profits and rents, was estimated in 1910 at $30,500,000,000. $8,000,000,000 in taxes would have been an enormous proportion to take from this. The appropriations now made by Congress for the fiscal year 1918-1919 substantially exceed the total income of the country for 1910. None the less, the country is bearing its burden of taxes and in addition is subscribing heavily to liberty loans. The First Liberty Loan, dated June 15,. 1917 (15-30 year loan)[1] amounted to $2,000,000,000; the Second Liberty Loan, dated November 15, 1917 (10-25 year loan) amounted to $3,808,766,150; the Third Liberty Loan, dated May 9, 1918 (10 year loan) amounted to $4,176,516,850; the Fourth Liberty Loan, dated October 24, 1918 (15-20 year loan) has exceeded $6,900,000,000, making a grand total of more than $16,900,000,000 raised in liberty loans by the end of October, 1918, with the certainty that further and even greater loans will come as long as the war continues.

[1] An excellent "conspectus" of the four liberty loans appears in the *Economic World* of October 12, 1918, page 523.

Yet another important source of income for the government has been in the sale of war savings stamps and thrift stamps, designed to reach the smallest savings. The total receipts from this source,[1] by October 23, 1918, were $807,222,544.

The explanation of the ability of the country to meet such extraordinary financial burdens is to be found in the figures which we have given before[2] for the growth in the income of the country. Under the joint influence of expanding physical volume of production and rising prices, the income of the country has risen from $30,500,000,000 in 1910 and $32,600,000,000 in 1914 to $49,200,000,000 in 1916, to $68,600,000,000 in 1917, and to well over $70,000,000,000 in 1918.[3]

But not even this great growth of the income of the people of the United States was sufficient to enable them to meet the whole burden of war finance without temporary resort to expansions of credit by the banks. The amounts involved were too great, and the shock to industry and trade of such subtractions taken in large blocks from the current incomes of the people or of businesses would have brought bankruptcies and demoralization. Expansions of credit, largely temporary, have for the most part eased the tension and made the process a wonderfully smooth and frictionless one. For this, the policy of the Treasury in anticipating tax payments and liberty loans by short term Treasury certificates is in large degree responsible, though, as we have seen, the machinery of the federal reserve system has ·also aided very greatly. The government has commonly spent the tax receipts and the liberty loans before the people have paid them. It has done this by selling in advance, very largely to the banks, short term Treasury certificates maturing about the time the tax payments or the liberty loan payments were due. The volume of these short term certificates has risen and fallen, rising to billions just before the tax payments or the liberty loan payments were due, and falling greatly as tax payments and liberty loan payments came in and the government returned to the

[1] New York *Evening Post*, October 26, 1918.
[2] Page 156.
[3] *Vide Value of Money*, pages 267-278, and *Annalist*, January 6, 1919, pages 5-6 and 61.

banks the short term advances made. In part, too, the Treasury certificates have been taken by large tax payers or prospective purchasers of large blocks of liberty bonds, and these Treasury certificates have been accepted by the government in lieu of cash in payment of taxes or in payments on liberty loans.

Further, however, the banks have been called upon to purchase the liberty bonds themselves and to make loans on liberty bond collateral to purchasers of these bonds. The extent of this will receive consideration below. Banks have, moreover, been obliged to no small extent to make temporary advances of funds and possibly even long time advances of funds to various businesses to enable them to meet the tax payments, particularly the excess profits tax payments of corporations whose " profits " have consisted, in part, of nonliquid assets.

The traditional policy of an American Congress in meeting a war emergency has been to rely largely on long time loans and only gradually and through a long period of years to raise the revenues required to pay them off. This tradition represents a great advance over the Civil War practice, when during the early period of the war much of the burden was carried by the issue of inconvertible paper money. It is probable that in the absence of vigorous action by certain American economists, the loan policy would have been pursued to extremes in the present war. At the outbreak of the war, however, a strong movement was begun to finance the war largely by taxes. The leading figure in this movement was Professor O. M. W. Sprague, whose writings during the winter and spring of 1917 had the significance of a great state paper. In our discussion of loans and taxes in France, we have criticised Professor Sprague's view as representing an exaggeration, and had his extreme program been carried out it would have been unfortunate. The significance of his work, however, is to be found in the fact that a much heavier taxation program than would otherwise have been employed was put through, and it is probably just to say that Professor Sprague purposely cast his argument in a somewhat extreme form, being well aware that the opponents of his plans would make all the qualifications that were necessary, and that the great danger was that taxes would be too light rather than that they would be too heavy.[1]

Among the arguments which have been offered against the employment of loans and bank credit in financing the war has been the contention that such a policy, leading to an expansion of bank credit, would force up prices—an argument commonly cast in the mold of the quantity theory, though not necessarily involving quantity theory reasoning. To the astonishment of most adherents of the quantity theory, the period since the great expansion of bank credit growing out of liberty loans has not been the period of rapidly rising prices. It will be most convenient to discuss this matter in connection with the discussion of prices in the United States. It is enough to point out at this time that commodity prices had their great rise between December, 1916, and June, 1917, that since June and July, 1917, the average of commodity prices has been fairly stable in the United States; and that from June, 1917, to the middle of 1918 stock and bond prices have had on the whole a steadily downward course, while there has been something approaching panic in the real estate markets in several of our greater cities.

Those writers who see nothing but " inflation " in expanding bank credit during periods of stress, emergency and rapid transition, fail wholly to take account of the essential functions of the bank credit. Bank credit expands when transitions are to be accomplished. An enormous volume of new bank credit has been required to finance the shifting of industry from peace occupations to war occupations, to finance the huge receipts and disbursements of the Treasury, to ease the tension of tax payments, to enable business men to liquidate slow assets while changing the character of their production and meeting the burden of taxes and loans. Expansion of bank credit is necessitated by the " hoarding " of deposits by business men who feel the necessity of keeping an unusually liquid position in times of stress and uncertainty. It is hard to understand what the " inflation-

---

[1] The present writer takes the greater pleasure in making this acknowledgment to Professor Sprague, inasmuch as he felt called upon to criticize in some measure Professor Sprague's plan in the spring of 1917. See " Conscription of Wealth," *Annalist,* April 16, 1917.

ist " theory would have banks do in a great emergency. It is certain that if banks refused to expand their credits in times of stress, we should have demoralization and chaos—as has been abundantly exemplified in our discussion of war time conditions in France.

It will be interesting to examine statistically the extent to which the war finance of the United States Government has been accompanied by bank expansion. Precise measurements appear at the present time to be impossible, but certain significant figures can be presented which will make it clear that the apprehensions expressed in the spring of 1917 that the loan policy would lead to excessive expansion were on the whole unfounded. The following figures dealing with bank resources are of course a crude index, but are none the less significant. They represent resources of all banks reporting to the Comptroller (including national, State, savings and private banks and trust and loan companies, but excluding federal reserve banks) and resources of federal reserve banks.

(In millions of francs)

	June 30 1914	June 23 1915	June 30 1916	June 30 1917	1918
National and State banks etc.	26,971	27,804	32,271	37,126	[a] 40,525
Federal reserve system..		381	625	2,000	[b] 3,806

[a] The figure for 1918 is based on the Comptroller's figures for national banks, as of May 10, and the figures for State institutions at about the same date, prepared by Mr. R. N. Sims, Examiner of State Banks in Louisiana. See *Annalist*, August 12, 1918, page 150. For other years, the Comptroller's figures are used. These figures are not the Comptroller's figures for "banking power," but for total resources.
[b] June 21, 1918.

The figures for the banks other than the federal reserve banks show that the great expansion of bank resources occurred before the entrance of the United States into the war. From June, 1915, to June, 1917, the expansion was nearly ten billions; from June, 1917, to June, 1918, the expansion was a little over three billions. The main expansion since the United States entered the war has been in the federal reserve banks themselves. But the figures for expansion by the federal reserve system do not represent net addition to the banking resources of the country. To the extent of over two billion dollars they represent gold transferred by the other banks to the federal reserve banks, and on the liability side, viewed from the standpoint of addition to the circulating currency of the country, the only items in the federal reserve banks' balance sheets which should be considered are the excess of federal reserve notes over the gains in gold and the government deposits subject to check.

Instead, therefore, of increasing the rate of expansion of bank resources, the entrance of the United States into the war and the vast loans of the government down to June, 1918, were accompanied by a marked reduction-in the rate of expansion.

The following charts, covering the period March 1 to October 11, 1918, tell a similar story for the member banks of the federal reserve system reporting to the federal reserve banks. The first chart shows the growth of demand deposits and of total loans, investments and Treasury certificates of indebtedness, together with the ratio between them, for the reporting member banks in all twelve districts and for the reporting member banks in the New York district. For the member banks in all twelve districts, demand deposits, including government deposits, show almost no increase during this period, while for the New York district, there appears even a slight decline. During this same period, the government deposits and deposits by foreign governments with the federal reserve banks have remained small, around $300,000,000. The second chart shows the amount of war obligations of the United States held by the reporting member banks, either owned outright or made the basis of loans, together with the total earning assets of these banks, and the proportion of total earning assets represented by United States war obligations. The black area, indicating United States bonds owned, exaggerates the outright ownership of liberty bonds, since it includes some hundreds of millions of the old bonds securing national bank note circulation. On the whole, the liberty bonds have been taken by the people. The area representing loans secured by United States obligations is again gratifyingly small. On the whole, the people have paid for their liberty bonds out of current income. The main item in the exten-

1918

RATIO OF LOANS AND INVESTMENTS (OTHER THAN U.S. GOV'T
LONG TERM SECURITIES)-TO- DEMAND DEPOSITS (INCLUSIVE
OF U.S. GOV'T DEPOSITS) OF REPORTING MEMBER BANKS.
RATIO
BILLIONS OF DOLLARS
MAR. APR. MAY JUNE JULY AUG. SEPT. OCT. NOV. DEC. JAN. FEB.
2.50 15
MEMBER BANKS
IN ALL 12 DISTRICTS
(A) TOTAL LOANS, INVESTMENTS AND CERTIFICATES OF INDEBTEDNESS
2.00 12
(A)
A
(B) TOTAL DEMAND DEPOSITS - INCLUDING GOVERNMENT DEPOSITS
1.50 9
(B)
B
(C) RATIO OF LOANS AND INVESTMENTS TO DEPOSITS
(C)
C
1.00 6
.50 3
0 0
MEMBER BANKS
IN NEW YORK DISTRICT
2.00 12
1.50 9
(F) RATIO OF LOANS AND INVESTMENTS TO DEPOSITS
(F)
F
(D) TOTAL LOANS, INVESTMENTS AND CERTIFICATES OF INDEBTEDNESS
1.00 6
(D)
D
(E)
E
(E) TOTAL DEMAND DEPOSITS - INCLUDING GOVERNMENT DEPOSITS
.50 3
0 0
MAR. APR. MAY JUNE JULY AUG. SEPT. OCT. NOV. DEC. JAN. FEB.

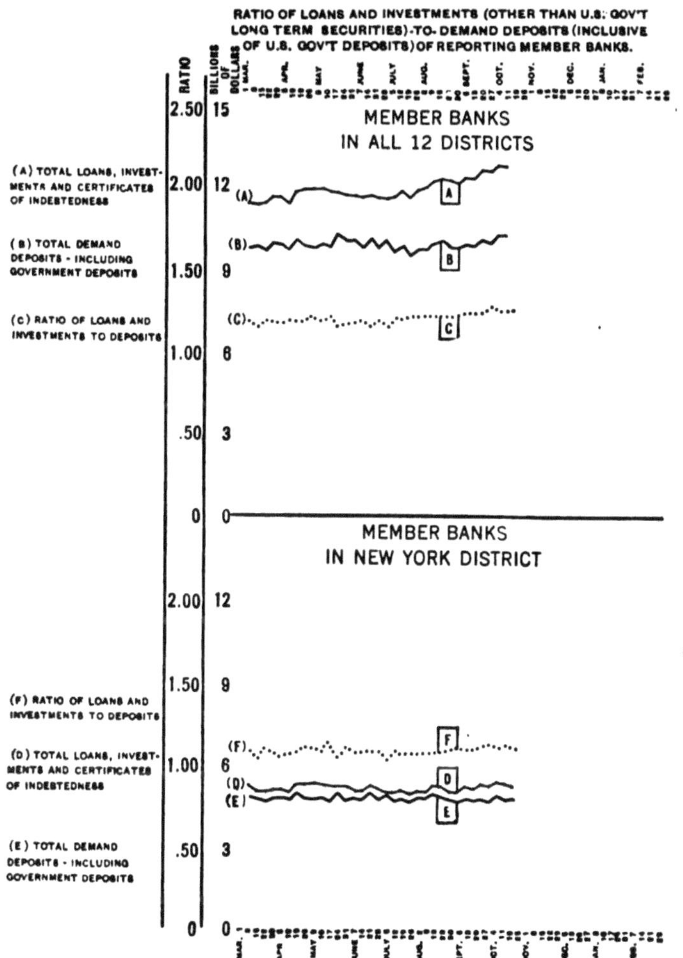

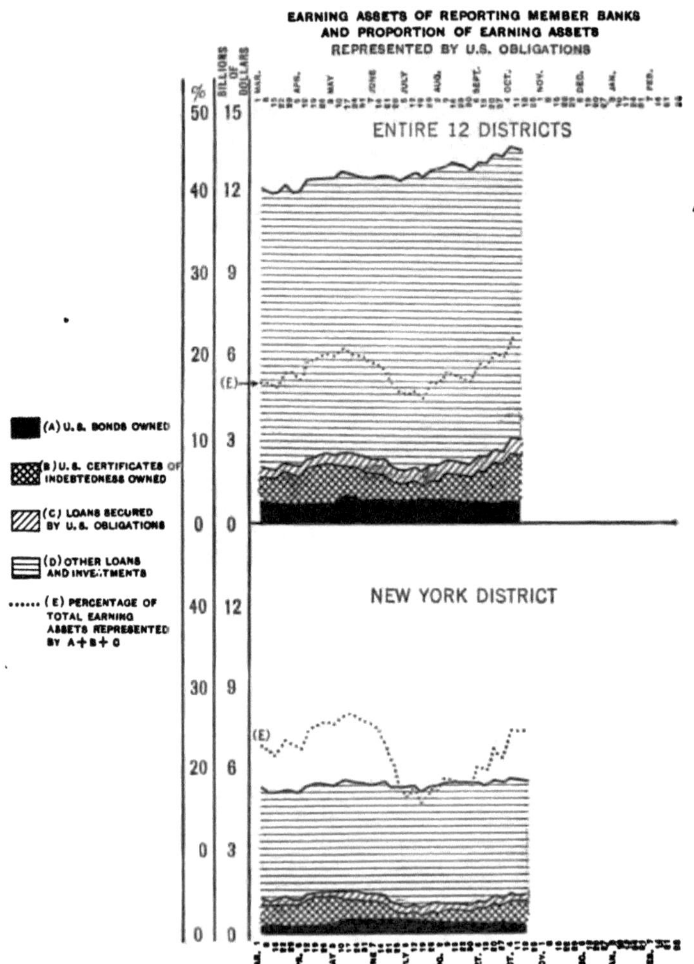
1918
EARNING ASSETS OF REPORTING MEMBER BANKS
AND PROPORTION OF EARNING ASSETS
REPRESENTED BY U.S. OBLIGATIONS
ENTIRE 12 DISTRICTS
NEW YORK DISTRICT
%
BILLIONS OF DOLLARS
(A) U.S. BONDS OWNED
(B) U.S. CERTIFICATES OF INDEBTEDNESS OWNED
(C) LOANS SECURED BY U.S. OBLIGATIONS
(D) OTHER LOANS AND INVESTMENTS
(E) PERCENTAGE OF TOTAL EARNING ASSETS REPRESENTED BY A+B+C
MAR. APR. MAY JUNE JULY AUG. SEPT. OCT. NOV. DEC. JAN. FEB.

sions of credit by these banks in connection with war finance has been in the short term certificates of indebtedness, issued by the Treasury in anticipation of loans and taxes. These have risen, as we have seen, to large proportions preceding loan or tax payments, and have declined as the government receipts from taxes and long term loans have come in. What extension has taken place between March 1, 1918, and October 11, 1918, has taken place in the federal reserve banks themselves and not in the main body of the banks which deal directly with the people. The expansion in the federal reserve banks connected with war finance during the period covered by these charts has been approximately a billion dollars, the main item being " bills discounted secured by government war obligations." Bearing in mind the tremendous operations involved in the period covered, which includes the Third Liberty Loan of $4,177,000,000, the payment of nearly $4,000,000,000 of taxes, and the issue of several billions of short term Treasury certificates in anticipation of the Fourth Liberty Loan, this is a showing which few would have been optimistic enough to expect a year before.

But this is not to discount the value of the forebodings issued by many economists at the outbreak of the war. By pointing out the danger of undue bank expansion, they have aided in preventing it, though the caution of bankers and business men would have largely done so in any case. Men do not pay interest at the banks for amusement. Banks do not extend their loans lightheartedly without seeing where they may expect to come out. With the tremendous uncertainties in the minds of both bankers and business men as to the future of business, with the grave uncertainties which have at times existed since our entry into the war as to the outcome of the war itself, with the certainty that perplexing problems, if not unmanageable problems, would have to be met at the end of the war, business men and bankers have both been cautious in accepting and in making loans.

People generally, moreover, have borrowed from the banks to a very small extent for the purpose of enabling them to continue ordinary consumption. It would be this kind of borrowing which would be most objectionable and which would have the greatest tendency to raise commodity prices. The essential thing in connection with war finance is that it shall provide a mechanism whereby the current flow of goods and services in the country may be diverted from the consumption of the people to the use of the government. If the people try to continue their customary consumption of goods and services at the same time that the government is enormously increasing its expenditures, so that the people are competing with the government in the markets for labor and supplies, the result will be, of course, assuming that the labor and other resources of the country are fully employed, to force prices up. But neither in normal times nor apparently at the present time are loans for ordinary consumption purposes important elements in the assets of American banks.[1]

In very large measure, moreover, as the government operations have made demands upon the loan funds of the banks, other borrowers have dropped out. Building operations have largely stopped. In general, long time construction for ordinary purposes has been greatly reduced. Few men would have the hardihood to build new plants at prevailing high costs with the practical certainty facing them that after the war competing plants can be built at much lower costs.

There has been, moreover, a very definite and vigorous effort on the part of the government and the banks to curtail credits to non-essential industries. This has been part of a large scheme whereby transportation facilities, coal, copper, steel, labor and other basic necessities of production have been diverted from non-essential industries to the industries needed for war. As early as January, 1915, the stock exchange in London issued orders in conjunction with the Treasury, limiting the issues of new securities in the United Kingdom during the war to such issues as could be shown to the Treasury to be advisable in the national interest; and a vigorous control on the part of the

[1] There really should not have been serious apprehensions that the American banks would lend or the American people try to borrow many billions of dollars to be spent on ordinary consumption. The people have curtailed consumption, particularly the buying of automobiles, pianos, furniture, expensive rugs, carpets, curtains and the like and also food and clothing.

Treasury, the banks and the stock exchange has since been exerted in Great Britain not only over the issues of new corporation securities, but also over ordinary loans at the banks. This was particularly easy in Great Britain since a small number of great joint stock banks with numerous branches largely dominated the banking situation.

With the outbreak of the war in the United States, it was at first thought that it would be difficult for the banks to develop an effective control in this matter, in view of the fact that we have many thousands of independent competing banks. A desirable customer, refused a loan at one bank, might take his account to another bank and there get the accommodation he wished. There is good reason to suppose, however, that informal control worked out through the banks under the guidance of the Federal Reserve Board and the federal reserve banks has now been made effective, particularly in the larger centers.

The Federal Reserve Board from the beginning of the war has with increasing emphasis and directness stressed the importance of this. Secretary McAdoo, in his annual report to Congress in December, 1917, foreshadowed a request for legislation dealing with this matter. Early in 1918, a Capital Issues Committee of the Federal Reserve Board, semi-official in character, was organized, whose function it was to pass on proposed new issues of securities. Lacking power to prohibit such issues, it none the less had such great influence through the effective cooperation of banks throughout the country that it was virtually able to boycott all issues of which it disapproved. Connected with it were local capital issues committees in each of the twelve federal reserve districts

The Capital Issues Committee of the Federal Reserve Board surrendered its functions upon the organization of the new War Finance Corporation in May, 1918, to the Capital Issues Committee of the War Finance Corporation, though in part the personnel of the two committees remained the same.

The War Finance Corporation, organized formally on May 20, 1918, under authority of Congress,[1] has a capital of $500,000,000

[1] Act approved April 5, 1918.

owned by the United States Government. It has a twofold function. One function is to continue the restrictive activities of the earlier Capital Issues Committee, passing upon and limiting new security issues. The other, supposed to be of special importance at the time the War Finance Corporation was organized, is to extend new credits to essential industries, and very specially to savings banks and public utilities, which had been suffering as a consequence of the changes of the past two or three years. Savings banks were suffering because of a decline in the market prices of the securities which they owned, and withdrawals by depositors to purchase liberty bonds. Public utilities, as gas plants, electric railways, electric light plants and the like, had been suffering because their rates were held stationary by law while their costs were rising. It was expected too that very many of the industries most vital to the war would need more new capital than they could get.through ordinary banking channels, particularly in view of the fact that the federal reserve banks are forbidden to rediscount stock and bond collateral loans.[1]

The machinery whereby credits were to be provided by the War Finance Corporation was complex. In general, they were expected to lend, not cash, but their own notes, maturing in from one to five years, eligible as collateral at the federal reserve banks, and it was expected that they would lend these notes, not directly to the enterprises which needed the accommodation, but rather to banks which represented these industries, and which would act as intermediaries between the industries and the War Finance Corporation. These notes were to be turned over to banks, in return for notes of the banks secured by stock and bond or other collateral. In other words, the War Finance Corporation would take over from the banks stock and bond collateral loans, not eligible for rediscount at the federal reserve

---

[1] The writer ventures to call attention to his contention in his *Value of Money*, pages 518-520, that the federal reserve banks should be authorized to rediscount stock and bond collateral loans and that without this power they could not provide their most effective aid in emergencies. The new War Finance Corporation is an indirect device for accomplishing just this end. The main war time function of the federal reserve banks has been to rediscount loans on collateral in any case, since loans on government securities (not included in the general prohibition) constitute their chief earning asset.

banks, and would give them in return its own securities which were eligible as collateral at the federal reserve banks. In exceptional cases, the War Finance Corporation was authorized to make advances directly to essential industries, including savings banks and public utilities, without the intermediation of banks, and even in the form of cash. The limitation upon the extensions of credit of the War Finance Corporation originally proposed was $4,500,000,000. This was subsequently reduced to $3,500,000,000.

In practice, the machinery has proved too complex and virtually all the extensions of credit made by the War Finance Corporation down to October 15, 1918, have been made without the intermediation of banks. The banks would have had to pay a higher rate, for one thing, in borrowing on War Finance Corporation collateral at the federal reserve banks than in borrowing on government war paper, or in rediscounting commercial paper. The total of all credits provided by that date was $43,202,592. The most important extensions of credit made by that date were $20,000,000 to the Bethlehem Steel Corporation, $17,320,000 to the Brooklyn Rapid Transit Company, $3,235,000 to the United Railways of St. Louis, and $1,000,000 to the Northwestern Electric Company.

Various efforts have been made by financiers in the course of the late summer and fall of 1918 to increase the usefulness of the War Finance Corporation, particularly by creating corporations of semi-banking character which should stand between public utilities and other needy borrowers and the War Finance Corporation. A ruling of the Attorney General to the effect that the War Finance Corporation could not lend more than $50,000,000 to any one borrower made it difficult for these plans to go through on the scale originally contemplated. One such organization, known as the Essential Industries Finance Corporation, incorporated under the laws of New York with an initial capital of $3,000,000, has been approved by the Capital Issues Committee of the War Finance Corporation.[1]

In the interval, the savings bank situation seems largely to

[1] *Chicago Banker*, September 28, 1918; *New York Times*, October 31, 1918.

have taken care of itself in view of the extension of such aid as was necessary by ordinary banks, and in view of the interruption of the downward course of investment bonds since December, 1917.

The too great complexity of the machinery has made it difficult for the War Finance Corporation to do, down to the end of October, a very important constructive work. It has, however, performed very important services on the negative side in supervising and limiting the issues of new securities. There was some discussion of a proposal to extend its functions in this matter to cover all loans made by banks exceeding $100,000, but after a conference with the leading bankers of the country this scheme seems to have been dropped. The banks themselves appear to be exercising sufficient control over loans, and the necessity of having the approval of the War Finance Corporation, or even of its local representatives, would introduce so much delay and friction in banking operations as probably to bring on a commercial crisis of the first order.

During late October and early November, 1918, there has been some discussion of extending the activities of the War Finance Corporation for a longer period than that originally contemplated, and of making it an important instrumentality in the after the war adjustment. Secretary McAdoo has been quoted as favoring such a proposal. It is not impossible that the organization might advantageously take over supervision of the delicate problem of readjusting government contracts with munition plants, aircraft plants, and other war industries whose operations must stop immediately after the war. If that adjustment is left to the slow machinery of the Court of Claims and congressional appropriations, very great delay, injustice and demoralization may ensue.

In additon to control, worked out informally by the individual banks, over extensions of credit, there was organized on September 17, 1917, a subcommittee on money rates of the New York liberty loan committee, composed of the leading bankers of the city. This committee has provided funds where necessary for the protection of the stock market and particularly of the liberty loans, and has also acted to check speculation, notably during

October, 1918, and especially by a ruling that banks should require a margin of 30 per cent on collateral loans made to stock brokers where an average of 20 per cent had been previously required.[1]

There has thus been an admirable dovetailing of efforts on the part of individual banks, federal reserve banks, and the Treasury, the various authorities concerned with the control of supplies of copper, steel, transportation and the like, and the ordinary individual consumer, all tending to transfer funds to the government without undue expansion of bank credit, all tending to lessen the competition of the general public in the market for goods and services as the government's expenditures have increased. On the whole, we have worked out, largely by informal organization, an admirably adjusted situation.

It may not be an unnecessary digression to point out here that our war experience goes far to prove that strong legal authority in the hands of the central government is unnecessary, that banking concentration in the French or English form is unnecessary as a means of controlling and mobilizing the resources of the country in time of stress. The common will and the common purpose, quick to respond to intelligent suggestion from trusted leaders, has probably proved more effective than any degree of rigid legal control could have proved. Our system of forty-eight autonomous States, and thirty thousand autonomous banks, has stood as severe a test as we have any reason to anticipate it will ever be subjected to in the future. Effective cooperation need not involve the destruction of individual and local liberties.

[1] New York *Journal of Commerce*, October 25, 1918.

CHAPTER XVII

Prices in the United States

No subject in the course of the war has been more eagerly discussed, whether by economists or by the masses of the people, than that of rising prices. There is a school of economists who have seen the whole cause of rising prices in the policy of the governments in borrowing instead of taxing, and in the policy of the banks in lending to the governments or to the holders of government war securities. This process, called "inflation," has been treated by many writers as an unmixed evil, and a very considerable part of the literature of war economics has consisted of invective against the stupidity of those whose policies led to "inflation." The economic problems of a great war would be beautifully simple if this sort of analysis were really fundamental!

To writers of this school, the terms "rising prices" and "depreciation of money" have been synonymous and the fundamental causation has been sought in monetary and banking phenomena.

To the present writer, it seems perfectly clear that the fundamental causation involved lies in the field of production and consumption and in the fields of public policy and social psychology, and that so far at least as the United States are concerned the phenomena of money and banking have been largely secondary and derived, adjusting themselves to, rather than causing, the more fundamental factors. This is not to deny that banking policy has had and has a considerable influence on the course of prices. It is rather to assert that the major influence is to be found in something more fundamental.

The fundamental explanation lies on the surface. Fifty to sixty million men, an enormous proportion of the labor force

of the civilized world. have been taken out of industry and put to
work in the most destructive kind of consumption of the products
of industry. Another and larger number of men have been
diverted from the production of goods for ordinary civilian
consumption to the production of munitions and army supplies,
to the production of shipping to replace the waste of the U-boat
campaign, to the building of airships and of elaborate plants for
the production of airships, and so on. The process began first,
of course, in the belligerent countries, where also it has gone
farthest, but no neutral country remains unaffected by the
demands for war materials and supplies, and in the United States,
first as a neutral and now as a belligerent, the process has gone
very far indeed. The following quotation contains the best
estimate the writer has found of the extent to which the resources
of the United States have been diverted from the production of
ordinary civilian goods to the prosecution of the war:

An examination of reports of the general participation of the American
people in the war leads to the conclusion that of the American population,
normally engaged in gainful occupations, fully one-half are devoting their
energies to the prosecution of the war, either by bearing arms or working
in industries charged with the production of war materials and performance
of war service.

According to the 1917 census estimate, the latest available,' the number of
men engaged in gainful occupation in the United States was 30,091,564 and
the number of women so engaged 8,075,772, or a total gainfully employed
of 38,167,336.

The military establishment now numbers approximately 5,000,000 men.
This includes army, navy and marine corps. On the government railroads
there are 2,300,000 employed and in the shipyards under government control
386,000. The list of civil service employes has sprung from 166,000 in 1917
to approximately 500,000. This makes a listed total of 8,186,000.

The government has taken over bodily many munitions plants and other
industrial enterprises. In addition, it has awarded contracts to many plants
in which 75 per cent and in many cases 100 per cent of the workers are
solely engaged in turning out government material. With the aid of the
Department of Labor and the United States Employment Service. it is estimated that the number of persons employed in these industries, operating
for government account, amounts to about 12,000,000.

A total of approximately 20,000,000 persons engaged in war work therefore is obtained. The men drafted into or enlisted in the military service
must be subtracted from the total of those normally engaged in gainful occupations. On the other hand, the stress of war has caused many persons
to enter gainful occupations not previously so employed.

It is believed fair and conservative to conclude that these elements equalize—if they do not increase—the proportion of war workers to more than 50 per cent.[1]

In these facts, we have an adequate explanation of the rise in commodity prices without ascribing it to the stupidity of the fiscal policy of the Treasury, without assigning it to the stupidity of the banks and without attributing it to monetary depreciation.

Outside the United States monetary depreciation has been substantial in many countries and very great indeed in some. There has been a collapse in the value of Russian money which has sent prices to unheard of heights. The same is true in Austria, Germany and Italy, in less degree and to no small extent in France, as we have found reason to believe. In all of these countries the paper money has depreciated, to greater or less degree, below the value of its nominal gold equivalent. The extent to which monetary depreciation is a factor in Great Britain, however, can not be so great, while in Canada the element of monetary depreciation is probably very slight.

The table on the following page presents an interesting comparison of various index numbers covering not only the United States, but Great Britain, Canada and Austria, as well.

For comparison, the figures of the *Bulletin de la Statistique Générale de la France* are repeated from our chapter on French prices:

FRANCE

	1901–1910	1912	1913	1916	1917	1918
Entire period	100	118	116	....	....	....
1st quarter	....	....	....	....	258	370
2d quarter	....	....	....	....	297	384
3d quarter	....	....	....	2:5	315	....
4th quarter	....	....	....	229	339	....

UNITED KINGDOM

	1901–1910	1912	1913	1916	1917	1918
Entire period	100	116	116	....	....	....
1st quarter	....	....	....	....	223	255
2d quarter	....	....	....	....	240	260
3d quarter	....	....	181	....	240	....
4th quarter	....	....	203	....	249	....

[1] Federal Trade Information Service, Wednesday, October 23, 1918, page 197. It is proper to reduce this estimate somewhat, in that not all of the railway employes are to be counted as doing war work. On the other hand, it is very questionable if the soldiers have been fully replaced by people not previously employed.

WHOLESALE PRICES IN THE UNITED STATES AND CERTAIN FOREIGN COUNTRIES [1]
(Index numbers expressed as percentages of the index number for 1913)

| Year and month | United States | | | | | United Kingdom | | Canada | Australia |
	Bureau of Labor Statistics: 294 commodities (variable)	Annalist: 25 commodities	Bradstreet: 96 commodities	Dun: 200 commodities	Gibson: 22 commodities	Economist: 44 commodities	Sauerbeck: 45 commodities	Department of Labor: 272 commodities (variable)	Bureau of Census and Statistics: 92 commodities
1890	81	78	......	[a]75	[a]75	[a]83	85	81	97
1895	70	68	70	[a]67	72	72	73	71	70
1900	80	71	86	77	76	82	88	80	82
1905	86	79	88	83	81	81	85	84	84
1910	100	98	98	98	102	90	92	92	92
1913	100	100	100	100	100	100	100	100	100
1914	99	104	97	101	105	99	100	100	106
1915	100	106	107	105	110	123	127	110	147
1916	123	126	128	123	129	160	160	134	138
1917	175	187	170	169	191	204	205	174	....
1914									
January	100	102	97	103	100	97	98	101	[b]100
April	98	101	95	99	99	96	96	101	[b]102
July	99	104	94	99	101	95	104	99	[b]109
October	99	107	100	102	108	101	106	102	[b]113
1915									
January	98	108	99	103	111	112	118	103	[b]127
April	99	109	106	103	117	124	125	108	[b]153
July	101	105	107	103	111	122	126	111	[b]167
October	101	101	108	105	103	125	134	112	[b]142
1916									
January	110	110	119	114	113	143	149	127	[b]138
April	116	118	128	121	123	156	157	132	[b]137
July	119	121	125	120	124	156	157	132	[b]138
October	133	136	131	126	141	171	175	138	[b]139
1917									
January	150	151	149	140	150	184	187	154	[b]140
February	155	159	151	146	156	188	193	160	....
March	160	170	154	154	166	197	199	163	....
April	171	188	158	157	188	200	203	169	[b]146
May	181	203	164	172	204	201	205	177	....
June	184	198	168	176	197	210	211	179	....
July	185	189	175	175	200	208	208	179	....
August	184	190	178	181	203	210	207	181	....
September	182	195	181	178	206	209	207	179	....
October	180	200	184	182	207	212	212	179	....
November	182	199	185	183	206	214	214	183	....
December	181	200	191	182	209	217	218	187	....
1918									
January	185	200	195	184	205	215	219	190	....
February	187	204	196	188	210	216	220	194	....
March	188	204	196	189	217	218	221	199	....
April	191	207	200	191	225	221	223	199	....
May	191	207	205	188	216	223	225	204	....
June	193	201	206	186	211	227	226	207	....

[a] Average for January and July.   [b] Quarter beginning in specified month.

[1] *Monthly Labor Review*, U. S. Bureau of Labor Statistics, September 7, 1918.

The agreement between the two index numbers for Great Britain is startlingly close. The divergence among American index numbers is somewhat greater, Gibson's showing the greatest rise by June, 1918, and Dun's the least increase by that date. The Annalist index number is based solely on foods and is thus less representative than the other index numbers. On the whole, the writer prefers to use the Bureau of Labor Statistics' index number, though it moves more slowly than Bradstreet's, and in the chart which follows that index is employed. We may continue the table for this index number through July and August; reaching 193 in June, 1918, it grows to 198 in July and to 203 in August.[1]

Commodity prices at wholesale in the United States have thus doubled since the outbreak of the great war, at the same time that the labor force available for producing ordinary civilian goods and service in the United States has been, as shown above, practically cut in two. The writer attaches no significance to this fortuitous exact coincidence of ratios. Social phenomena rarely obey the law of simple quantitative proportionality between any two factors. But the writer does maintain that in the enormous reduction of available goods and services for civilian consumption, we have an adequate explanation of the 100 per cent rise in the wholesale commodity prices, and that no further recondite explanation based on a " quantity theory of money " is called for as an additional principle.

It is not necessary for present purposes to undertake to show the relation between the reasoning of those who see the explanation of price changes primarily in monetary and banking phenomena, and the reasoning employed in the present chapter. In part, the two methods of reasoning deal with the same fundamental factors, using different language and different modes of presentation. For detailed discussion and defense of the theory underlying the present chapter, the reader is referred to the writer's *Value of Money.*

---

[1] I am informed by a careful student in the Bureau of Labor Statistics, who has watched in detail the elements entering into the index number, that the rise in the summer of 1918 is directly and obviously due primarily to the increase in railway freight rates.

We shall distinguish four ideas which have been to a considerable extent confused in current discussion of price changes:

    (a) A general rise in prices
    (b) A rise in commodity prices at wholesale
    (c) A rise in "cost of living"
    (d) A fall in the value of money

Before one can assert that there has been a general rise in prices, one must take account not only of commodity prices, but also of stocks and bonds, real estate and other long time income bearers. The country has seen a great rise in commodity prices, but it has also seen a fall in stocks, bonds and real estate.

Cost of living has not risen as high as commodity prices at wholesale. Cost of living is concerned with retail prices and with certain other items, as house rents, which enter into the budget of a family. Commonly, one has the family of a laborer in mind when speaking of cost of living, which still further limits the items that will enter. Retail prices have risen much less than wholesale prices. House and apartment rents, taking the country as a whole, have risen little if at all, and the general rise in cost of living was estimated in the middle of the summer of 1918 at rather less than 50 per cent by a government official peculiarly qualified to give an estimate on this point. The best general figures to be found dealing with cost of living are those published by the United States Bureau of Labor Statistics in the *Monthly Review*, covering the shipbuilding districts of New York, Philadelphia and various south Atlantic and Gulf ports. A general summary of these results would indicate slight if any rise in house rents (with actual decline in many of the southern centers) down through 1917, with a considerable rise in house rents in a number of them during 1918, as congestion at these points increased. Satisfactory general studies of cost of living, however, covering the country as a whole, have not yet been made.

Under ordinary conditions, a marked rise in commodity prices may be taken as an index of a fall in the value of money. Under ordinary conditions if the value of money is constant, the probabilities are that the general average of commodities will bear a fairly constant relation to money. Some commodities may fall in value and consequently in price, but other commodities will be likely to rise in value and consequently in price, and, in the great average, changes on the part of one commodity will be offset by opposite changes on the part of other commodities. It is more probable that three hundred commodities will, on the average, remain stable in value than that one commodity, gold, will do so. But this reasoning may very well be upset by the conditions of a great war. Commodities in general may grow scarce and increase in value, and under such circumstances a general rise in commodity prices indicates, not a fall in value of money, but a rise in the value of goods. Where goods are as abundant for ordinary civilian consumption as they were before 1914, they have not risen in price. Coffee is a case in point. Coffee sold for 13 cents in 1913; it has sold for less than 9 cents through 1915, 1916, 1917 and the greater part of 1918. India rubber is another illustration. House and apartment rents would illustrate the same proposition. In certain sections, like Washington, where there has been a great increase in population, rents have naturally risen, and in many growing cities there has been some tendency to a rise in the fall of 1918, since building operations had been suspended for a considerable period preceding that. There had been, however, little if any rise in house and apartment rents through the country down to the early part of 1918, despite the check in building operations, and in those communities where the population has remained stationary there has been no rise at all. Had the rise in prices been due to depreciation of money, house and apartment rents would have risen with other prices.

It can not be said that the failure of rents to advance earlier was due to any inertia or to a failure of landlords to take quick advantage of opportunities. The writer has made rather careful investigation in certain centers, notably the East Side of New York, and is assured by real estate men that the situation is a fluid one, that landlords are quick to take advantage of opportunities to increase their rents.

There has not even been a general rise in prices. What has

happened rather is a transformation in the price system, under which certain prices have risen and other prices have fallen. Labor and its current products, scarce and dear, have risen markedly under the pressure of war demands; stocks, bonds and real estate and other long time income bearers have fallen drastically, as men and governments have sacrificed them to obtain the vitally needed present goods. The future has been ruthlessly sacrificed to the present. Coming with this change, and part and parcel of it, has come a marked rise in the long time rate of interest, symptomatic of the emphasis on the present and the .discount on the future. These three changes: (1) a rise in present goods and services; (2) a fall in long time income bearers; and (3) a rise in the long time interest rate, are merely different aspects of the same general fundamental fact.

In the midst of these changes, gold has remained fairly stable · in value, and has proved itself a good measure of values, an accurate monetary yardstick. It has correctly registered the rise in present goods and services; it has correctly registered the fall in long time income bearers. We may picture the situation by the figure of a seesaw, at one end of which are placed labor and commodities currently produced, at the other end, stocks, bonds and real estate, while gold stands at the center. In 1914 our seesaw was in equilibrium. The war has tilted the plank, raising labor and commodities and depressing stocks and bonds. Gold stands in the center, where it stood before, substantially unchanged in value.

The United States have gained, as we have seen, over a billion dollars in gold during the war. Under ordinary conditions, such an increase in the gold of the country, if expected to be permanent, would lead to a great decline in the value of gold. But the conditions are extraordinary. Emergencies of the war have led, as we saw in an introductory chapter of this monograph, to a greatly increased significance of one function of gold, namely, the "bearer of options" function. Ready gold, the one sure liquid asset to which men can always turn in times of stress and emergency, has been more eagerly sought for during the war than in the years preceding. The increased value coming to gold from this war time cause, has offset the tendency to decline in the value of gold in the United States, caused by the increased quantity of gold.

Parenthetically, it may be noticed that price changes in different parts of the world seem to have had no close connection with the actual movements of gold. Gold came to the United States and prices rose in the United States, but gold left England and France, and prices rose in those countries even more. The effort to work out any definite correlation between gold and prices on the basis of " normal laws " in these wholly abnormal times appears to the present writer to be futile.

Viewed in fundamental, psychological terms, the rise in the values of labor and commodities is inevitable under such conditions as we have had. In the first place, as we have seen, they have grown scarce. In the second place, they have attained an unusual significance owing to the intensity of our concern over the outcome of the war. All the ideal values of our civilization, dependent on the outcome of the war, have attached themselves to the guns and cannon, powder and shells, food stuffs, carriers and other things, an abundant supply of which is essential to the winning of the war. And all the economic values that men and nations could command in the future, ordinarily largely dormant in their influence at present market values, have been brought in to reinforce the values of these vitally necessary present goods.

To these fundamental changes in the technological and psychological factors, money, banking and public finance have adjusted themselves, bank credit has expanded as it has been necessary to accomplish the transformations, and as prices have risen. After the war, when commodity prices and wages come down again—as they inevitably will in terms of gold—bank expansion will also diminish.[1]

---

[1] No discussion of price fixing is given in this chapter, as the matter is to be dealt with in detail in another monograph in the present series. *Vide* the present writer's paper " Value and Price Theory in Relation to Price Fixing and War Finance," *American Economic Review*, Supplement, March, 1918.

COMMODITIES AND SECURITIES

The story of price changes in the United States is not complete without an account of the course of the stock market. The following chart exhibits the relation of stock prices to commodity prices during the war.

It will be observed that stock prices fell sharply where commodity prices changed little at the outbreak of the war; that stock prices recovered markedly and rose high in 1915, before the movement of commodity prices got well under way; that beginning with November, 1916, at a time when commodity prices had still made only a moderate rise, stock prices began their great and drastic fall, during which commodity prices soared to new and unheard of levels.[1] The two lines crossed in our diagram of April, 1917. It will be observed that while commodity prices start on a base of 100 per cent in January, 1914, stock prices start at the actual average figure of the fifty stocks chosen. It will be noticed too that the scale for stock prices, indicated in our first vertical column of figures, is twice that of commodity prices. The stock prices run in terms of actual dollars per share; the commodity prices run in terms of percentages of 1913 prices.

A more detailed picture of the course of stock prices during the war is given in our second chart, which distinguishes bonds, railroad stocks and industrial stocks, giving also the combined curve for rails and industrials. The scale of this chart is only half that of the curve for stock prices in the preceding diagram.

Following the sharp drop in stock prices at the outbreak of the war and the closing of the stock exchange, there are no quotations of significance to be had until the stock exchange opened again in November for bonds, and in December for

---

[1] The great rise from August, 1916, to June, 1917, in commodity prices—over sixty points—constitutes by far the major portion of the rise for the whole war. Forty points of this came between December and June, the sharpest rise of all being from March to May. Much of this was a speculative rise, in anticipation of war expenditure. All of it preceded the actual getting under way of the main financial operations of the United States Government.

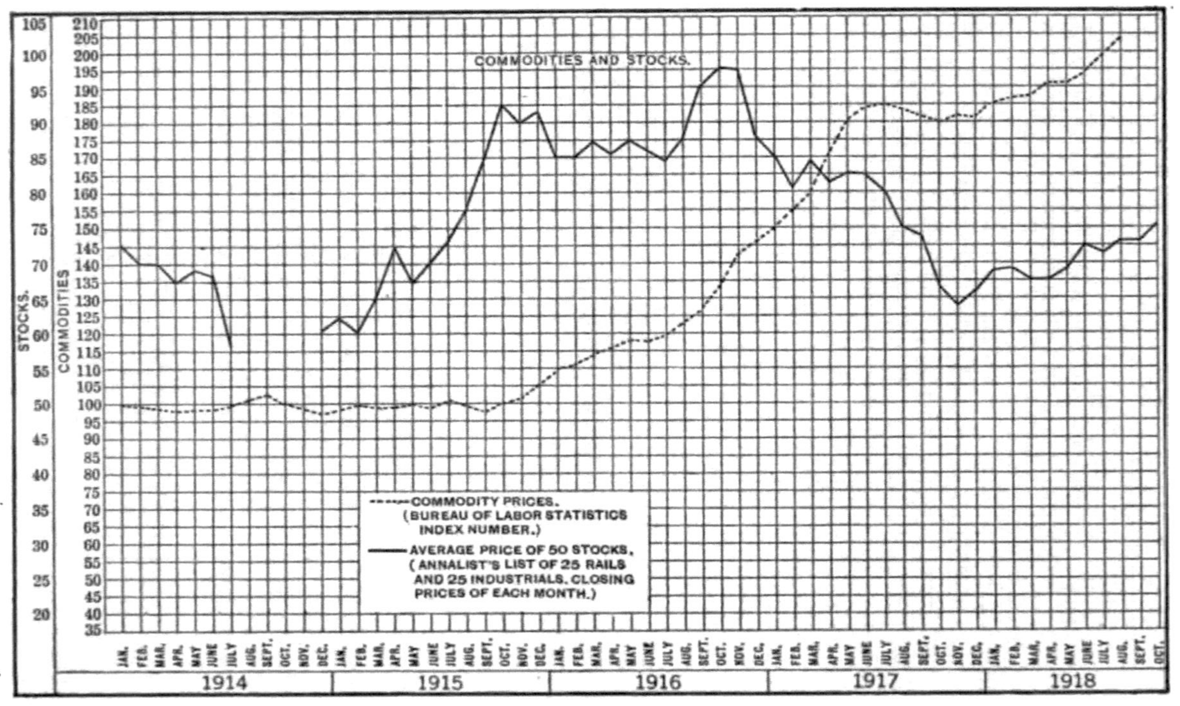
COMMODITIES AND STOCKS.
STOCKS.
COMMODITIES
COMMODITY PRICES.
(BUREAU OF LABOR STATISTICS
INDEX NUMBER.)
AVERAGE PRICE OF 50 STOCKS,
(ANNALIST'S LIST OF 25 RAILS
AND 25 INDUSTRIALS. CLOSING
PRICES OF EACH MONTH.)
1914
1915
1916
1917
1918

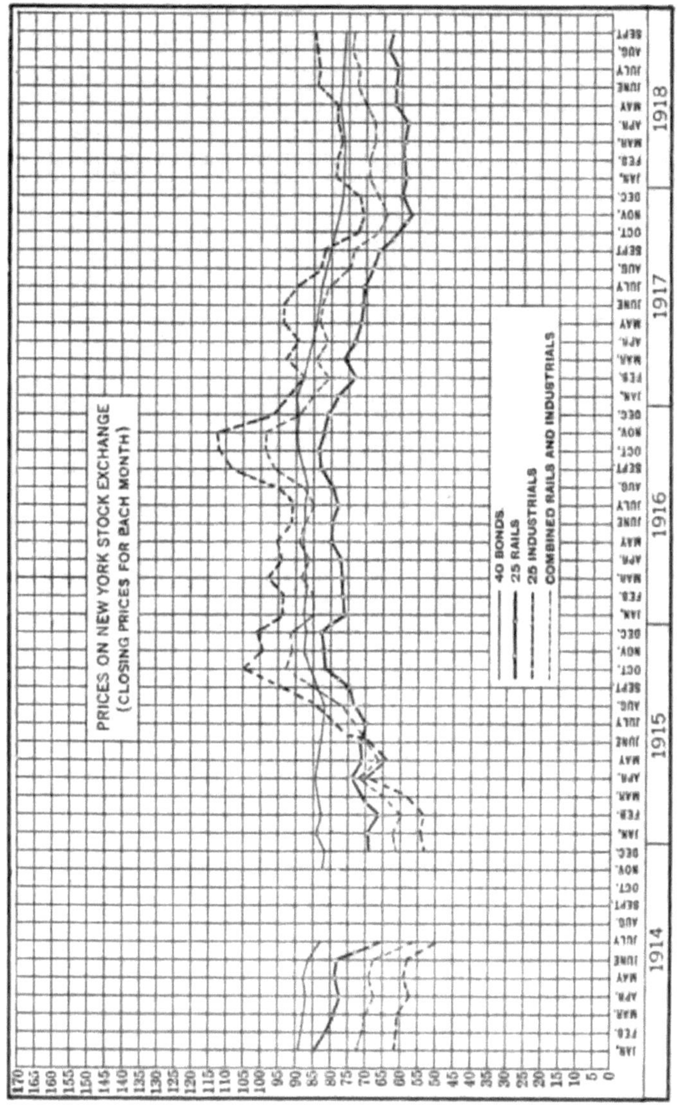
PRICES ON NEW YORK STOCK EXCHANGE
(CLOSING PRICES FOR EACH MONTH)
40 BONDS
25 RAILS
25 INDUSTRIALS
COMBINED RAILS AND INDUSTRIALS
1914
1915
1916
1917
1918

stocks. Prices remained low until May, 1915, when there began an extraordinary rise in the industrial list, chiefly connected with the " war babies," or stocks of corporations which were beneficiaries of the European demand for munitions and war supplies. Among these were Butte and Superior, whose shares rose early on the great demand for zinc, Westinghouse Electric and, most conspicuous of all, Bethelehem Steel. The price of the industrials crossed the price of the rails in June, 1915, and the stock exchange thrilled with the excitement of frequent million share days for a prolonged period. Though the crest for this curve was reached in October, great activity continued through the year, and December 31, 1915, on which day Austria's note to the President acceding to an ultimatum by the United States was received, was a million share day with substantial gains in many securities, notably Mexican Petroleum. In the phrase of one habitué of the ticker, 1915 went out in a " blaze of glory." The year 1915 also saw a substantial rise in the rails. The bears controlled the market through the earlier months of 1916, and there was a sharp drop in April of that year over the prospect of war with Germany, at the time of the sinking of the *Sussex*. The German assurance of cessation of illegal submarine activities restored confidence in some measure, and after a few more months of gloom a rise began in July under the leadership of United States Steel, which carried the industrial list and the whole list to the high peak of the war in November, 1916. In the course of this move, General Motors went to its dizzy high of $800 a share.

A substantial rise in the rails during 1916 also took place under the influence of great increase in both their gross and their net earnings. By October, 1916, however, it had become clear to careful students of the railroads that expenses of operation were growing as rapidly as gross receipts, that they would soon be outrunning them, and that a decline in net revenues of the railroads was in early prospect. This did take place, except for Southern Pacific and one or two other fortunately situated railroads, by the end of the year.

In December, 1916, rumors of peace led to a sharp break in

the price of all stocks, while rumors of the entrance of the United States into the war led to a further drastic decline, and the end of the year saw stocks lower by far than they had been at the beginning of the year. Early in 1917, the renewal of Germany's submarine warfare and the diplomatic break of the United States with Germany led to new low levels.

The day on which Ambassador Bernstorff was sent home presented a particularly dramatic episode in the stock market. All securities fell heavily until suddenly the news ticker announced that the President had handed Germany's ambassador his passports. Instantly, flags flew out throughout the financial districts in New York and Boston and in other centers, while bidding for all securities began. It lifted the general list two points or more above the low for the day, and lifted many securities eight or ten points above their low price for the day. It was the stock market's method of giving expression to its patriotism and its confidence in the success and righteousness of the American cause.

For some months following the dismissal of the German ambassador, there was recovery in the industrials, though the rails continued to sag, but by June, 1917, as the market began to realize the drastic taxation and heavy bond issues that were coming and the fundamental readjustments that were to be gone through with, all kinds of securities fell, and fell heavily. The climax was reached in December, 1917.

The course of the rails through 1917 is probably as significant as any other feature of the market, although bonds also took the same course. With rates fixed under legal control and with costs mounting, the railroads of the country were in a desperate plight. By December, their credit was in a very unfortunate condition and railroad prices seemed to have no bottom. A speech of President Wilson to Congress in December, 1917, announcing that the government would take over the railroads on favorable terms, primarily for the purpose of protecting their credit, though also for the purpose of enabling them to be utilized more effectively for the war emergency, explains the sharp rise indicated in our stock curves at that time.

In 1918 stocks rose during the early months, were depressed in March, April and May under the influence of the terrible German drive, and subsequently rose fairly steadily to the end of October, discounting successful peace. The increase of railway rates in 1918 explains one substantial sharp movement in the railway curve.

The decline of bond prices from a high of 90 in December, 1916, to a low of 80 in September, 1917, is significant of the growing scarcity of capital and the rise in long time interest rates. This factor is strongly evidenced in the prices of all securities, especially the rails and preferred stocks of all kinds. In the case of the bond list, however, it constitutes virtually the . whole explanation of their course from the beginning of 1917.

APPENDIX

LONDON STOCK EXCHANGE VALUES [1]

(In thousands of pounds sterling)

	9 British and Indian Funds. (Par Value 862,786)	26 British Ry. Ord. Stocks. (Par Value 310,750)	14 British Bank Shares. (Par Value 29,338)	38 Comm. Ind. Shares. (Par Value 36,701)	7 Shipping Shares. (Par Value 7,200)	15 South African Mines, etc. (Par Value 20,704)	Total of all Securities. (Par Value 3,424,586)
Dec. 18, 1913...	653,948	271,693	178,139	81,259	14,022	55,209	3,341,085
Jan. 20, 1914...	673,520	278,940	180,050	83,942	14,165	56,434	3,389,478
Feb. 20, 1914...	693,845	286,577	180,625	85,683	14,577	58,964	3,455,452
Mar. 20, 1914...	682,221	276,145	179,484	84,081	14,351	56,216	3,407,840
Apr. 20, 1914...	688,616	273,798	181,167	84,063	14,355	58,680	3,406,191
May 20, 1914...	683,452	269,149	181,670	83,236	14,326	55,877	3,385,562
June 20, 1914...	684,499	269,032	182,195	83,244	14,543	55,104	3,383,128
July 20, 1914...	690,355	269,513	182,650	81,662	14,546	55,458	3,370,709
July 30, 1914[a]..	646,101	255,866	177,514	77,063	13,604	45,699	3,182,717
Jan. 20, 1915...	632,188	254,422	175,824	69,954	14,352	41,362	3,114,027
Feb. 19, 1915...	632,406	251,255	74,756	69,548	14,011	40,631	3,092,243
Mar. 20, 1915...	616,812	243,682	172,834	68,837	14,100	41,815	3,017,660
Apr. 20, 1915...	615,883	243,227	173,478	69,100	14,831	45,189	3,052,996
May 20, 1915...	615,300	241,563	173,107	68,351	14,388	43,205	3,025,592
June 21, 1915...	614,964	237,624	170,684	66,684	14,059	43,230	3,008,578
July 19, 1915...	603,373	226,069	163,949	60,804	13,818	40,830	2,909,989
Aug. 21, 1915...	602,833	216,635	156,783	57,883	14,613	39,744	2,907,091
Sept. 21, 1915...	602,833	216,635	156,783	57,883	14,613	39,744	2,906,032
Oct. 21, 1915...	603,778	211,916	154,987	57,537	14,658	39,157	2,925,698
Nov. 19, 1915...	603,616	214,395	157,222	59,008	15,299	41,135	2,968,459
Dec. 17, 1915...	579,527	216,030	159,537	60,326	15,869	41,131	2,907,281
Feb. 21, 1916[b]..	577,334	216,804	58,613	63,501	16,035	40,220	2,888,559
Mar. 21, 1916...	571,247	213,050	56,850	61,617	16,199	40,126	2,862,454
Apr. 19, 1916...	570,034	213,110	59,055	61,890	16,985	39,472	2,855,386
May 19, 1916...	569,783	216,354	160,211	62,119	18,334	38,788	2,838,989
June 21, 1916...	581,430	225,412	164,059	67,465	18,812	41,870	2,912,501
July 21, 1916...	558,351	228,295	164,613	72,332	19,266	41,147	2,893,182
Aug. 19, 1916...	557,268	227,803	163,694	71,756	19,874	43,144	2,898,496
Sept. 20, 1916...	561,438	217,520	162,230	70,789	19,818	44,605	2,896,390
Oct. 20, 1916...	542,840	208,681	161,425	66,644	19,685	44,455	2,831,082
Nov. 20, 1916...	529,443	205,856	160,865	68,954	20,012	44,617	2,797,782
Dec. 18, 1916...	526,141	204,078	161,359	67,781	19,709	43,939	2,758,349
Jan. 22, 1917...	513,623	205,893	161,077	66,611	18,801	45,301	2,746,793
Feb. 19, 1917...	504,915	207,306	158,931	66,683	19,067	43,712	2,652,388
Mar. 20, 1917...	513,825	204,556	158,603	67,807	18,964	44,583	2,669,377
Apr. 21, 1917...	526,402	207,168	161,364	68,392	19,617	44,036	2,713,005
May 21, 1917...	525,476	202,532	161,347	68,641	19,683	45,412	2,710,465
June 21, 1917...	524,037	203,666	162,469	68,225	19,999	45,995	2,717,316
July 20, 1917...	528,069	206,809	162,662	70,441	20,541	45,037	2,729,992
Aug. 20, 1917...	529,017	204,411	161,444	70,868	20,410	44,443	2,728,193
Sept. 20, 1917...	523,357	197,976	161,823	70,405	20,196	45,906	2,690,337
Oct. 20, 1917...	530,656	201,126	162,027	70,040	20,791	46,341	2,688,395
Nov. 17, 1917...	525,143	198,716	162,881	71,045	21,120	44,558	2,634,633
Dec. 17, 1917...	520,281	195,263	163,623	71,647	21,440	43,796	2,600,653
Jan. 18, 1918...	519,984	200,131	165,987	72,087	23,018	44,378	2,622,516
Feb. 18, 1918...	517,048	199,675	165,904	72,469	22,820	44,066	2,619,780
Mar. 18, 1918...	510,879	187,679	165,513	69,701	22,691	44,021	2,592,215
Apr. 18, 1918...	514,870	185,272	165,601	68,189	22,351	41,221	2,571,612
May 17, 1918...	524,238	189,310	167,181	67,856	22,470	43,705	2,614,394
June 19, 1918...	525,054	193,876	167,640	69,446	22,745	45,536	2,633,824

[a] Stock exchange closed.

[b] Values for January not given in *Bankers' Magazine.*

[1] London *Bankers' Magazine.* The *Bankers' Magazine* figures are for the total values of the issues, rather than for prices per share.

PRICES OF BRITISH WAR LOANS [1]

	3½% 1925-28	4½% 1925-45	5% 1929-47	4% 1929-42	CONSOLS
Jan. 31, 1914	....	....	....	....	75¾-76
Feb. 28, 1914	....	....	....	....	75½-76
Mar. 28, 1914	....	....	....	....	75¼-75¾
Apr. 25, 1914	....	....	....	....	74⅝-74⅞
May 30, 1914	....	....	....	....	74⅞-75⅛
June 27, 1914[a]	....	....	....	....	74⅜-75⅛
Jan. 30, 1915	$94\frac{9}{16}$	....	....	....	68½
Feb. 27, 1915	$94\frac{1}{16}$	....	....	....	68½
Mar. 27, 1915	$94\frac{5}{16}$	....	....	....	$66\frac{9}{16}$
Apr. 24, 1915	94⅜	....	....	....	$66\frac{9}{16}$
May 29, 1915	$94\frac{3}{16}$	....	....	....	$66\frac{9}{16}$
June 26, 1915	93⅞	....	....	....	65
July 31, 1915	92⅞	97¼	....	....	65
Aug. 28, 1915	92⅛	98	....	....	$65\frac{1}{16}$
Sept. 25, 1915	$92\frac{1}{16}$	$97\frac{9}{16}$	....	....	65
Oct. 30, 1915	92¾	98⅛	....	....	$65\frac{1}{16}$
Nov. 27, 1915	89¾	$97\frac{11}{16}$	....	....	60
Dec. 31, 1915	89½	97¼	....	....	58½
Jan. 29, 1916	89¾	$96\frac{15}{16}$	....	....	59¼
Feb. 26, 1916	88⅛	97	....	....	58⅛
Mar. 25, 1916	87¼	96¾	....	....	57¼
Apr. 29, 1916	87⅝	$96\frac{11}{16}$	....	....	57⅛
May 27, 1916	88⅜	95⅛	....	....	57⅝
June 24, 1916	89¼	$96\frac{1}{16}$	....	....	59¼
July 29, 1916	88	$95\frac{15}{16}$	....	....	59½
Aug. 26, 1916	86½	96⅜	....	....	59
Sept. 30, 1916	85½	94¾	....	....	59¾
Oct. 28, 1916	84¼	95½	....	....	56¼
Nov. 25, 1916	83½	95½	....	....	55¾
Dec. 30, 1916	85¼	96	....	....	55¼
Jan. 27, 1917	85¾	99¾	....	....	51¾
Feb. 24, 1917	84½	89¾	....	....	52
Mar. 31, 1917	85¾	92¼	94⅞	99½	53⅛
Apr. 27, 1917	87	91½	94	100½	55
May 26, 1917	87	91¾	94¾	100½	55½
June 30, 1917	86¾	94	94½	101	54¼
July 26, 1917	87½	94½	94½	102	55¾
Aug. 25, 1917	87¼	97¾	94½	102¾	56¼
Sept. 29, 1917	86¼	101	94¼	100	54⅝
Oct. 26, 1917	85½	99⅜	$93\frac{11}{16}$	99¾	56¼
Nov. 30, 1917	85¼	99½	$93\frac{13}{16}$	100¾	56
Dec. 29, 1917	85	99½	$93\frac{13}{16}$	101	54¼
Jan. 26, 1918	86⅜	99⅞	93⅜	101½	54⅝
Feb. 28, 1918	86¼	100⅝	93¼	102	54½
Mar 27, 1918	85¾	100¾	93¾	100¼	54¾
Apr. 26, 1918	87	99½	93⅛	100¾	55⅜
May 31, 1918	87⅞	99⅝	$93\frac{13}{16}$	101¾	56⅜
June 29, 1918	87⅞	99¾	$93\frac{13}{16}$	108½	56

[a] Stock exchange closed.

[1] London *Economist*.

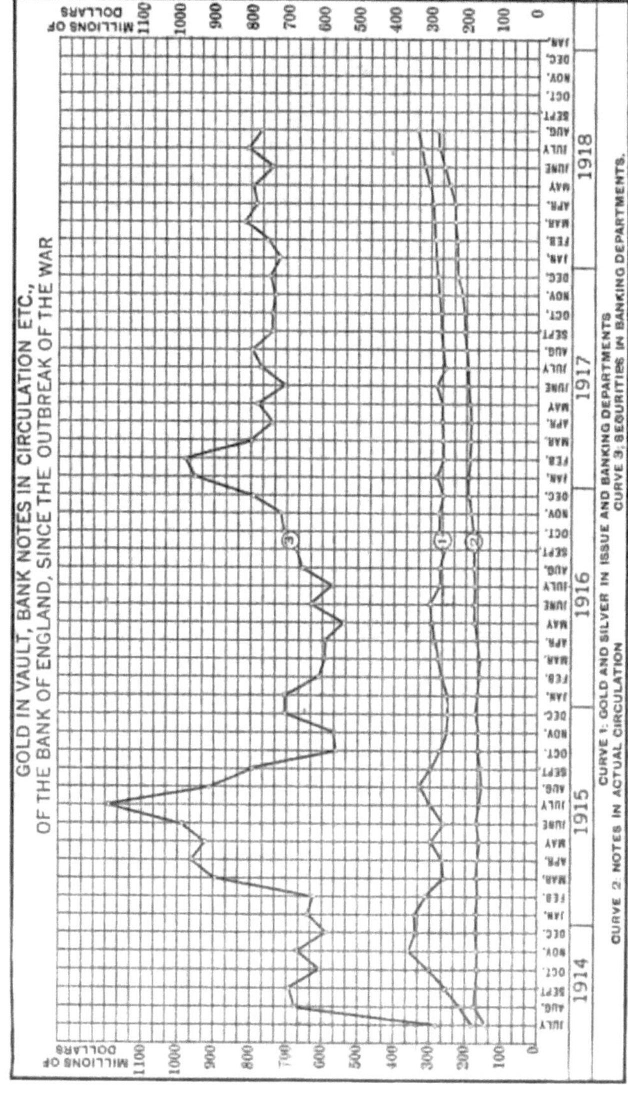

Reproduced from *Federal Reserve Bulletin*, October 1, 1918, page 999.

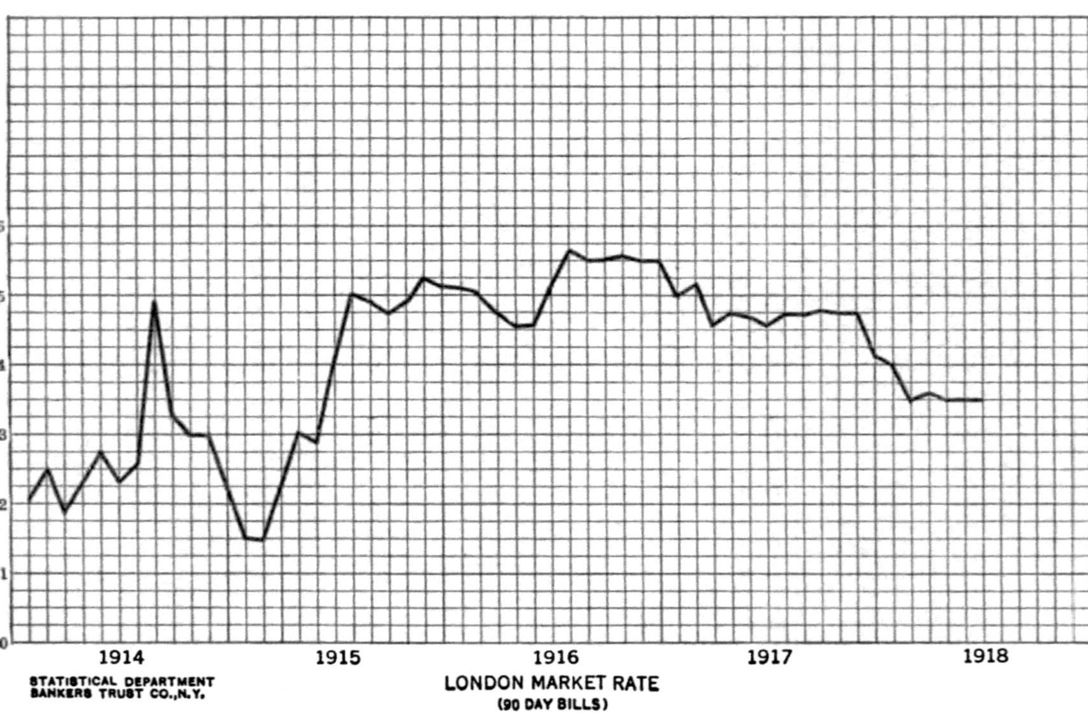

6
5
4
3
2
1
0
1914
1915
1916
1917
1918
LONDON MARKET RATE
(90 DAY BILLS)
STATISTICAL DEPARTMENT
BANKERS TRUST CO., N.Y.

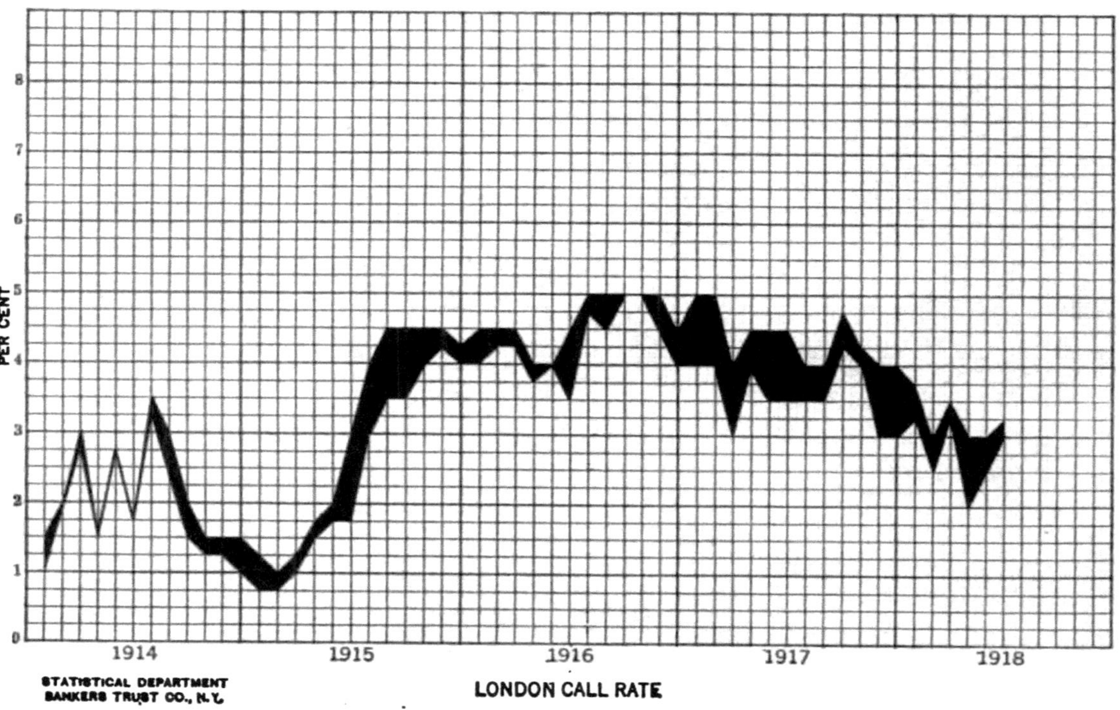
LONDON CALL RATE
PER CENT
8
7
6
5
4
3
2
1
0
1914
1915
1916
1917
1918
STATISTICAL DEPARTMENT
BANKERS TRUST CO., N.Y.

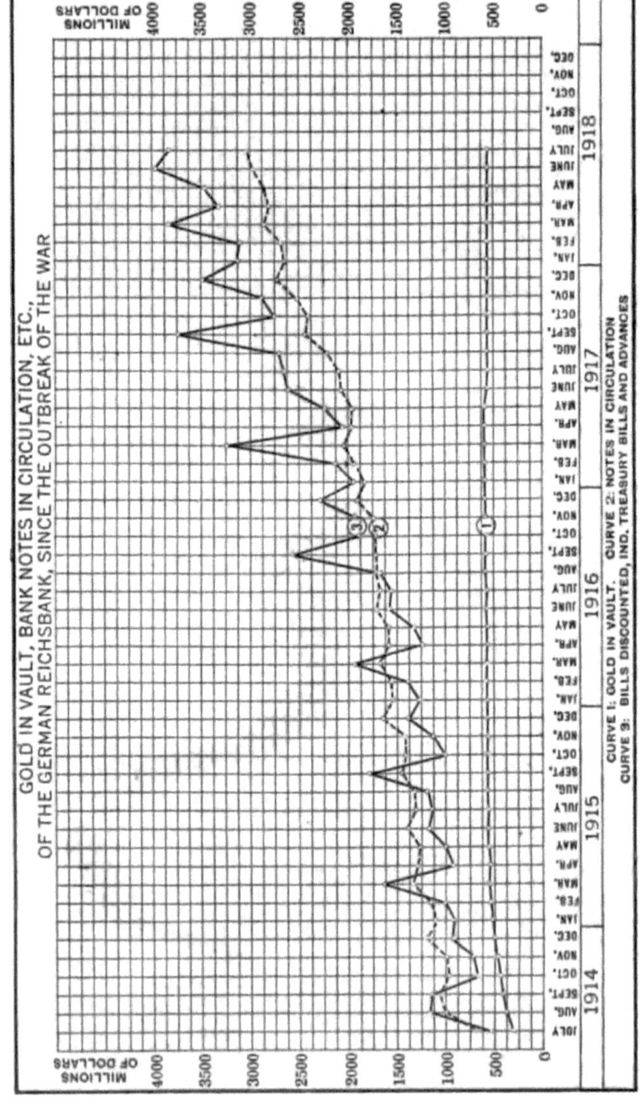

Reproduced from *Federal Reserve Bulletin*, October 1, 1918, page 1001.

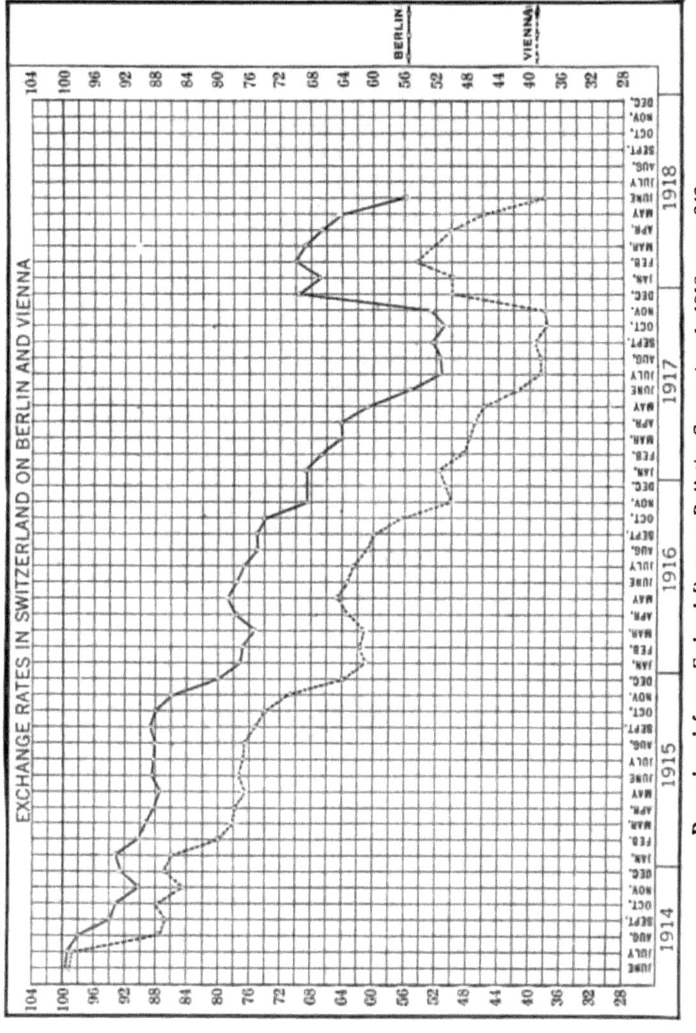

Reproduced from *Federal Reserve Bulletin*, September 1, 1918, page 842.

INDEX

Acceptances—*see* Bills of exchange.

Aldrich-Vreeland Act, 10, 150, 151, 165.

Allies, The: increase in American exports, 4; adverse balance of trade, 11; increasing shipments of goods from United States, 12; loans by United States, 180.

American National Monetary Commission, 37, 53.

Austin, O. P., 159.

Austria: national banks, 10.

Bank credits: efforts to convert to gold, 5; Germany, France and Russia, 6; contraction, 11; expansion, 12, 13; France, 28, 32, 109-110, 126; transfers without use of checks, 30; German "giro system," 30; in time of panic, 52-54; increase, France, 68; United States, 170; expansion, 182-195; Treasury certificates of indebtedness, 182, 183; loans on liberty bonds, 183; loans to tax payers, 183; effect on prices, 184; necessity for expansion during transition periods, 184-185; effect of loan policy of United States, 185; control over extensions, 172-174, 190-194; subcommittee on money rates of New York liberty loan committee organized, 194. *See also* Credit.

Bank notes: usage in England, France and America, 29; velocity of circulation, France, 31; hoarding, in France, 45, 78, 85, 110; depreciation of French, 79, 83, 84, 85; comparison between bank note issue and deposit and check system, 89-90; issue of Banque de France, 110, 112; raising legal limit of issue, table, 111; issue of Banque de l'Algérie, 111; of federal reserve bank notes, 163; federal reserve notes as legal reserve, 169. *See also* Currency; Money; Paper money.

Bank of England: depository at Ottawa, 12; discounted heavily for London banks, 1914, 53; all lawful demands for gold paid, 106; gold reserve policy, 174, 175; agency for federal reserve banks, 178; gold in vault, bank notes in circulation, etc., since outbreak of the war, chart, 215.

Bank of France—*see* Banque de France.

Banking systems: lack of French statistical material, 19; character and operation of French banks, 19-23; contrast between French and American, 19, 24-25, 27, 29, 31, 34, 53-54; French terms explained, 20-23; centralization in France, 24-26; evils accentuated by centralization, 39; marketing operations of private banks, 36; testimony of officers of Crédit Lyonnais as to marketing operations, 37; deposit and current account banking, 27, 30, 31, 32, 33, 34; in America, 33, 34; branch banking in Canada, France, etc., 40; investments, loans, etc., banks of various countries, 40-42; French system, 43;

United States federal reserve system, 165-178.

Banks: efforts to increase gold reserve, 6; central, suspend gold redemption, 6, protected by closing of stock exchanges, 8-9; central, aid in meeting collapse of credit system, 9; issue of emergency currency, 10-11; character of French banks, 19, 27, 28; resemble American bond houses, 37-38; investment of funds, 38-40; manufacturing enterprises financed by German, 40, 41; assets of German banks not liquid, 41; French, heavy lenders to German banks until 1911, 41-42; runs on French banks, 44; shares decrease in value on French exchange, 45; recovery in shares of Banque de France, 48; great credit houses of France, 45, 49, 52; assets not liquid, 50; American, in times of panic, 53; London joint stock banks curtail loans, 53; clearing house certificates in time of panic, 54; Banque de France, 105-113; banks in France, 114-121; difficulties due to moratorium, 54, 55, 122, 124, 126; banks of France supporting American loan, 137; United States, drains on cash reserves in July, 1914, 150; clearing house certificates, 150; United States, legal reserve, 169; State, response to President's appeal to join federal reserve system, 177; resources, 1914-1918, 185. *See also* Private banks; Savings banks.

Banque de France: note issue, 10, 22, 24, 27, 112; legal limit increased, 51, 111; table, 1915-1918, 111; issue expanded to meet emergencies, 109, 110; value of notes, 107; amount in circulation, 108; Chamber of Commerce notes secured by notes of, 88; credits, 11, 13, 29, 30, 32, 33; plans for relief of Parquet, 123; steady rise in shares from 1915, 127; chart, 128; the great central bank, France, 24; gold reserve, 24, 35, 107-108, 143; assets limited to liquid items, 42; stops runs on Société Générale by statement of bank's status, 44; initial burden of war on, 45; selected items from balance sheets, 1914-1918, table, 113; suspension of specie payments, 50; rediscounting for private banks, 52, 54, 111, 126; decline in moratorium bills and gain in new bills, 67-68; advantage taken of moratorium, 85; receives hoarded gold for Treasury notes, 86; advances to the government, 70, 100, 101, 108, 109, 112; redemption of notes, 79; silver reserve, 83; silver affected as legal tender by suspension of gold payments, 84; gold supply protected, 87; attitude toward use of checks, 90, 91; clearing operations, 91; heroic rôle during the war, 105; gold policy, 105-107; methods to reduce State's debt, 109; current accounts ex-